THE

GOOD

GIFT

OF

WEAKNESS

ERIC M. SCHUMACHER

HARVEST HOUSE PUBLISHERS
EUGENE, OREGON

Cover design by Faceout Studio, Molly von Borstel
Cover art © donatas1205 (texture); GreenArtStory (art) / Shutterstock
Interior design by KUHN Design Group

For bulk, special sales, or ministry purchases, please call 1-800-547-8979.
Email: CustomerService@hhpbooks.com

THE GOOD GIFT OF WEAKNESS
Copyright © 2024 by Eric M. Schumacher
Published by Harvest House Publishers
Eugene, Oregon 97408
www.harvesthousepublishers.com

ISBN 978-0-7369-8866-7 (pbk.)
ISBN 978-0-7369-8867-4 (eBook)

Library of Congress Control Number: 2023950729

"This book helped me see God's good purpose in making us creatures of weakness and dependence. You will be filled with wonder that Jesus became weak, and encouraged in the weak places of life as you see that Jesus doesn't despise weakness. Indeed, he's drawn to it." 				**—Nancy Guthrie,** author and Bible teacher

"Eric Schumacher takes us on a tour of the entire Bible as he explores the theme of weakness, imprinting on us that without Christ we can do nothing. I am grateful for the biblical faithfulness and the honest vulnerability that characterize this wonderful book." 				**—Thomas R. Schreiner,** author, associate dean at
The Southern Baptist Theological Seminary

"Nothing feels more shameful in our culture than weakness, so we hide it and pretend we are strong. Eric Schumacher, with the insight of a trusted scholar and the grace of a trusted friend, deconstructs that self-defeating shame. This book points us to the Christ whose glory shines through our vulnerability." **—Russell Moore,** editor in chief of *Christianity Today*

"Compelling, convicting, and comforting, this book will guide your weak and weary soul toward the true, persevering strength found only in Jesus Christ."
—Gretchen Saffles, bestselling author of *The Well-Watered Woman*

"With refreshing honesty and a good dose of humor, Eric's words remind us we're not alone." 		**—Laura Wifler,** author, podcaster, and cofounder of Risen Motherhood

"I would expect any book written by my friend Eric to be filled with deep wisdom and Biblical clarity. What I didn't expect was the depth of his own weakness transparently put on display for us. It's my privilege to recommend his work to you."
—Elyse Fitzpatrick, author and counselor

"In *The Good Gift of Weakness*, Eric explores the implications of the dazzling reality that God's power is made perfect in weakness." **—Justin S. Holcomb,** Bishop of the Episcopal
Diocese of Central Florida, author, and seminary professor

"Reading Eric Schumacher's book *The Good Gift of Weakness* was a paradigm shift for me. It challenges everything most Christians think about, well, everything. It is thoroughly Biblical, surprisingly comprehensive, and amazingly authentic."
—Steve Brown, author, professor, and radio broadcaster

"God's power is manifested precisely in the midst of our weaknesses because it's then that we lean on his power. I'm so grateful for Eric's work to trace for us throughout Scripture how God has always operated by this mysterious truth."
—Ashfin Ziafat, lead pastor of Providence Church in Frisco, Texas

"In a world where strength is heralded, Eric gives us a sobering and yet liberating reminder that it's not our talent or ingenuity but rather our shortcomings that God uses the most."
—**Davey Blackburn,** author and founder of Nothing is Wasted

"Scripture emphasizes weakness as a path for living a life pleasing to Jesus, yet few works have been given wholly to the significance of this trait. Schumacher fills this gap with a look at how weakness is an integral part of the plan of redemption."
—**Eric C. Redmond,** Professor of Bible, Moody Bible Institute

"Eric does a beautiful job of pointing us back to our true source of strength: Christ, and Christ alone."
—**Jerrad Lopes,** author and founder of Dad Tired

"*The Good Gift of Weakness* is deeply encouraging, especially for those of us who have come to the end of our strength, cleverness, or goodness." —**Barnabas Piper,** pastor and author

"In a world that focuses on strength and accomplishment, *The Good Gift of Weakness* is a great reminder that weakness is a gift that draws us to God."
—**Vaneetha Risner,** author of *Desperate for Hope* and *Walking Through Fire*

"Eric's words bring me so much comfort and hope. He helps us understand the good gift of weakness—in God's original design and in the (still) nail-pierced hands of our risen Savior. I think this book should be read by every Christian."
—**Quina Aragon,** author of *Love Has a Story*

"The profound biblical wisdom I gleaned from this helpful resource will surely influence not only my ministry but also the way I personally engage my own weaknesses."
—**Christine M. Chappell,** author of *Midnight Mercies*, biblical counselor, and host of the *Hope + Help* podcast

"I left this book humbled, comforted, and deeply grateful for God's perfect strength."
—**Emily A. Jensen,** author of *He is Strong*

"This book will encourage you to see weakness not as a liability but as a way to glimpse the glory of God."
—**Phylicia Masonheimer,** founder and CEO of Every Woman a Theologian

"The Good Gift of Weakness is rich with biblical theology and practical application but is also written with a pastoral sensitivity that makes this book accessible to anyone. I recommend every pastor read this book."
—**Brian Croft,** Founder and Executive Director, Practical Shepherding

For my pastor, Michael Felkins.
Stay weak, my friend.

Contents

FOREWORD

I sat in my chair, physically unable to move. Multiple surgeries had rendered me weaker than I'd ever been in my life, and I was in the chair for one reason: I simply didn't have the strength to get out of it. That chair was not my comfortable place to relax—no, it was my prison. I hated how weak I was. I hated my inability to do what I normally do. I hated how completely dependent I was on my dear wife, Luella, for just about everything. And my weakness made no sense to me. Here I was at the highest point of my ministry influence, yet unable to do the thing God had called and gifted me to do. I spent day after day in the chair, for two long months, before I had the strength to move around a little bit. But during those two months, a realization slowly dawned on me: I would be sick and weak for the rest of my life. The damage done to my body would not go away. There was a new normal and it was called "weak."

What I'm about to say may surprise you. I'm very thankful for the travail that locked me into that chair. I'm very thankful that I was rendered that weak. In those two months, something wonderful and transformational took place. I began to understand that much of what I thought was faith in Jesus, in truth, wasn't. What I would have named as trust in him was actually self-reliance. I had spent my life healthy and strong. I had enjoyed the ability to do things quickly and produce much. I was proud of both my productivity and my strength. But it was all a self-congratulatory delusion. I had no independent strength to be proud of. Everything I had ever produced was the result of the intervention of divine grace. In that chair, I began to acknowledge and confess my weakness. No, not just the present condition of weakness, but the weakness that was the story of my entire life. You see, my suffering hadn't made me something different—it exposed what I had been denying about who I really was all along.

It is embarrassing to admit that, after all my years in ministry, it was only in those months that I began to understand and experience what it really means to rest in weakness and to trust Jesus for the strength that he, and only he, can give. Because of that, if I had to go through again all the suffering that locked me in that chair, I would gladly do it, because I now know—experientially know—the grace and glory of weakness. I had to come to the place of giving up hope in my strength in order to truly experience the transforming beauty of hope in Jesus.

Perhaps it is my own story that makes me love the book you are about to read so much. We are bombarded by stories of human strength, stories of self-made people who accomplish great things. And we are tempted to buy into the fantasy that we could be one of those heroes. But it is a delusion. There is no such thing as an independent human being. God created us to be dependent on him and on one another. Even in the utter perfection of the Garden of Eden, Adam and Eve were dependent. Yes, they were perfect people, living in a perfect relationship with God, but they were hardwired to be dependent on their Creator and one another.

So I am very thankful that my friend Eric Schumacher wrote a book, one not about the glories of human strength but about the grace and glory that is ours in our weakness. This book will confront your delusion of independent strength, it will comfort you with the amazing things God does in and through those who are weak, and it will remind you that Jesus stepped into your weakness so that you would know the strength that comes only from him.

There is one particular element that I love about Eric Schumacher books. He doesn't just approach a topic from the perspective of the Bible. No, he unpacks the topic by giving you a tour of the Bible from Genesis to Revelation. This book helps you to examine each step of the biblical narrative through the lens of weakness. And because it does this, it enables you to see things in Scripture, perhaps for the first time or in ways you have never seen them before.

You may not think that you need to read a book about weakness—but you do, and here is why. One of Satan's most powerful and deceptive tools is the delusion of independent human strength. If you buy into this delusion and think you are strong, then you won't seek God's help and strength and you won't seek and celebrate the grace that makes that help available. The enemy of your soul will gladly give you your formal religion, with its theology, Sunday service attendance, small group studies, personal Bible reading and prayer, and episodic moments of ministry, if he can keep you from being humbly and completely dependent on the Savior for everything you are and have and do. Denial of weakness always means devaluing the grace of Jesus, that grace that is meant to be our only hope in this life and the life to come.

I am very thankful for this book. I have been convicted by its confrontation and encouraged by its comfort, and I think you will be too. It is only when we abandon our hope in our strength that we can begin to rest in the strength that is ours by means of divine grace alone.

Paul David Tripp
October 16, 2023

CHAPTER 1

WEAKNESS IN CREATION

For from him and through him and to him are all things.
To him be the glory forever. Amen.

ROMANS 11:36

I t was 1980-something. I was in the seventh grade, taking my spot on the field for the opening kickoff of a small-town junior high football game. I knew my assignment: I was to run directly downfield at kickoff, getting past the blockers to tackle the player with the ball. As I looked straight ahead, I saw him, the player we'd been warned about—the Man-Boy.

Legend had it the Man-Boy had repeated junior high multiple times, making him the only eighth grader in the county old enough to register for the draft. He had a visible five-o'clock shadow, bulky muscles, and forearms so hairy that his grandmother could shave them and use the hair to knit cardigans for her church's missionary society. You could picture him puffing a cigarette while lifting engines out of small cars in his father's auto shop. There he was, directly before me, the blocker assigned to stop me, with a twenty-yard running start.

The Man-Boy sprinted toward me like a semitruck barreling down on a BMX bike, a raging bull charging a scarecrow. Though he was twice my size, I determined not to flinch. I would hit him head-on, as hard as I could. Twenty yards separated us. Then fifteen. Ten. Five. I lowered my shoulder and…I don't recall what happened next—not the impact, not a feeling, not even a sound. I don't remember anything between him being five yards away and me looking up at the blue sky.

I had zero effect on the Man-Boy. None. I hadn't slowed him down. I didn't hinder him. I didn't move him an inch. He ran through me like a locomotive passing through the fog. I was, in a word, weak. And running to the sideline, I was ashamed, wondering who had seen whatever had just happened, praying I'd never hear a word of it.

Humiliated, defeated, and wanting to hide—that's how most of us feel about weakness. We want to get as far away from it as possible. But we shouldn't feel that way. There's nothing inherently wrong about being weak. Weakness isn't a bug in the design of the universe; it's a feature. It's how God made us.

WHAT IS WEAKNESS?

At some point—after Harvest House accepted my book proposal but before I started writing this book—I realized it might be a good idea to know what I mean by *weakness*. (That's probably a good thing for you to know, too, before we get much further.) So I did what elementary kids did when stuck inside for recess in the days before the internet—I went dictionary surfing. (Online Merriam-Webster.com dictionary surfing, because there's the internet now and I don't own an actual physical dictionary.)

Merriam-Webster defines *weakness* as "the quality or state of being weak." Thank you, Captain Obvious. What does it mean to be weak? "Lacking strength." Well, duh. What's strength? "The quality or state of being strong." Fine. I'll play along…What's it mean to be strong? "Having or marked by great physical power." This is so pointless I think I'll stick a pencil in my eye (the other great pre-internet stuck-inside-at-recess pastime) because, hey, at least a pencil has a point.

What's power? The "ability to act or produce an effect." Having surfed five word-waves, I finally reached the sandy beach of understanding. Weakness is the inability to act or produce an effect. In short, a weak person is one who cannot do things or make things happen. That's us—weak.

There are three types of weakness we'll encounter in this book (and in the Bible): natural, consequential, and relative. By natural weakness, I mean our inherent inability as created beings. This is a good weakness—a gift—which we'll cover in chapter 1 (creation). By consequential weakness, I mean weaknesses introduced or magnified by the entrance of sin, which we'll cover in chapter 2 (the Fall). A derivative of consequential weakness is moral weakness, our moral depravity resulting from the Fall. By relative weakness, I mean our inability in comparison to others (for example, people, animals, or forces of nature). Relative weakness will pop up throughout the Bible as we think about "the weak" in contrast to "the strong" in human terms.

ONLY GOD IS NOT WEAK

The opening line of the Bible impresses upon us the fact that God—and God alone—is not weak. In the beginning, God existed. He did not begin; he always was. No one created God. His existence—past, present, and future—owes itself to nothing. He depends on nothing. Nothing started him. Nothing sustains him. He has no need, weakness, or vulnerability. Nothing can end him. He simply is. That's not true of anyone or anything else. Any semblance of power in a creature is a derived and dependent strength: It comes from God and depends on him to sustain it. Therefore, every created thing has an inescapable weakness: It cannot exist or continue existing apart from God's will. Every creature is inherently vulnerable: It could cease to exist at any moment if God so willed, and it can do nothing to prevent it.

Those are staggering thoughts, impossible for us to fathom because we're not God. We can't begin to imagine what it is to be uncreated, unsustained, entirely independent, all-powerful, and eternal. But these are the first truths of the Bible, nonnegotiable and foundational to everything that follows. Understanding the storyline of the Bible—and, therefore, the storyline of each of our lives—is impossible apart from grappling with the colossal distinction between Creator and creature. We are weak; he is strong.

WE ARE WEAK

We are weak. That is good. God made us weak—and everything that God made was good. Before sin and death entered the world, weakness existed. It's not a result of the Fall. The creation story drives this point home as it highlights the creation of human beings. We depend entirely upon God for our place, presence, purpose, provision, protection, and partners.

We depend entirely upon God for our place.

"Now the earth was formless and empty, darkness covered the surface of the watery depths, and the Spirit of God was hovering over the surface of the waters" (Genesis 1:2). Theologians and scholars have debated what's going on in this verse for centuries. We may not know every detail of the earth's condition before God created life, but we know that these conditions aren't conducive to life. (How's that for weakness? We're so weak that we have needs before we even exist!) In what follows, God brings about an environment in which life not only exists but can thrive as a testament to his glory. He speaks light into darkness, binds the waters, fashions the sky, brings forth dry land, calls forth vegetation, and orders celestial lights to rule the night and day. After the place is ready, God fills it with blessed living creatures.

The Lord provided the first humans with a particular place, a home. "The Lord God planted a garden in Eden, in the east, and there he placed the man he had formed" (Genesis 2:8). And what a place it is! A garden of gorgeous trees bearing good fruit, watered by a river that flowed down into the surrounding lands filled with gold and precious stones. But as lavish as this place is, there is something even better: God was there, walking with his people.[1] Isn't that incredible? God doesn't just give us a place to live; he provides us with a place to live with him.

Life with God is neither a luxury nor a bonus. It's a rock-bottom, nonnegotiable need. God is life—"the Father has life in himself" (John 5:26). As we've seen, God doesn't get life from anywhere. He *is* life—and he alone gives life. Apart from him, we have no life. To be banished from his presence is to die forever.

Life with God is a need, and it's also a gift. Unless God gives us himself, we can't have him. We didn't earn life with God in the beginning. He gave it to us. We don't earn it now. He comes down to us in free grace. We won't deserve it in the end—it will be given to us without cost. Every grace from creation to new creation is nothing short of God living with us so that we might live in him—"for in him we live and move and have our being" (Acts 17:28).

We depend entirely upon God for our presence.

Who are we apart from God? Simply put, we aren't. Humanity didn't exist. "Then God said, 'Let us make man'" (Genesis 1:26). At his word, we existed "remarkably and wondrously made" (Psalm 139:14). Our presence in creation begins and continues only through God's will and work. "The life of every living thing is in his hand, as well as the breath of all humanity" (Job 12:10).

We exist, but what are we exactly? Remarkably weak stuff, it turns out. "Then the LORD God formed the man out of the dust from the

---

1. See Genesis 3:8.

ground" (Genesis 2:7). Go run your hand across the top of your refrigerator and look at your fingers. Now take that dust and make a fully functional human body. You didn't try it, did you? No worries, I didn't either. I can't make a fully functioning human being out of dust, and neither can you. But God can. That's the point. No matter how we may feature in God's plan, our usefulness and accomplishments don't rest in what we are. We're dust.

Why dust? In Scripture, dust represents a lowly status: "I raised you up from the dust and made you ruler over my people Israel" (1 Kings 16:2). Dust signifies poverty and humiliation: "He raises the poor from the dust and lifts the needy from the trash heap" (1 Samuel 2:8). Dust is death: "Your dead will live; their bodies will rise. Awake and sing, you who dwell in the dust!" (Isaiah 26:19). God made us from dust to teach us to walk with him in humility.[2]

How can dust come to life? When God formed the first man out of dust, he was only a "lifeless corpse."[3] But then God "breathed the breath of life into his nostrils, and the man became a living being" (Genesis 2:7). Isn't that a strange yet wonderful image? The all-powerful God of the universe stooping to put his lips to the face of a dead body, gently and lovingly filling it with new life. This isn't the last time God will draw near to the dead with tender, life-giving love. The Bible is the story of God raising the dead from creation to new creation.

We are fragile earthen vessels that God filled with life. The apostle Paul meditates on this in the New Testament: "Now we have this treasure in clay jars, so that this extraordinary power may be from God and not from us" (2 Corinthians 4:7). The treasure Paul refers to is the gospel, the message of Jesus Christ crucified for our sins and raised from the dead. We'll dig deeper into that in a few chapters.

---

2. Victor Hamilton, *The Book of Genesis: Chapters 1–17* (Grand Rapids: Eerdmans, 1990), 158.
3. Hamilton, *Genesis*, 159.

For now, notice this: God ordained that the message of his saving glory would be transported in ordinary, fragile containers—clay jars (that's us!). That's not a new idea. We didn't become clay jars when we received the gospel. No, we were already clay pots, ordinary and fragile vessels from the beginning. Before sin and death entered the world, God chose to display his life-giving glory to the world through fragile earthen vessels.

We depend entirely upon God for our purpose.

We do not determine or create our purpose; the meaning of life doesn't come from us. Rather, God gives us our purpose. That's good news because his purpose for us is better than anything we could imagine. "Then God said, 'Let us make man in our image, according to our likeness. They will rule the fish of the sea, the birds of the sky, the livestock, the whole earth, and the creatures that crawl on the earth'" (Genesis 1:26). Did you catch that? God created us to rule "the whole earth"! If you ask a college graduate what she plans to do with her life and she replies, "I want to rule the world," don't laugh. Congratulate her—she's on the right path. (How she gets there is another matter entirely!)

God made human beings to rule the earth: "They will rule...the whole earth." So we read, "God created man in his own image; he created him in the image of God; he created them male and female" (Genesis 1:27). What does that mean? In the ancient Near East (the context in which Moses wrote Genesis), an image represented a god; "the image functions in the place of the deity."[4] A king was also considered to be the image of a god, "ruling on the god's behalf."[5] The Lord forbade his people from making an image of him, not because

---

4. Bruce K. Waltke, *Genesis: A Commentary* (Grand Rapids: Zondervan, 2001), 65–66.

5. I. Hart, as quoted in Waltke, *Genesis*, 66.

he was against images of himself but because he had already made them—human beings. In God's plan, his image wasn't a carved statue. Nor was it limited to a singular king. The image of God was "democratized to all humanity."[6] God designed humans to cooperate in exercising his royal authority on the earth. That's amazing, but it doesn't end there.

Genesis 2 zooms in on the creation of humans. After the Lord formed the first man and breathed life into him, "the LORD God took the man and placed him in the garden of Eden to work it and watch over it" (verse 15). There's another specific assignment—to work and watch over God's garden. There's more going on here than horticulture. There are only two other places where Moses uses *work* and *watch over* as a pair—Numbers 3:7-8 and 8:25-26, where they refer to priestly service in the tabernacle sanctuary. That leads us to understand that humans were to serve as priests to God in the garden sanctuary in Eden.

Rulers of the whole earth and priestly servants of God. That's a high calling. But notice that—it's a calling. It's not something we won in battle, purchased with wealth, earned with service, or obtained through a popular vote. It's a purpose bestowed upon us by God. Apart from his declaration, we have no purpose. Our purpose, like our existence, comes from outside us, from God. God alone possesses ruling authority in himself. Any we have comes from him. God alone determines who serves in his presence. If we find ourselves there, it is a gracious gift.

We depend entirely upon God for our provision.

One of my sons enjoys watching survivalist shows, particularly those about people living off the grid in the Alaskan wilderness. It's not uncommon to hear them talk about being self-sufficient, depending

---

6. Waltke, *Genesis*, 66.

only on themselves for their livelihood. But even if we hunt, gather, and grow everything we eat, sew our clothes, and build our own shelters, self-sufficiency is always an illusion. We hunt and gather what already exists. We grow crops from seeds that are already there. We sew and build with preexisting materials. We do it all with bodies that God formed and sustains with life. We depend on him for all we need all the time.

Human beings love food. We love to talk about it, prepare it, buy it, and post pictures of it online. Most of all, we love to eat it! So it should not surprise us that the first subject God speaks to after creating humans is food:

> Look, I have given you every seed-bearing plant on the surface of the entire earth and every tree whose fruit contains seed. This will be food for you, for all the wildlife of the earth, for every bird of the sky, and for every creature that crawls on the earth—everything having the breath of life in it—I have given every green plant for food (Genesis 1:29-30).

The need for food isn't discussed; it's just assumed. To live, we need to eat. To eat, we need food. To have food, we need God.

We need food. We derive strength from food. Without food, our power fades, and ultimately, we die. The need for food isn't a product of the Fall; it's a product of design. God didn't have to make us this way, but he did. In doing so, he reminds us daily that we're not self-sustaining. The living God does not eat. So, when we eat, we remember that we're not God. We repeatedly eat throughout life to remember that we always have needs that God alone can provide. Food helps us recognize that life comes from and is sustained by God. "He gives food to every creature" (Psalm 136:25).

When I was a child, our school cafeteria offered only one meal option each day. If you didn't like it, you didn't eat (except you had to because the teachers made you). But God isn't like the grumpy lunch lady slapping mystery meat onto your tray with a "you're gonna eat it, and you're gonna like it" look in her eye. "The LORD God planted a garden in Eden, in the east, and there he placed the man he had formed. The LORD God caused to grow out of the ground every tree pleasing in appearance and good for food, including the tree of life in the middle of the garden, as well as the tree of the knowledge of good and evil" (Genesis 2:8-9). Did you catch the description of the trees in God's orchard? "Every tree pleasing in appearance and good for food." God could have whipped up some bland, gelatinous all-in-one food source, something straight out of a dystopian sci-fi flick. But he didn't. He gave us variety, beauty, and nutrition! God's provision is like the charcuterie boards so popular these days—an assortment of meats and cheeses, breads and crackers, fruits and nuts, vegetables and chocolates offered in abundance and displayed with beauty.

Why is God's provision so lavish? Because food exists to give us something more than physical strength (Psalm 104:14-15):

> He causes grass to grow for the livestock
> and provides crops for man to cultivate,
> producing food from the earth,
> wine that makes human hearts glad—
> making his face shine with oil—
> and bread that sustains human hearts.

Why does God cause grass and crops to grow? Why does he produce food from the earth? So that wine can make our hearts happy. So that oil can make our skin shine. So that bread can sustain not merely our bodies but our hearts.

God's provision isn't utilitarian. It's designed to function and to please, to go beyond our needs so that we remember "life is more than food and the body more than clothing" (Luke 12:23). God provides in pleasing ways so that we won't forget he's the source of all our happiness.

We depend entirely upon God for our protection.

When we bought our first house, my wife discovered a plant with poisonous berries growing in the fence around our garden. When our young son became mobile, the presence of those berries posed a dangerous threat. Seeing us eat the fruit in the garden, he'd assume he could eat the berries on the fence. Unable to discern safe fruit from toxic fruit, he could make a lethal mistake. So we took pains to remove the plant and guard against its return. We also taught our son, as he grew, not to eat berries and plants unless we'd given our permission. Our son depended on us not only for provision but for protection.

So far, we've seen that the Lord provided the first man with a lavish, appetizing orchard. What we haven't seen is that eating from one of those trees would result in death. So the Lord gave the man both permission and a prohibition: "You are free to eat from any tree of the garden, but you must not eat from the tree of the knowledge of good and evil, for on the day you eat from it, you will certainly die" (Genesis 2:16-17). Not a few scholars have debated the exact meaning of "the knowledge of good and evil." For our purposes, it's important to notice that (1) the man was able to die and (2) eating from this tree would result in death.

We were created mortal—we can die. Only God is immortal (see 1 Timothy 6:16). It's always true that life is a gift from God to us, as is the ongoing preservation of life. (Genesis 3:22 seems to imply that living forever depends on taking from the tree of life, something God provides or withholds.) The first man, like our son, had no way of knowing which plants were safe and which one was life-threatening unless his parent told him.

Here's our weakness: We're incapable of discerning what is safe and what is deadly, what is good and what is evil, unless the Lord tells us. This is one more way we're incapable of living and being without God's gracious gift. That gift, in this situation and throughout the Scripture, is his Word. We're not wise in ourselves; we're born lacking wisdom. "The fear of the LORD is the beginning of wisdom" (Proverbs 9:10). From the very beginning, we're taught not to lean on our own understanding but to live by faith, trusting God for protection.

We depend entirely upon God for our partners.

"Can you help me?" That's a question we learn to avoid from an early age. If you've been around children, you know that point in development where they insist, "Me do it!" Unfortunately, that stubborn independence rarely fades with age. Asking for help is a confession of weakness, an acknowledgment that we can't do something alone. It's a humbling truth to admit. Perhaps that's why the Lord chose to end the creation story with a slow, extended observation of our need for help.

Throughout Genesis 1, we read a repeated refrain: God saw that it was good.[7] That refrain culminates with the announcement "God saw all that he had made, and it was very good indeed" (Genesis 1:31). So, in Genesis 2, it's shocking to read, "It is not good for the man to be alone. I will make a helper corresponding to him" (verse 18). "It is not good"—that's no soft statement of disappointment; it's "highly emphatic."[8] God's stressing the point: This is really bad.

Why is it not good for the man to be alone? Is it because he's lonely? No, it can't be that, because he has God. Is it because there's safety in numbers? No, he has the Lord as his protector and provider. God's remedy reveals the answer: "I will make a helper corresponding

---

7. Genesis 1:4, 10, 12, 18, 21, 25.
8. Waltke, *Genesis*, 88.

to him." It's not good for the man to be alone, because he needs a human helper. A helper comes alongside another to lend strength and assistance in a task.[9] The man needs a helper because he needs help. He's incapable of ruling the earth or serving in the garden alone. God designed the first human being with a deficiency, a weakness. Before the Fall, sin, and death, God made us weak.

Weakness itself is not what the Lord declares not good. It's not wrong that the man needs help. If that were the case, the Lord would have altered him so he could fulfill his calling alone. But the Lord doesn't do that. Instead, he makes another human (the woman) so that they can accomplish their purpose together, her adding her strength to his. No man or woman can independently fulfill God's purpose on the earth; rather, "both sexes are mutually dependent on each other."[10]

The Lord really, really wants us to see this weakness. That's why he saved this bit for the end. Among God's last recorded words in the creation story are "It is not good for the man to be alone" (Genesis 2:18). It is as though God shouts, "Humans. Are. Weak!" The sentence that follows in the same verse is just as important: "I will make a helper corresponding to him." The woman is God's solution—but she's *God's* solution. The remedy isn't provided by the man or the woman. The help only arrives because the Lord supplies it. God's the one who delivers strength for our every weakness. The Lord alone enables us to do the work he gave us. "It is not good for the man to be alone" isn't an assessment limited to the creation of the first man. It's an ongoing, by-design, good reality that continues today.

9. The word translated as "helper" (*ēzer*) is most frequently used to describe the Lord's relationship to Israel. See, for example, Exodus 18:4; Deuteronomy 33:7, 26, 29; Psalms 33:20; 115:9-11; 124:8; 146:5.

10. Waltke, *Genesis*, 88.

WHY WEAKNESS?

I hope you've begun to see why we're studying weakness. Weakness matters because it's the backdrop against which God displays his strength. "Weakness is a prominent image in the Bible, for weakness stands in contrast with the surpassing strength of the principal character of the biblical story, God."[11] When we deny our weakness, we reject God's power. When we boast in ourselves, we deny God's provision. Weakness exists to display God's glory in everything.

Weakness is God's good gift because it's the context in which he gives us himself. If we weren't weak, we wouldn't need God—we would rival him. "What do you have that you didn't receive? If, in fact, you did receive it, why do you boast as if you hadn't received it?" (1 Corinthians 4:7). Embracing our weakness trains us to humble ourselves and to boast in God. Such weakness is good news because God loves the weak, and only the weak can genuinely love God. "Weakness is a holy invitation to allow grace to do its work."[12]

God loves the weak. As we've seen in this chapter, all creation is ultimately weak—especially us. But God isn't looking down his nose, despising his creatures for needing him. No, he approves of it! "God saw all that he had made, and it was very good indeed" (Genesis 1:31). God loves his weak creation! He enjoys supplying us with good things from his hand to give us strength and gladden our hearts. God's love for the weak doesn't change when sin enters the picture. He continues to love the humble, the lowly, the poor, and the downcast. He satisfies the hungry with good things.[13] "He raises the poor from the dust and lifts the needy from the trash heap" (Psalm 113:7).

---

11. Leland Ryken, James C. Wilhoit, and Tremper Longman III, eds., "Weak, Weakness," in *Dictionary of Biblical Imagery* (Downers Grove, IL: InterVarsity Press, 1998), 932–934.
12. Alia Joy, *Glorious Weakness: Discovering God in All We Lack* (Grand Rapids: Baker Books, 2019), 163.
13. Luke 1:53.

Only the weak can genuinely love God. "God resists the proud but gives grace to the humble" (James 4:6). God resists the proud because they resist him. The proud person cannot admit he's weak; he can't accept that he has needs only God can supply. Therefore, he cannot trust God. But the humble know who they are before the Lord; apart from him, they are and have nothing. Consequently, they seek him and trust him to provide.

Weakness reminds us that God designed all of life to be lived by faith. He didn't create us to live by our own power, only introducing the need for faith once we needed to be saved from sin and death. Life, liberty, and happiness aren't found in our independence. They're rooted entirely in our dependence on the Lord. From the beginning, God made us look to him for all we are and all we need. Weakness is the soil in which faith grows—and faith is where life flourishes.

So, friend, don't be ashamed of your weakness. Don't hide it. Don't think it makes you unable to approach God. Don't despair, thinking it means that true strength is not available. Let's embrace and celebrate weakness so we can embrace and celebrate all that God is for us and gives to us in Jesus Christ.

> Jesus loves me—this I know,
> For the Bible tells me so:
> Little ones to him belong—
> They are weak, but he is strong.[14]

---

14. Anna Bartlett Warner, "Jesus Loves Me," originally published as a song in *Bradbury's Golden Shower of S.S. Melodies: A New Collection of Hymns and Tunes for the Sabbath School*, ed. William B. Bradbury (New York, 1862).

CHAPTER 2

WEAKNESS IN THE FALL

For you are dust, and you will return to dust.

GENESIS 3:19

E ric!" my mother gasped in horror when she entered the kitchen. It looked like a scene from a slasher movie. Dark red splatter covered the kitchen cupboards, dripped from the ceiling, and pooled on the counter. I stood there in shock, literally red-handed, wiping my face, staring down at my stained T-shirt, wondering what had just happened.

We had been unpacking groceries when I spotted something fascinating—a plastic bottle of Cookies Original BBQ Sauce. Up to this point in my childhood, condiments came in glass containers. But companies were beginning to introduce squeezable bottles. And the label on this bottle highlighted the new packaging with the words "Shatterproof Bottle!" So I did what any self-respecting eight-year-old boy would do: I grabbed it by the neck, hoisted it over my head, and shouted, "Unbreakable bottle!" before bringing it down with all my might onto the edge of the kitchen counter. The bottle did not shatter. It exploded, covering every kitchen surface with the sweet and smoky smell of an Iowa summertime.

What went wrong? I deceived myself into believing that *shatterproof* and *unbreakable* were synonyms. I wanted the bottle to be something more, something stronger than what it was. My deception and consequent action resulted in an incredible mess (and a family legend I have never lived down). In many ways, that's the story of humanity. The first humans overestimated their strength, so God's good and perfect creation became a grotesque mess. Our first parents wanted to be more than what they were—and we've been following their example ever since.

DEADLY DECEPTION

The Garden of Eden came with a warning label: "You are free to eat from any tree of the garden, but you must not eat from the tree of the knowledge of good and evil, for on the day you eat from it, you will certainly die" (Genesis 2:16-17). If the man and woman trusted God's promise and warning, they would live happily ever after.

In the first verse of Genesis 3, we meet the serpent, the "most cunning of all the wild animals that the LORD God had made." He approached the woman, masking his wicked shrewdness in a seemingly innocent question: "Did God really say, 'You can't eat from any tree in the garden'?" She responded with a summary of God's word and warning. They would die if they ate from the tree in the middle of the garden.

The serpent replied to the woman with a flat contradiction: "No! You will certainly not die" (verse 4). He mixed this lie with equal parts truth: "In fact, God knows that when you eat it your eyes will be opened and you will be like God, knowing good and evil" (verse 5). That sentence is true; God says as much at the end of the chapter after they eat: "The man has become like one of us, knowing good and evil" (verse 22).

Knowing good and evil refers to moral autonomy—the ability to decide for oneself what is right and wrong and choose a course of proper action.[1] Here is another weakness: Humans aren't able to decide for themselves what is good or evil, nor do we have the ability to determine how to live as a result of such judgments. That capacity belongs to God alone. Our moral strength comes only through the word he speaks to us, so we must live by faith in his Word and not by our inherent understanding.

Humans were made in God's image—to rule together on earth as God's representatives. God decides what is good and evil, right and wrong, and how we should live. We're designed to "image forth" wisdom that originates in God alone (and not in ourselves). We weren't made with the knowledge of good and evil. Eating from the forbidden tree would turn humans into creatures with a corrupted and rebellious capacity to decide right from wrong and how to live accordingly. That capacity belongs to God alone. In our hands, it explodes into a mess.

What follows the serpent's suggestion is one of the most tragic lines in human history: "So she took some of its fruit and ate it; she also gave some to her husband, who was with her, and he ate it" (verse 6). Notice the word *so*. *So* indicates motivation, linking the action to the reason. What motivated her to reach out, take the fruit, and eat it? "The woman saw that the tree was good for food and delightful to look at, and that it was desirable for obtaining wisdom. So she took some of its fruit and ate it; she also gave some to her husband, who was with her, and he ate it" (verse 6). She took and ate because she wanted knowledge of good and evil. Her husband followed suit.

The man and woman weren't content to be made in God's likeness. They wanted to be gods themselves. Grasping for moral autonomy is nothing short of attempting to usurp God. "Man has indeed

1. "What is forbidden to man is the power to decide for himself what is in his best interests and what is not. This is a decision God has not delegated to the earthling." Victor Hamilton, *The Book of Genesis: Chapters 1–17* (Grand Rapids: Eerdmans, 1990), 166.

become a god whenever he makes his own self the center, the spring-board, and the only frame of reference for moral guidelines. When man attempts to act autonomously, he is indeed attempting to be godlike."[2] Plucking that fruit was an act of treason, which is why doing so came with the death penalty.

The woman took and ate because she was deceived.[3] She put her faith in the serpent's promise that she would not die. Believing herself to be strong—immune from death—she took, ate, and gave some to her husband who was with her, and he ate it. While the woman transgressed the commandment out of deception, the man sinned with eyes wide open. He knew firsthand, having received the promise directly from God, that eating would result in death. His eating was an act of high-handed, deliberate rebellion. Somehow, he looked at God's warning and believed he could escape the punishment. He thought he was stronger than God. The man and the woman forgot their weakness, and their rebellion exploded into a mess they could never clean up, a mess that exists in our world and our flesh to this very day.

CONSEQUENTIAL WEAKNESS

In the previous chapter, we observed our natural weaknesses, which exist because we're creatures, not God. These are good gifts of God's design, gifts that invite and require us to live by faith in him to supply our needs. We embrace these weaknesses and gladly continue in them so that God's strength might be displayed in us.[4]

Adam's rebellion introduced a new type of weakness: *consequential weaknesses*. These result from the corruption that entered the world

---

2. Hamilton, *Genesis*, 166.

3. See 1 Timothy 2:14.

4. "Some kinds of weakness are of God's appointment, and necessarily incident to manhood; they are not sinful, and, therefore, we may continue to be subject to them without regret." C.H. Spurgeon, "God's Cure for Man's Weakness," in *The Metropolitan Tabernacle Pulpit Sermons*, vol. 12 (London: Passmore & Alabaster, 1866), 349.

through sin. As Paul explains, "Sin entered the world through one man, and death through sin, in this way death spread to all people, because all sinned" (Romans 5:12). The moment Adam sinned, death entered the world. Everyone experiences this death because we're all born with a corrupted nature that sins. Though we know better through what God has revealed, we seek to pull God off the throne and take his place. Therefore, we all experience sin's consequences. We die—and this death is far worse than the immediate cessation of life.

Consequence #1: Knowledge of Nakedness

You've probably had that dream where you find yourself standing in front of a crowd of people, only to realize you're completely naked. It's horrifying and thoroughly embarrassing. There's no feeling of relief quite like waking up and realizing it was just a dream. Adam and Eve had quite the opposite experience. After eating the fruit, they woke up to a living nightmare: "Then the eyes of both of them were opened, and they knew they were naked" (Genesis 3:7).

Nakedness is exposure. Before sin entered the picture, "both the man and his wife were naked, yet felt no shame" (2:25). Pre-sin, this nakedness represented humanity's "complete openness and innocence."[5] In their innocence, they lived without "shame and temptation and so no need to protect their vulnerability by the barrier of clothing."[6] Before the Fall, no thorns, thistles, sinful neighbors, or curses existed. They lived exposed. They were weak but safe—without the threat of harm from each other, their environment, or God.

After the Fall, their eyes were opened to what they'd done and who they now were outside God's grace. This newfound awareness represents a realization that they were guilty and death had entered

---

5. John D. Currid, *Genesis: Volume 1* (Holywell, UK: Evangelical Press, 2003), 119.
6. Bruce K. Waltke, *Genesis: A Commentary* (Grand Rapids: Zondervan, 2001), 90.

the world.[7] They now lived in a dangerous world, "exposed in every conceivable way to the possibility of loss."[8] They were vulnerable to harm from each other, their environment, and the God they offended. Choosing to live outside God's strength, they became weak and unsafe—exposed to present danger in manifold ways.

Consequence #2: The Delusion of Self-Sufficiency

When the man and woman realized they were naked, they sought a solution. "They sewed fig leaves together and made coverings for themselves" (Genesis 3:7). I'll leave it to your imagination to understand the inadequacy of leafy loincloths to cover human nakedness. Their attempt at clothing was pathetic, not merely because they used leaves to cover minimal bits of their bodies, but because they attempted to fix the problem.

As foolish as the man and woman were in thinking they could hide their nakedness from each other with foliage, it's surpassed by what they did next. "Then the man and his wife heard the sound of the LORD God walking in the garden at the time of the evening breeze, and they hid from the LORD God among the trees of the garden" (verse 8). If it's foolish to think that leaves are adequate to hide our nakedness from one another, how much more so to believe that trees can hide us from God!

When the Lord called out to the man, "Where are you?" the man replied, "I heard you in the garden, and I was afraid because I was naked, so I hid" (verses 9-10). Evidently, he understood the insufficiency of his frond-thong. Since the leaves didn't cover his nakedness, he'd try whole trees. Sadly, his awareness of guilt and shame still didn't drive him to God's mercy. Instead, it caused him to hide from God.

---

7. Hamilton, *Genesis*, 181.

8. Andy Crouch, *Strong and Weak: Embracing a Life of Love, Risk, and True Flourishing* (Downers Grove, IL: InterVarsity, 2016), 44.

And the foolishness didn't stop with the trees. When God asked him directly about his sin, rather than repenting, the man tried to hide behind his wife: "The woman you gave to be with me—she gave me some fruit from the tree, and I ate" (verse 12). When confronted with her trespass, the woman had the sense to confess to eating but attempted to hide behind the serpent: "The serpent deceived me, and I ate" (verse 13). Though both spoke some truth about what happened, neither was willing to humble themselves and say, "God, be merciful to me, a sinner!"[9]

If the first sin was believing they could be like God and live, the second sin was thinking they could protect themselves from the consequences. They could have turned to God (who we soon learn walks with them in the garden). They could have confessed their sin and asked their Creator for mercy. They could have acknowledged their weakness and sought his strength to save them. Instead, "their guilt leads them into a self-atoning, self-protecting procedure: they must cover themselves."[10] They embraced the deadly delusion of self-sufficiency—they thought they could save themselves.

Self-sufficiency is a deadly delusion. Yet the belief that we can redeem ourselves from sin still plagues today's world. It's present in false religions and systems of thought that tell us we can become good enough to earn forgiveness, to merit our way into heaven. It's found when we try to hide our guilt behind good deeds. It's there when we attempt to dodge conviction by throwing someone else under the bus. Had I tried to clean up the kitchen with hands covered in barbecue sauce, I would have succeeded only in spreading the mess around. Our attempts at saving ourselves are no better—we're only finger painting with our sin.

---

9. See Luke 18:13.

10. Hamilton, *Genesis*, 191.

Consequence #3: Spiritual Disruption

What we just witnessed highlights another consequential weakness: Our relationship with God is disrupted. As we'll see throughout this book, God mercifully continues pursuing his sinful creatures. Yet, apart from a miraculous and gracious intervention, humans refuse to relate to God on his terms. "Claiming to be wise, they became fools" and instead seek salvation in created things (see Romans 1:22-23).

We see this spiritual disruption in the man and woman attempting to hide their nakedness behind fig leaves. We see it in their scapegoating attempts to avoid acknowledging guilt. Ultimately, we see it in a profound separation from God, the end of fellowship in paradise. The consequences of sin culminated in the Lord sending them away from the garden in Eden. He drove them out, stationing a heavenly being with a flaming sword at the entrance to ensure that none may reenter.[11] No longer would they walk with God in his sanctuary, serving him in harmony and joy. Now they're sent away from Eden, away from God's presence, into a wilderness of pain.

Lest we think this condition was limited to Adam and Eve, we immediately encounter the heartbreaking story of their firstborn son, Cain.[12] One day, Cain and his brother Abel presented offerings to the Lord. The Lord received Abel's offering but did not have regard for Cain's offering, because Abel brought his in faith while Cain did not.[13] "Cain's sin is tokenism. He looks religious, but in his heart is not totally dependent on God, childlike, or grateful."[14]

Rather than turn from sin and trust the Lord, Cain responded in furious despondency. Despite God's gracious invitation to do what is right and be accepted, he chose to murder his brother. This act

---

11. See Genesis 3:22-24.
12. See Genesis 4:1-24.
13. See Hebrews 11:4.
14. Waltke, *Genesis*, 97.

betrayed Cain's lack of regard for God. How we treat God's image reveals what we think of God. Cain destroyed God's image because he hated God.

In response to Cain's sin, the Lord declared that Cain was cursed. Alienated from the ground he once farmed and unable to grow crops, he would be "a restless wanderer on earth" (Genesis 4:10-12). Instead of responding in repentance and seeking God's grace, Cain objected, "My punishment is too great to bear! Since you are banishing me today from the face of the earth, and I must hide from your presence and become a restless wanderer on the earth, whoever finds me will kill me" (verses 13-14). Thus Cain remained unconcerned with God's glory and grace, caring only about his well-being.

Notice how Cain understood his destiny: "I must hide from your presence and become a restless wanderer on the earth." Being a restless wanderer on earth is parallel to (or synonymous with) hiding from God's presence. Cursed and entrenched in unbelief, Cain would spend his life trying to hide from God: "Then Cain went out from the LORD's presence and lived in the land of Nod, east of Eden" (verse 16). Cain literally walked away from God and produced a line of descendants characterized by sin, selfishness, and hatred of God.

Consequence #4: A Depraved Nature

Cain's depravity wasn't limited to him or his immediate line of descendants. Sin corrupted every human (see Genesis 6:3)—so much so that "when the LORD saw that human wickedness was widespread on the earth and that every inclination of the human mind was nothing but evil all the time, the LORD regretted that he had made man on the earth, and he was deeply grieved" (verses 5-6). Notice sin's exhaustive corruption: "**Every** inclination of the human mind was **nothing but evil all the time**" (emphasis added). In our fallen state, we never have a single inclination that isn't evil. Lest we think this only describes those living before the great flood, Paul reminds us that this describes everyone:

> There is no one righteous, not even one.
> There is no one who understands;
> there is no one who seeks God.
> All have turned away;
> all alike have become worthless.
> There is no one who does what is good,
> not even one (Romans 3:10-12).

"There is no one righteous, not even one." Fallen humanity is exhaustively wicked all the time—depraved by nature, dead in sin, enemies of God.[15] This depraved nature, our "moral weakness," is far and away our greatest weakness. In and of ourselves, we're incapable of doing good, loving God, or redeeming ourselves. Only God's free grace can save us.[16]

Consequence #5: Relational Disruption

When our relationship with God is disrupted, and our hearts are depraved, the resulting dysfunction spills over into how we treat each other. As mentioned above, how we relate to God's image (our neighbor) flows from how we relate to God. We saw a hint of this when the man pointed a finger at his wife when confronted with his sin. We see this relational discord amplified when God spells out the consequences of sin.

The Lord tells the woman, "Your desire will be for your husband, yet he will rule over you" (Genesis 3:16). Scholars debate the meaning of "your desire will be for your husband." Some take that to mean

---

15. See Ephesians 2:1-3; Romans 5:10.
16. See Genesis 6:8; Ephesians 2:4-10.

a sinful desire to dominate her husband in the same sense that sin desires to overtake Cain in Genesis 4:7. Others understand it to be a good desire, as found in Song of Songs 7:10: "I am my love's, and his desire is for me." The immediate context favors the latter interpretation. The man and woman desire to do what they were created to do—fill the earth and exercise dominion over it and its creatures. But those desires are met with frustration. The proper desire to work the soil now meets thorns, thistles, and sweat (Genesis 3:17-19). The good desire to have children is now met with intense labor pains and painful effort (verse 16). The good desire to live is met with death and decay (verse 19). In the same vein, the woman's good desire to cooperate with her husband in living out God's purposes will be met with his rule.

"He will rule over you" communicates sinful dominance over his wife. Instead of exercising dominion with her, according to God's design,[17] he'll dominate her. That domination is illustrated in Cain's descendant Lamech, who threatened his wives with a lethal vengeance should they dare offend him.[18] It's seen throughout the Bible and today in all manner of interpersonal wickedness—abuse, rape, murder, human trafficking, theft, deception, greed, and things like these. Hating God and wanting to overthrow him, we hate our neighbors and seek to rule them.

Another regrettable weakness resulting from sin is the corruption of our ability to cooperate in God's purposes. Instead, humans collaborate to oppose God's purposes.[19] The creation of a people who come together to glorify God takes an act of sovereign grace.[20] We lack the strength and ability to live out our purpose apart from God's grace.

---

17. See Genesis 1:26-28.
18. See Genesis 4:23-24.
19. See the Tower of Babel incident recorded in Genesis 11:1-9.
20. See God's covenant with Abraham in Genesis 12:1-3 and everything that follows.

Consequence #6: Spiritual Warfare

Our sinful nature isn't the only enemy working against our flourishing. The spiritual warfare that began in the garden is intensified in the Fall. The Lord told the serpent, "I will put hostility between you and the woman, and between your offspring and her offspring" (Genesis 3:15). Our enemy is "the ancient serpent, who is called the devil and Satan, the one who deceives the whole world" (Revelation 12:9). Moreover, we have a collective enemy in his offspring, made up of those who are evil and don't submit to God: "Cain, who was of the evil one and murdered his brother" (1 John 3:12).

In general, Satan hates humans (God's image) because he hates God and wants to destroy him. In particular, Satan hates the "offspring of the woman" because that offspring will destroy him. "The Son of God was revealed for this purpose: to destroy the devil's works" (1 John 3:8). Collectively, the woman's offspring refers to all those who belong to God through the Son of God (see 3:9-10). "The God of peace will soon crush Satan under [their] feet" (Romans 16:20).

Spiritual warfare exposes and exploits our moral weakness (depravity). So weak are we in our fallen state that Satan is called "the ruler of this world" (John 12:31). God made humans to rule the earth. But, taking advantage of our weakness, Satan usurped our role.

We should not underestimate Satan's power and pervasive effort to destroy us. Before we're saved, we live "according to the ways of this world, according to the ruler of the power of the air, the spirit now working in the disobedient" (Ephesians 2:2). As God's people, we live the reality that "our struggle is not against flesh and blood, but against the rulers, against the authorities, against the cosmic powers of this darkness, against evil, spiritual forces in the heavens" (Ephesians 6:12). The only way we can "stand against the schemes of the devil" is to be "strengthened by the Lord and by his vast strength" (verses 10-11). The might needed to overcome our spiritual enemy isn't ours by nature. It's alien to us, belonging to God and coming from God to clothe us. We stand victorious only by faith in God's promised Son.[21] Apart from God's strength, we're utterly weak, unable to stand against our foe and overcome by him.

Consequence #7: Painful Labor

It's bad enough to be weakened by sin and the devil, but now we see that creation itself resists us. God summarized his purpose for humanity this way: "God blessed them, and God said to them, 'Be fruitful, multiply, fill the earth, and subdue it'" (Genesis 1:28). These tasks—multiplying and subduing the earth—were blessings. But as a consequence of sin, those tasks now feel like burdens. Creation—including our physical bodies and the earth itself—will resist our efforts to fill the world and subdue it.

God said to the woman, "I will intensify your labor pains; you will bear children with painful effort" (3:16). Filling the earth would now be an intense and painful effort. It certainly includes the pain of labor and delivery. In the grand scheme, it includes the new realities of infertility (which can have its source in the female or male body), miscarriage, stillbirth, the deaths of laboring mothers, and the heartbreak of rebellious children (like Cain). Childbearing won't be easy. It will be painful, frustrating, and feel futile at times.

Likewise, subduing the earth will be frustrating to the point of death. To the man, God said, "The ground is cursed because of you. You will eat from it by means of painful labor all the days of your life. It will produce thorns and thistles for you, and you will eat the plants of the field. You will eat bread by the sweat of your brow" (3:17-19).

No longer would they enjoy the pleasant task of working and keeping the garden in Eden. Outside the garden, the ground is cursed,

---

21. See 1 John 5:4; Revelation 12:11.

producing thorns and thistles that assault the farmer and choke out the crop. Food comes only through painful labor and sweat. Work won't be easy. It will be painful, frustrating, and seemingly futile.

These consequences reveal newfound weaknesses in our bodies. Cut off from the tree of life, exposed to harsh elements, and destined to die, human bodies no longer exist in the ideal conditions in which they were created. Weakened, they experience intense pain in the struggle to survive. Our corrupted, dying human bodies lack the strength to overcome the effects of the Fall.

Consequence #8: Decay and Death

All this weakness and suffering brings us to the final consequence God promised in the original prohibition—death. "You will eat bread by the sweat of your brow until you return to the ground, since you were taken from it. For you are dust, and you will return to dust" (Genesis 3:19). Adam and Eve, and all their descendants, would toil in pain and sweat every day of their lives until they returned to the dust from which they were made.

In the previous chapter, we considered the weakness of dust. Dust is lifeless in itself. Humans aren't merely made from dust; they *are* dust and return to dust. Due to sin, we humans are sentenced to death—and dust cannot make itself live.

Death, however, would not be instantaneous disintegration. Returning to dust, like working the soil and having children, would be painful. We're not merely born sinful; we're born dying. Every human body enters the world corrupted, in the process of decay. For some, it's the long, slow process of the body wearing out over eighty years. For others, this decay manifests in genetic abnormalities of various sorts, which may appear at birth or wait decades to show up. Some encounter the scourge of terminal disease or chronic pain. Most of us will experience the invasion of harmful viruses and germs, resulting in various degrees of illness or even death. Many will suffer mental illness in their lifetime, whether from genetics, traumatic experiences, or other causes. And after all that suffering, we die.

Consequence #9: Eternal Death

Physical death, however, isn't the end of the story. We know that "it is appointed for people to die once—and after this, judgment" (Hebrews 9:27). "For we must all appear before the judgment seat of Christ, so that each may be repaid for what he has done in the body, whether good or evil" (2 Corinthians 5:10). After physical death, there is another more significant and far more horrific death that awaits rebellious humans—God's eternal wrath. The prophet Daniel writes that the wicked will awake to "disgrace and eternal contempt" (12:2). And Jesus described hell as "the unquenchable fire," "where their worm does not die, and the fire is not quenched" (Mark 9:43-48). At the final judgment, the guilty will be thrown into "the second death, the lake of fire" (Revelation 20:14-15). We should not fear people who can kill us but God, "who has authority to throw people into hell after death" (Luke 12:5). The ultimate death is eternal separation from God's blessed presence to suffer under his wrath forever.

Because of sin, to quote the uncouth colloquialism, "life sucks, and then you die." Only it's worse than that. Apart from God's saving grace, life sucks, and then you die, and then you die again and never stop dying. We weak, sinful creatures cannot save ourselves from this fate.

Can it get any worse than all that? No, it can't. That means the only place we can go from here is up. And up we shall go! One more thing follows the Fall—not because of it so much as in spite of it. It's God's glorious, Satan-crushing, sin-forgiving, death-reversing saving grace. It's his message is good news, the best news—it doesn't get any better than this. (So, what are you waiting for? Turn the page already!)

CHAPTER 3

WEAKNESS IN THE PROMISE

He will strike your head, and you will strike his heel.

GENESIS 3:15

G rowing up, my two younger brothers and I had a knack for getting into trouble. I once asked my mother why my friends had
regular babysitters throughout their childhood but we had a revolving
door of different sitters. Apparently, she had trouble getting them to
come back after babysitting us once or twice. That probably explains
why I was babysitting my brothers the night the youngest one put
his head through the picture window.

Our television received a total of four broadcast channels. The
remote control was whichever person walked to the TV to adjust
the controls. Being the oldest and left in charge, I picked the chan-
nel and forbade the other two from changing it. "Don't even touch
it!" were my exact words.

My brothers, being younger and more foolish, didn't respect the
superior wisdom and authority of their eldest brother. The youngest
one darted to the TV and touched it. I sprang up and chased him
as he sprinted back to his seat. He moved so rapidly his momentum
carried him over the back of the couch, headfirst into the curtain that
covered a large plate-glass picture window. We heard the glass break

and opened the curtain to find a hole in the glass the exact size of his gigantic cranium (which was protected from harm by the thick curtain and his thick skull).

But now we had a problem: There was a hole in the picture window, and my parents were returning soon. I was responsible for what happened while they were away, so this needed to be solved, and quickly. Fortunately, being the oldest and wisest, I had a plan. I instructed my brothers to go find their wallets and piggy banks and bring back all the money they had. We would combine our life savings so that when our parents returned, we could explain what happened and present them with full payment for a new window. Everything would be fine. Nobody would get in trouble.

The benefit of your brother putting his head through a plate-glass window is that when you tell your parents what happened, they're immediately concerned about whether he's okay. That he was unscathed brought a sigh of relief. I seized that moment to explain that all was well—we had pooled our money to pay for the window. Then I presented them with a bag containing almost seven dollars in bills and change. Come to find out, picture windows cost more than seven dollars. Who knew?

Unfortunately, that incident would not be the last time I would attempt to fix a wrong in a woefully insufficient manner. I've spent a lifetime trying to cover up my sins with good works, external appearances, blame-shifting, and flat-out denial. It's something I inherited from my first parents—as did you.

In the last chapter, we observed the sinful delusion of self-sufficiency in Adam and Eve as it appeared in the organic underpants and their blame-shifting. In the end, they couldn't escape the consequences of sin through their efforts. Only God could provide redemption and restoration, which is why we read, "The LORD God made clothing from skins for the man and his wife, and he clothed them" (Genesis

3:21). The Lord provided a fitting covering for their sin and its consequences through the death of another.

THE PROMISE

The first promise of redemption in the Bible isn't made to God's people. Rather, it's made to God's enemy. His people are saved through the judgment of God's enemies—even when they're his enemies! The Lord pronounced his judgment on the serpent in Genesis 3:14:

> Because you have done this,
> you are cursed more than any livestock
> and more than any wild animal.
> You will move on your belly
> and eat dust all the days of your life.

For instigating this wickedness, the serpent was damned to utter humiliation all his days. If returning to dust meant death, he would eat death all his life without the possibility of redemption. But there was more in the next verse:

> I will put hostility between you and the woman,
> and between your offspring and her offspring.
> He will strike your head,
> and you will strike his heel.

The serpent's days would consist of relentless hostility with the woman he deceived. This warfare would pass down through their respective offspring.

The Hebrew word for *seed* translates to "offspring," which frequently refers to descendants. As in English, the word *seed* can represent a single seed ("a mustard seed") or a large group of seeds ("a bag of seed"). Throughout the Old Testament, this word will refer to both a singular figure and a family of descendants. In Genesis 3:15, *offspring* alludes to both.[1] Later in this chapter, we'll look at the family of descendants and how they wage warfare. But for now, we'll consider the singular "offspring of the woman."

The apex of the aforementioned hostility isn't a standoff between the serpent and the woman. Rather, the enmity culminates in a confrontation between the serpent and the woman's son. "He"—an individual male descendant—will strike the serpent's head. At the same time, the serpent will strike the son's heel. What's going on here? Imagine this scene:

> A mother sits outside the tent mending clothes and humming to herself as her young children play in the dirt at the edge of camp. She knows they'll need a bath later but hearing their laughter and squeals of joy is worth it.
>
> Suddenly it's silent. Then a low whine, the beginning of a scream, arises from her youngest. She looks up, and her heart stops. A few feet from her young ones is a large serpent. It raises its head in the air, agitated and ready to strike a toddler. There's nothing she can do. They're too far away. She can't make it in time.
>
> From seemingly out of nowhere, her teenage son steps between the serpent and her other children. There's a flash of motion too quick to take in, then a cloud of dust. When the air clears, she sees her teenage son standing with his heel on the serpent's head; its body is lifeless. Blood soaks into the surrounding earth. She breathes a sigh of relief. The serpent is dead, her children are saved.

1. Bruce K. Waltke, *Genesis: A Commentary* (Grand Rapids: Zondervan, 2001), 93.

As her son lifts his heel, she notices the serpent's head rising with it, attached to his foot. Then she understands what happened. She can't breathe. It's as though a sword has pierced through her very soul. At the moment her son's heel struck the serpent's head, the serpent struck his heel, driving in his fangs to deliver a lethal injection of venom.

Her son would not survive this. The serpent's death came about through her son's death. He had saved her offspring but only at the cost of his own life. He was pierced and died so that they could live.

That's what's happening in Genesis 3:15. It's not a matter of the serpent receiving a greater wound and the son receiving a lesser wound. They both deliver and receive a mortal strike. A man kills a serpent by striking its head with his heel. A serpent kills a man by striking his heel with its head. The death of the woman's son would bring an end to hostility between her and the serpent, between her offspring and the serpent's offspring. That's God's promise of redemption. That's our deliverance from the curse of death, from sin, and from the devil.

Where is weakness in the promise? It's staring us in the face. The reception of a mortal wound. Death. The promised Son enters into a conflict in which he not only can be wounded and killed, but he is. The ultimate weakness resulting from sin is death—and the Promised One receives death in his own flesh so that his brothers and sisters might live.

THE PROMISE REVEALED

In Genesis 3, the promise is delivered in a somewhat cryptic manner. We know that a man will arrive to defeat the serpent at the cost of his own life. We gather from the context that this act will bring an end to the hostility between the serpent and the woman, between its offspring and her offspring. It will remove the curse that followed the sin instigated by the serpent's temptation. We don't know much more than that—not yet anyway. But I don't want to make you read five more chapters to learn who this offspring is. I want to make that crystal clear right now.

This promised one is Jesus Christ, the Son of God. "When the time came to completion, God sent his Son, born of a woman" (Galatians 4:4). He's the "offspring of the woman" in a unique and miraculous manner. Indeed, conceived by the Holy Spirit and born of the virgin Mary, with no biological father, he's uniquely "offspring of the woman."[2] God is his true and ultimate Father.[3] Being the eternal second person of the Trinity (Father, Son, Holy Spirit), he's both fully God and fully man.[4]

Taking on human nature meant assuming human weakness. It's a rather stunning thought, isn't it? When we think of God coming to save us, weakness isn't the first thing that comes to mind. But that's the picture we get in Scripture. When Jesus arrived, he looked weak: "He didn't have an impressive form or majesty that we should look at him, no appearance that we should desire him" (Isaiah 53:2). That wasn't limited to external appearances.

Jesus actually took on the weakness of human nature and experienced a life of weakness: "He emptied himself by assuming the form of a servant, taking on the likeness of humanity" (Philippians 2:7). What's more, he died as a result of weakness, for "he was crucified in weakness" (2 Corinthians 13:4). That weakness is the revelation and completion of God's strength: "Christ is the power of God and the wisdom of God, because God's foolishness is wiser than human wisdom, and God's weakness is stronger than human strength"

---

2. See Matthew 1:20; Luke 1:30-33; Isaiah 7:14.

3. See Matthew 3:17; Luke 9:35.

4. See Philippians 2:5-7; Colossians 1:15-20.

(1 Corinthians 1:24-25). It's that weakness that conquers the power of sin, death, and the devil.

The truth is, Jesus came to destroy the devil's works.[5] He crushed the devil's head through his own death. In the final days of his earthly ministry, Jesus told the crowds, "Now the ruler of this world will be cast out. As for me, if I am lifted up from the earth I will draw all people to myself" (John 12:31-32). John tells us "he said this to indicate what kind of death he was about to die" (verse 33). Jesus was lifted up through crucifixion, pierced with nails that held him to the cross. Jesus crushed the serpent's head, receiving a mortal piercing resulting in his own death. And as a result, the ruler of the world (the devil) was defeated when Jesus died.

In a certain sense, Satan was operative in the events of the crucifixion. The devil "put it into the heart of Judas" to betray Jesus (13:2). Later "Satan entered Judas," setting in motion the betrayal, arrest, and trial of Jesus (Luke 22:3-6). Yet, ultimately, the ruler of the world had no power over Jesus (John 14:30), for Jesus would not die by the hand of Satan but by voluntarily laying down his own life.[6]

Explaining Jesus's death, the prophet Isaiah wrote that "the LORD was pleased to crush him severely" (Isaiah 53:10). God's wrath crushed Jesus. That's why Jesus cried out, "My God, my God, why have you abandoned me?" (Matthew 27:46). But why would the Father mortally strike his Son on the cross? Not because he was a sinner who deserved it. After all, Jesus "did not commit sin" (1 Peter 2:22). He was without sin (Hebrews 4:15). On the cross, Jesus was a sacrifice offered to pay for sin, for "Christ died for our sins according to the Scriptures" (1 Corinthians 15:3). That consisted of a glorious exchange: God "made the one who did not know sin to be sin for us, so that

---

5. See 1 John 3:8.
6. See John 10:15-18.

in him we might become the righteousness of God" (2 Corinthians 5:21). He received our sin and was counted as guilty so that we could receive his righteousness and be counted as righteous before God.

Our justification (being declared righteous) is a glorious gift for us—and a glorious gift for Jesus! Again, Isaiah writes:

> When you make him a guilt offering,
>   he will see his seed, he will prolong his days,
>   and by his hand, the LORD's pleasure will be accomplished.
> After his anguish,
>   he will see light and be satisfied.
> By his knowledge,
>   my righteous servant will justify many,
>   and he will carry their iniquities.
> Therefore I will give him the many as a portion,
>   and he will receive the mighty as spoil,
>   because he willingly submitted to death,
>   and was counted among the rebels;
> yet he bore the sin of many
>   and interceded for the rebels (53:10-12).

The first thing we notice is that after he dies, *he will see*, clearly indicating a resurrection from the dead. So, while the serpent is cursed to the dust, to die and never rise again, it's not so for the offspring of the woman. After dying, he'll live again. In his new life, he'll give eternal life to all his people.

After Jesus dies and rises, "he will see his seed." Here we find the concept of *offspring* (seed) central to the promise in Genesis 3. Only now, it's his offspring, which seems odd because Jesus fathered no biological children. But we soon learn that his *seed* is the *many* that he justifies (verse 11) and receives as a reward for his victory (verse

12). Jesus explained how he produced seed when he said, "Truly I tell you, unless a grain of wheat falls to the ground and dies, it remains by itself. But if it dies, it produces much fruit" (John 12:24).

So, here in the death and resurrection of Jesus Christ, the mystery of the woman's offspring is revealed and explained. On the cross, the (singular) seed falls to the ground and dies. But once buried in death, it rises to life and produces much seed. Jesus—the offspring of the woman—redeems and receives a glorious offspring through his death and resurrection.

That's how the promise is fulfilled: The redeeming power promised in the serpent-crushing son is brought to completion in the weakness of the cross. How should we respond to this incredibly good news?

THE PROMISE RECEIVED

When the Lord spoke of the coming Redeemer, he divided humanity into two camps: the serpent's offspring and the woman's offspring. Obviously, the serpent's offspring constitute God's enemies. Likewise, the woman's offspring constitute God's people, those aligned with Jesus Christ, the offspring of the woman. If we know what's good for us, we want to be counted among his number.

So, what does it mean to be counted among "the offspring of the woman"? Obviously, all humanity descends from Adam and Eve. Thus, in a biological sense, every human is her offspring. Yet, spiritually, not all are her offspring; some are the serpent's offspring.[7] Physical birth and natural descent aren't the determining factors for who does and does not belong to the offspring of the woman. So how does one become "the offspring of the woman"? We learn, as the story unfolds, it's through faith in God's promise.

---

7. See 1 John 3:10.

Adam's faith in God's promise is hinted at in Genesis 3:20: "The man named his wife Eve because she was the mother of all the living." Evidently, he believed that they would live and she would have children as God promised. Why else call her Eve (meaning *living* or *life*), "the mother of all the living"? Though Adam's faith is implied, it's the woman's faith that shines explicitly.

"The man was intimate with his wife Eve, and she conceived and gave birth to Cain" (Genesis 4:1). In response, Eve said, "I have had a male child with the Lord's help" (literally, with the Lord). Eve's response is noteworthy for several reasons. First, she acknowledges that the Lord gave her this child. Though we're told she conceived in the normal manner, she attributes her conception and the birth to the Lord's help.[8] Second, she notes it's a male child. Both of these observations connect to the promise—the Lord would bring redemption through the male offspring of the woman. Eve's statement reveals her faith that the Lord is keeping his promise.

Adam and Eve eventually had a second son, Abel. These brothers grew up and took on vocations. "Abel became a shepherd of flocks, but Cain worked the ground" (verse 2). At some point, both brothers presented offerings, portions of the fruit of their labors, to the Lord. "The Lord had regard for Abel and his offering, but he did not have regard for Cain and his offering" (verses 4-5). What made the difference? "By faith Abel offered to God a more acceptable sacrifice than Cain, through which he was commended as righteous, God commending him by accepting his gifts" (Hebrews 11:4 ESV).

Abel worshipped the Lord by faith. Cain did not. Abel is the offspring of the woman, not because he shares her DNA but because he shares her faith. Cain is not the offspring of the woman (despite

---

8. Her statement is the first recorded instance of a person calling God "the Lord" (*Yahweh*), the personal, covenantal name that is later revealed to Moses and Israel.

sharing her DNA), because he does not share her faith. Cain is one of "the devil's children," the offspring "of the evil one" (1 John 3:10, 12). Faith in God's saving promises is what makes one the offspring of the woman, while unbelief characterizes the offspring of the serpent. The closing of Genesis 4 drives home that truth.

Eve gave birth to another son and named him Seth, saying, "God has given me another offspring in place of Abel, since Cain killed him" (verse 25). That brief sentence is brimming with astute theological observation. Notice the word *offspring*—it's the same word used in the promise we've been examining. Eve recognizes that Seth is her offspring (the offspring of the woman). Not only that, but she sees that he's *another offspring*, a replacement for Abel. Why did she need another offspring in Abel's place? She still had Cain. Except she didn't—he wasn't her true offspring and she knew it. Abel was no longer her offspring because he was physically dead. Cain was no longer her offspring because he was spiritually dead. If the Lord was to keep his promise, he would need to give her another offspring. She recognized and received this son from him by faith.

Seth proved to be "another offspring," his mother's true son by faith. Seth had a son named Enosh, and "at that time people began to call on the name of the LORD" (verse 26).[9] That likely means that religious worship of the Lord first became an organized observance. Through Seth, faith in the Lord and in his promise was passed down—a faith that continues today in all who call upon Jesus. So, how does faith connect with weakness?

WHAT IS WEAK IN THE WORLD

Faith highlights the central role that weakness plays in our salvation. We'll see this throughout the Bible in the chapters that follow. We see it in two distinct ways in the story we've been examining.

---

9. In English translations LORD (in small caps) translates "Yahweh."

Faith highlights God's choice to display his strength through the weakness of his people.

Something unexpected happened in the story of Cain and Abel. Had we not been familiar with that story, we would read of Cain's birth and naturally conclude he was the promised offspring. The Lord promised a son to the woman. The next thing we know, she's having a son. It must be him—right? Besides, in an ancient Near Eastern culture (to which Moses wrote Genesis), favoring the firstborn son was expected. Culture aside, simply by virtue of his being older, we might expect him to have more experience, wisdom, and strength than his little brother. But that's not how God works.

From the very beginning, God flips human expectations of strength and advantage on their heads. He chooses the younger of the sons—and it's not the last time this will happen in the storyline of redemption. Not at all! Repeatedly, the Lord will choose the weaker, smaller, overlooked, and unexpected of men and women to receive his promise and carry along the lineage of the Redeemer. That continues today in those God calls to himself through faith in Jesus. The apostle Paul reminds his readers (and us) in 1 Corinthians 1:26-29:

> Brothers and sisters, consider your calling: Not many were wise from a human perspective, not many powerful, not many of noble birth. Instead, God has chosen what is foolish in the world to shame the wise, and God has chosen what is weak in the world to shame the strong. God has chosen what is insignificant and despised in the world—what is viewed as nothing—to bring to nothing what is viewed as something, so that no one may boast in his presence.

God intentionally chooses the weak to put the strong to shame. Why? Because the weaker the person that God chooses, the more his strength is put on display. When he saves the weak, it's obvious that they didn't save themselves. Therefore no one can boast about anything but him! We get his salvation. He gets the glory.

Faith is how we wage war against the serpent and his offspring.

In Cain and Abel, we saw not only the offspring of the serpent and the offspring of the woman but also the hostility the Lord promised between them. This enmity appeared immediately. Cain, furious and despondent, lured his brother out to the field where he attacked and killed him. That's how the serpent and his offspring wage war to this very day—through lies and murder. Jesus told a group of unbelieving Jews (who thought they were Abraham's children because they descended from him), "You are of your father the devil, and you want to carry out your father's desires. He was a murderer from the beginning and does not stand in the truth, because there is no truth in him" (John 8:44). If the serpent and his offspring wage war with lies, threats, and murder, how do we wage war as children of faith?

Peter warns believers, "Your adversary the devil is prowling around like a roaring lion, looking for anyone he can devour" (1 Peter 5:8). How are we to defend ourselves? "Resist him, firm in the faith, knowing that the same kind of sufferings are being experienced by your fellow believers throughout the world" (verse 9). We defend ourselves against the serpent's attacks not through physical prowess but by believing the gospel. Satan tempts us to believe that our afflictions are an indication that God has abandoned us. But *the faith*—the message of the gospel—tells us the truth. "The God of all grace, who called you to his eternal glory in Christ, will himself restore, establish, strengthen, and support you after you have suffered a little while" (verses 10-11). When we resist the devil by believing the gospel, he flees.[10]

---

10. See James 4:7.

The world and the devil battle through confidence in their own strength. If we don't believe that God has our back, then it's every man (or demon) for himself. If anyone threatens our power, wealth, or reputation, then they must die. We must lie, steal, murder, and destroy by whatever means necessary in lives characterized by hate and selfishness. But if we believe that God does have our back, then we don't have to fight as the world does. Because we know that Christ laid down his life for us, we're free to lay down our lives for our neighbor. We embrace weakness, freely surrendering our lives for one another, because we trust that God will raise and reward us in eternal glory.

Saving faith is weakness dressed in God's strength. We're "strengthened by the Lord and by his vast strength" (Ephesians 6:10). We "put on the full armor of God" so that we "can stand against the schemes of the devil" (verse 11). We do battle against cosmic power by standing in God's armor (verses 12-17). What is God's armor? The belt of truth—the true word of the promise fulfilled in Jesus. The armor of righteousness—the righteousness of Jesus that we receive by grace through faith. The sandals of the gospel of peace—the declaration that we have peace with God through Jesus crucified and risen. The shield of faith—our confidence that Christ has died for our sin and risen from the dead to make us his own regardless of what lies Satan tells. The helmet of salvation—no condemnation can fall on our head because Jesus died in our place. The sword of the Spirit, which is the word of God—the Scripture tells us the story of how God promised his Son and kept his promise. Every piece of armor is simply a facet of the single jewel that is the gospel of Jesus Christ, crucified for our sins and raised from the dead to forgive and redeem all those who trust in him.

Spiritual warfare—and victory in the battle—is nothing less (and nothing more) than faith in the person and work of Jesus Christ the promised Son. "Everyone who has been born of God conquers the world. This is the victory that has conquered the world: our faith.

Who is the one who conquers the world but the one who believes that Jesus is the Son of God?" (1 John 5:4-5). Yes, hear it again:

> The salvation and the power
> and the kingdom of our God
> and the authority of his Christ
> have now come,
> because the accuser of our brothers and sisters,
> who accuses them
> before our God day and night,
> has been thrown down.
> They conquered him
> by the blood of the Lamb
> and by the word of their testimony;
> for they did not love their lives
> to the point of death (Revelation 12:10-11).

Satan is thrown down and conquered by Christ's blood and our testimony of faith in him. Yes, believer, "the God of peace will soon crush Satan under your feet" (Romans 16:20). So we say with all the saints, "Thanks be to God, who gives us the victory through our Lord Jesus Christ!" (1 Corinthians 15:57).

Friend, if you feel too weak to be saved, I have good news for you. Even better, God has good news for you: He only saves the weak. That's what he asks of you—to confess your weakness: your sin, your guilt, your inability to save yourself. He calls you to see the strength he has supplied in the weakness of Christ crucified. Jesus, insignificant and despised in the world, has become our righteousness, sanctification, and redemption.[11] We're called to humble ourselves and boast in Christ alone.

---

11. See 1 Corinthians 1:26-31.

CHAPTER 4

WEAKNESS IN ISRAEL'S HISTORY

"Not by strength or by might, but by my Spirit," says the LORD *of Armies.*

ZECHARIAH 4:6

If you ask me what I remember from two years of high school Spanish classes, it's this command: *"¡Siéntate!* Sit down!" I remember that word because our teacher said it multiple times in every class for two years. Some members of our class had trouble staying in their seats, opting instead to get up, roam about the room, and cause trouble. (Not me, of course, as you've probably gathered that I was a perfect child that never got into any trouble at all.) Because ~~we~~ they were so frequently out of ~~our~~ their seats, she was always telling ~~us~~ them, *"¡Siéntate!* Sit down!" She had to make her point over and over because ~~we~~ they never seemed to get it. (That's the problem with giving commands in Spanish to Spanish students who aren't paying attention to the Spanish lessons…) Ironically, because of the repetition, I now understand what *siéntate* means!

The Old Testament story is a lot like my high school Spanish class. The same point is shouted at us over and over because God's people just couldn't seem to get it right. Only this time, the command isn't

"Sit down!" Instead, it's "Trust in the Lord!" In Genesis 3, the Lord promised a Redeemer. The rest of Scripture is about God keeping that promise—and calling a people to trust him to do so.

Far too often, we make the Bible more complicated than it needs to be. Instead of searching for hidden codes or settling for surface-level moral examples, we should read it as a single, unified story that began in Genesis 1–3. The key to understanding the Old Testament is to "follow the offspring," paying close attention to the family line that the Scripture highlights, noting the progressively revealed information about who the Savior will be. With every figure that appears, we should ask, "Is this him?" At every turn in the story, we should ask, "Where's the Promised One? Is he here yet?"

To help us see the point, we're going to take a 40,000-foot flight over Old Testament history, beginning with Abraham. We can't cover every detail in the story. That would take a whole series of books! But, since the focus of our exploration is the place of weakness in God's plan of redemption, we'll keep asking, "How does weakness show up here?" As your tour guide, I'll point out the major landmarks in the storyline. We'll see again and again that the Lord calls his people to embrace their weakness, look to his strength, and trust him to save them as he promised. So, *siéntate*, put up your feet, and enjoy your flight!

ABRAHAM

In Genesis 12, the story focuses on Abram and his wife Sarai (later renamed Abraham and Sarah). The Lord appeared to Abram, commanding him to leave his father's house and go to the land God would show him, promising to bless him and make him the father of a great nation that would bring blessing to all the people of the earth.[1]

---

1. See Genesis 12:2-3.

When Abram arrived in Canaan, the Lord appeared to him and said, "To your offspring I will give this land" (verse 7). He later told him, "I will give you and your offspring forever all the land that you see. I will make your offspring like the dust of the earth, so that if anyone could count the dust of the earth, then your offspring could be counted" (13:15-16). Did you catch all that? It's all there, the stuff of the promise in Genesis 3: Promised offspring. Blessing. Relief from the curse. Life in the land—forever. We are right if we suspect God's saving promises are coming to fruition in Abram's offspring. But it seems there's a catch.

One night, the Lord spoke to Abram in a vision: "Do not be afraid, Abram. I am your shield; your reward will be very great" (15:1). But Abram questioned whether the Lord could reward him: "Look, you have given me no offspring, so a slave born in my house will be my heir" (verse 3). Abram understood his weakness as an elderly, childless man with a barren old wife. God promised him uncountable offspring inhabiting the Promised Land forever. At this point, however, God hadn't given him even one offspring—and that seemed impossible. But the Lord insisted, "One who comes from your own body will be your heir" (verse 4). He took Abram outside and told him to count the stars, insisting that his physical, biological offspring would be that numerous.

Then we read, "Abraham believed the LORD, and he credited it to him as righteousness" (verse 6). Righteousness signifies conformity to a covenant and its instruction. To be righteous is to have a right standing in the eyes of the law. The Lord counted Abram's belief—his confidence that the Lord would keep his promise—as righteousness. Seeing Abram's faith, the Lord replied, "I am the LORD who brought you from Ur of the Chaldeans to give you this land to possess" (verse 7). That's a strange word of reassurance. The Lord doesn't directly say, "Here's what I'll do." He says, "Here's who I am." The

Lord pulled Abram's eyes off his childless, aged flesh. His weak body wasn't the source of his salvation. God wanted Abram to look at him, the Lord, who was all he needed to be assured of the promise.

When Abram responded, "Lord GOD, how can I know that I will possess it?" the Lord instructed him to gather animals, cut them in half, and lay the pieces opposite one another (verses 8-10). When two parties entered a covenant, they did this and walked together through the middle of the divided animals. It signified the solemnness of the agreement, each party essentially saying, "Let this be done to me if I do not keep my covenant promises."

Only now, the Lord didn't walk through the pieces with Abram. Instead, a deep sleep came over Abram. In the darkness, the Lord reiterated his promises to Abram, then "a smoking fire pot and a flaming torch appeared and passed between the divided animals" (verse 17). The Lord assumed the place of both parties to the covenant, indicating that he would keep every aspect of the covenant. While Abram slept, the Lord did all the work. This covenant didn't depend on Abram's works or strength. It was a covenant of God's grace, which Abram entered into and received by faith.

Where is weakness?

God's choice of Abram highlights weakness at every turn. When the Lord called Abram, he lived in Ur and worshipped other false gods. Moreover, he and his wife, Sarai, were childless and elderly. An old, childless pagan with an old, barren wife isn't exactly the number-one draft pick when it comes to parents-of-the-promised-offspring candidates. Why would God choose such a weak man to receive this promise?

The Lord chose a specimen of weakness to display his power as "the one who gives life to the dead and calls things into existence that do not exist" (Romans 4:17). In Abraham, the Lord reveals where true strength is found—not in the flesh, but through faith:

He did not weaken in faith when he considered his own body to be already dead (since he was about a hundred years old) and also the deadness of Sarah's womb. He did not waver in unbelief at God's promise but was strengthened in his faith and gave glory to God, because he was fully convinced that what God had promised, he was also able to do. Therefore, it was credited to him for righteousness (Romans 4:19-22).

That's how we are saved: "Now 'it was credited to him' was not written for Abraham alone, but also for us. It will be credited to us who believe in him who raised Jesus our Lord from the dead. He was delivered up for our trespasses and raised for our justification" (verses 23-25).

ISAAC

The first thing we read after God vowed to give Abram offspring from his own body is this: "Abram's wife, Sarai, had not borne any children for him" (Genesis 16:1). Nevertheless, she had a plan. Sarai told her husband, "Since the LORD has prevented me from bearing children, go to my slave; perhaps through her I can build a family" (verse 2). Abram did what his wife told him. His firstborn son, Ishmael, came through Sarai's slave Hagar.

After this incident, the Lord appeared to Abraham again, reiterating everything he'd promised, emphasizing that Abraham would have a son with Sarah. Hearing this, Abraham fell on his face laughing: "Can a child be born to a hundred-year-old man? Can Sarah, a ninety-year-old woman, give birth?" (17:17). Sarah responded the same way. But the Lord's answer remained the same: "Is anything impossible for the LORD?" (18:13-14). Eventually, as the Lord promised, they had a son, whom they named Isaac. As with Cain and Abel (and Seth), the *offspring* wasn't the culturally expected firstborn but the one connected with faith and God's promise.

Where is weakness?

Sarai said to Abram, "Since the LORD has prevented me from bearing children, go to my slave; perhaps through her I can build a family" (Genesis 16:2). Sarai rightly believed the Lord prevented her from conceiving (the power to give conception is in his hands!). Yet she didn't believe he would give her a child. Sarai's confidence was in herself: "I can build a family." She believed that she could build a family without the Lord's help. Ultimately, she doubted God's promise and trusted her own strength. The Lord reminds them (and us) that faith is hoping in the Lord's power to keep his promise, even in the face of our own absolute weakness.

JACOB (ISRAEL)

Like Abraham, Isaac also had two sons—twins, Esau and Jacob. The promises and the lineage of the promised Redeemer would pass through the young brother, Jacob, later renamed Israel, who fathered the twelve tribes that became the nation of Israel.

Where is weakness?

"Isaac prayed to the LORD on behalf of his wife because she was childless. The LORD was receptive to his prayer, and his wife Rebekah conceived" (Genesis 25:21). Like Sarah, Rebekah was childless. Like Eve, Rebekah had sons with the help of the Lord, who responded to Isaac's faith (prayer). Thus, Jacob isn't the product of strength (fecundity) but of God's strength perfected in weakness (infertility).

When Rebekah's twin boys wrestled with each other in the womb, she asked the Lord, "Why is this happening to me?" (verse 22). He replied, "Two nations are in your womb; two peoples will come from you and be separated. One people will be stronger than the other, and the older will serve the younger" (verse 23). From her sons, Esau and Jacob, would come the nations of Edom and Israel, respectively. Like the brothers, these peoples would wrestle. But one nation (Israel) would be stronger than the other (Edom), such that "the older will serve the younger."

Though Jacob's offspring would be stronger than Esau's, we should not take it to mean that God's purposes are accomplished by means of human strength. Quite the opposite: Jacob's offspring prevailed not by Israel's greatness but by God's choice. The Lord chose Jacob and his offspring when he was a weak baby in his mother's womb. "For though her sons had not been born yet or done anything good or bad, so that God's purpose according to election might stand—not from works but from the one who calls—she was told, 'The older will serve the younger'" (Romans 9:11-12). As with Abraham, Jacob's election showcases the Lord's power.

From birth into adulthood, Jacob was the weaker brother. Esau modeled traditional masculinity, "covered with hair like a fur coat" and "an expert hunter, an outdoorsman" (Genesis 25:25, 27). He was his father's favorite because Isaac enjoyed eating the wild game he prepared. Jacob, on the other hand, "was a quiet man who stayed at home" (verse 27), his mother's favorite. These twin brothers—a man's man and a mama's boy—couldn't be more different.

If you had to wager on who would produce a nation that rules the other, you'd bet on the hairy hunter who is skilled at killing things. If you had to guess which son would inherit the promises given to his father, you'd pick the firstborn, the favorite son. Esau is a natural choice because he embodies worldly strength and advantage. But, if you've been reading the Bible, you might go with the younger, weaker of the two—Jacob. And you would be right. The "offspring of the woman" is, so to speak, the mother's son.

Through exploitation and deception, Jacob stole his brother's birthright and blessing. But even here, we should not conclude that Jacob prevailed by the strength of shrewdness and cunning behavior. He didn't need to exploit his brother's vulnerability or deceive Isaac to inherit the promises. The Lord promised the blessing to Jacob while he was in Rebekah's womb—and told Rebekah! Their unethical behavior sprang from unbelief. Unwilling to trust the Lord to do what he said, they sought to gain the blessing through the strength of human scheming. The Lord made no mention of these events when he appeared to Jacob at Bethel, telling him that the covenant promises belonged to his offspring. God's covenant promises are neither earned nor captured by human strength. They are gifts of grace given to weak people.

After much conflict between Jacob and Esau (and their respective families), the day came for them to meet. Jacob feared how Esau would receive him. At stake was God's promise: Would the older serve the younger—or would he destroy him? The night before their meeting, a man attacked Jacob and wrestled with him all night. During this encounter, the stranger spoke to Jacob. "Your name will no longer be Jacob," he told him. "It will be Israel because you have struggled with God and with men and have prevailed" (Genesis 32:28). These words and the blessing to follow reinforced that God's promise would stand; Esau would not prevail over Jacob. Though the stranger would not reveal his name, Jacob understood that it was the Lord.

There is a sentence in this story that should give us pause: "When the man saw that he could not defeat him, he struck Jacob's hip socket as they wrestled and dislocated his hip" (verse 25). Does that mean Jacob prevailed by his own strength, that he was the Lord's equal? Not at all. At every turn in the encounter, the Lord had the position of strength over Jacob. Yes, Jacob must have possessed remarkable physical strength and endurance to struggle all night (no doubt gained by years of hard shepherding). Yet, when his opponent decided it was time to be done, he simply struck and debilitated Jacob, giving the impression he could have done this at any time. The Lord could wrest Jacob's name from him, but Jacob could not force his opponent to reveal his identity. Jacob's summary of the event indicates he understood that he didn't prevail in human strength: "'I have seen God face to face,' he said, 'yet my life has been spared.'" (verse 30). He was spared—the Lord showed him mercy. So now the question is, why did the Lord present himself as a figure who could not defeat Jacob? What is he teaching us?

> Here the paradox of the human condition is vividly summed up. On the one hand, God allows, even puts his people into, difficult or impossible situations, but it is the same God who delivers us from them... This experience of Jacob at the Jabbok summed up his career. It was God who had brought him to this crisis situation, confronting Esau, but it was the same God who would bring him through victoriously.[2]

Jacob prevailed and would prevail, not by his own strength but by God's grace.

ISRAEL (THE NATION)

When he was about seventy-eight, Jacob married sisters Leah and Rachel. The Lord "opened" Leah's womb first, while Rachel remained unable to conceive (Genesis 29:31). Leah gave birth to four sons—Reuben, Simeon, Levi, and Judah—before she stopped having children (verses 32-35). Jealous of her sister, Rachel gave her slave Bilhah to Jacob as a wife. Bilhah gave birth to two sons, Dan and Naphtali

---

2. Gordon J. Wenham, "Genesis," in *New Bible Commentary: 21st Century Edition*, ed. D.A. Carson et al., 4th ed. (Leicester, UK; Downers Grove, IL: InterVarsity Press, 1994), 82.

(30:1-8). Unable to have more children, Leah gave her slave Zilpah to Jacob as a wife, and Zilpah bore sons Gad and Asher (verses 9-13). Then, through a bitter and bizarre encounter that involved buying sex with mandrakes, Leah gave birth to a son, Issachar, followed by their son Zebulun and daughter Dinah (verses 14-21). Finally, "God remembered Rachel" and opened her womb, and she gave birth to Joseph (verses 22-24). Later, after a difficult labor, Rachel gave birth to another son, whom she named Ben-oni with her dying breath— Jacob called him Benjamin (35:16-20).

By means of famine and miraculous intervention, Jacob's household ended up in Egypt, where they numbered only seventy persons. They found reception and kindness in Egypt through the intervention of Rachel's son Joseph, whose brothers had sold him to slave traders. After the twelve sons all died, the Lord kept his promise to Abraham, Isaac, and Jacob and made their offspring into a great nation that none could count. In Egypt, by God's favor, "the Israelites were fruitful, increased rapidly, multiplied, and became extremely numerous so that the land was filled with them" (Exodus 1:7). The twelve tribes bearing their fathers' names now constituted the nation bearing the (new) name of their father—Israel.

Where is weakness?

The twelve tribes of Israel, as far back as Israel's twelve sons, have their origin in weakness. Like Sarah and Rebekah before them, both Leah and Rachel experienced the weakness of barrenness. What's the deal with infertility in the storyline anyway? Jacob revealed the point when he lashed out at Rachel, "Am I in the place of God? He has withheld offspring from you!" (Genesis 30:2). God is the one who promised "the offspring of the woman." The power to produce offspring—whether to fill the earth or to fulfill the promise—does not reside in humans. God alone has the power to bring about his promise of redemption. Infertility is a powerful and obvious display of that truth. Like Eve, Sarah, and Rebekah, these women bore male offspring with the Lord's help.[3] Infertility is a painful yet potent gift of weakness in and through which God puts his power into full display.

Jacob's twelve sons shared the moral weakness of their father (and mothers). They were conceived in situations involving polygamy, an unloved wife, jealousy, envy, bitterness, anger, sex with slaves, and exchanging mandrakes to procure conjugal privileges. The boys grew into men who shared the same proclivity toward envy and hatred. They plotted to kill their brother Joseph and cover up the murder, only to settle on selling him to slave traders, who took him to Egypt. If you're looking for a family in the Bible that merits God's blessing on the basis of their righteousness, it's not this one. The only thing they've earned is their own cringeworthy reality TV show.

When famine struck and threatened to end Israel, the line of the offspring was saved through an unlikely hero who arose from places of weakness. Joseph was raised from a cistern tomb to become Israel's savior—the slave became second in command, ascending from the dungeon to be the deliverer. This is the weakness in which God displayed his saving power, the weakness of the seed of the woman: An unwanted brother, sold for coins, falsely accused, forgotten, and left for dead, was raised up by God to reign over his enemies and his family.

EGYPTIAN SLAVERY AND THE EXODUS

Israel arrived in Egypt a puny nation. But after Joseph and all that generation died, "the Israelites were fruitful, increased rapidly, multiplied, and became extremely numerous so that the land was filled with them" (Exodus 1:7). This concerned the new king, who saw that the Israelites were "more numerous and powerful" than the Egyptians

---

3. See Genesis 29:31; 30:17, 22; cf 4:1, 25.

(verse 9). So he launched a population-control initiative. Phase one involved enslaving the Israelites. It failed: "The more they oppressed them, the more they multiplied and spread so that the Egyptians came to dread the Israelites" (verse 12). Phase two was infanticide; the king of Egypt commanded the Hebrew midwives to kill every Hebrew son upon delivery. When the Hebrew midwives (who feared God) let the boys live, Pharaoh commanded all his people to throw every newborn Hebrew son into the Nile. This, too, failed in dramatic fashion. Pharaoh's own daughter received a Hebrew boy out of the Nile and brought him into her home as her adopted son, naming him Moses.[4]

Though the Egyptian oppression didn't slow the multiplication of the Hebrews, it did make their lives bitter. So the Israelites groaned and cried out for help. "God heard their groaning, and God remembered his covenant with Abraham, with Isaac, and with Jacob. God saw the Israelites, and God knew" (Exodus 2:24-25). In response, the Lord called Moses to lead his people out of Egypt. When Pharaoh refused to release the Israelites, the Lord sent plagues to afflict the Egyptians, which culminated in the death of every firstborn in the land. The Israelites were spared through the Passover meal at which each household slaughtered a lamb, painted its blood on their doorposts, and ate its meat for dinner with unleavened bread. After the final plague, Pharaoh released the Israelites, who plundered Egypt's wealth as they left on foot. But Pharaoh quickly regretted freeing the Israelites. He and his army soon caught up with the Israelites, who were camped at the edge of the Red Sea. The Lord famously parted the sea, allowing his people a way of escape. When Pharaoh's army pursued them, the Lord closed the sea and drowned them while Israel watched from the opposite shore.[5]

---

4. For these events, see Exodus 1–2.

5. For these events, see Exodus 3–15.

Where is weakness?

Moses's narration of the Exodus event ends with these words: "When Israel saw the great power that the LORD used against the Egyptians, the people feared the LORD and believed in him and in his servant Moses" (14:31). Then Moses and the Israelites sang a song to the Lord, recounting his deeds. Its main point is "The LORD is my strength and my song; he has become my salvation" (15:2). The purpose of the Exodus story is to showcase the Lord's strength.

Exodus opens with the king observing that the Israelites were more "powerful" than the Egyptians. We might expect the more powerful nation to rise up and free itself. Yet at no point was Israel's size or strength the source of their salvation. Despite Israel's greater strength, they remained unable to free themselves. They groaned and cried out for deliverance. Salvation had to come from outside them.

The plan of the powerful, unnamed king was thwarted by two named women—Shiphrah and Puah—and other midwives like them who feared the Lord. Israel didn't multiply by natural fertility but by the power of God's goodness.[6]

The Lord defeated Pharaoh (a god to the Egyptians) through Moses, a model of human weakness. Though he killed an Egyptian for beating a Hebrew, Moses didn't free the people by becoming a warrior. Rather, he reluctantly became the mouthpiece of the Lord who "is a warrior" (15:3). Even as a spokesman, Moses wasn't a naturally strong speaker; his mouth and tongue were so sluggish that the Lord appointed Aaron to be "a mouth" for him (4:10-16). Though weak in speech, the Lord made Moses—a slave's child—"like God to Pharaoh" (7:1).

The Israelites left Egypt in military formation,[7] but this army didn't prevail in human strength. They plundered Egypt without

---

6. See Exodus 1:15-21.
7. See Exodus 14:41.

lifting a finger, simply asking for Egypt's wealth.[8] The Israelites knew their weakness compared to Pharaoh's army. They needed to be saved from the power of the Egyptians, which is why they were terrified when they saw Pharaoh's army approaching.[9] Moses didn't comfort the Israelites by telling them how strong they were but instead said, "Don't be afraid. Stand firm and see the LORD's salvation that he will accomplish for you today; for the Egyptians you see today, you will never see again. The LORD will fight for you, and you must be quiet" (14:13-14). The Lord would do all the fighting; they only had to be quiet and watch him work.

THE WILDERNESS WANDERING

After the Exodus, the Lord led the Israelites through "the great and terrible wilderness with its poisonous snakes and scorpions, a thirsty land where there was no water" (Deuteronomy 8:15). During their first year and a half, the Lord gave them water from a rock, manna from heaven, quail from the sky, and the Law from Mount Sinai. Then he commanded Moses to send men, one from each of the tribes, to scout out the land of Canaan. When they returned, they reported that the land was abundantly fruitful and the inhabitants incredibly strong. Caleb, one of the scouts, encouraged the people to go immediately and take the land. The others objected, saying they seemed like grasshoppers compared to the giant inhabitants.[10]

The negative report so frightened the Israelites that they refused to enter the land. They threatened to stone Caleb and Joshua for encouraging them not to be afraid. That unbelief provoked the Lord's judgment. He killed the unbelieving scouts, declared that the nation would wander the wilderness for forty years until the unbelieving

---

8. See Exodus 12:35-36; 3:22; 11:2.
9. See Exodus 14:10-12, 30.
10. For these events, see Numbers 13.

generation died (except for Joshua and Caleb), and let the Israelites suffer a brutal military defeat.[11] The Israelites would go on to spend forty years in the wilderness.[12]

Where is weakness?

Weakness first appears in the Israelites' inability to keep themselves alive. A land without water is a land without life—especially for a nation numbering in the millions. Without water, you cannot live long, not to mention grow crops or raise livestock. If they lived, it would be by God's provision, which Moses emphasized at the end of their wanderings: "He humbled you by letting you go hungry; then he gave you manna to eat…so that you might learn that man does not live on bread alone but on every word that comes from the mouth of the LORD" (Deuteronomy 8:3). The Lord brought the Israelites through the wilderness to teach them to confess their weakness and to live by faith in God's promise. The Lord taught them that lesson in the wilderness because it would be necessary for their survival in paradise.

> He fed you in the wilderness with manna…in order to humble and test you, so that in the end he might cause you to prosper. You may say to yourself, "My power and my own ability have gained this wealth for me," but remember that the LORD your God gives you the power to gain wealth, in order to confirm his covenant he swore to your ancestors, as it is today (verses 16-18).

In the Promised Land, the Israelites would be tempted to trust their own strength: "My power and my own ability have gained this

---

11. For these events, see Numbers 14.

12. See Exodus 15–40; Leviticus; Numbers; Deuteronomy.

wealth for me." They must remember that "God gives you the power to gain wealth." Moses warned that if they forgot their weakness—if they forgot the Lord—they would "certainly perish" (verse 19). We are weak; the Lord is strong—salvation always depends on embracing those two truths.

Weakness also appears in the report of the unbelieving scouts: "We can't attack the people because they are stronger than we are!" (Numbers 13:31). They judged their ability to take the land by human strength. Ultimately, such a perspective believes that the Lord is weak—"Why is the LORD bringing us into this land to die by the sword?" (14:3) That implies the Lord's ability to fulfill his promises depends on human strength: If they were weaker than the Canaanites, the Lord could not keep them from dying. A god who depends on the strength of his creatures is a weak god. But that's not Yahweh—with him, the salvation of his weak people depends entirely on his strength.

ENTERING THE PROMISED LAND

After Moses died, the Lord called Joshua to prepare the Israelites to enter the Promised Land. Under Joshua's leadership, the twelve tribes passed through the Jordan River (which the Lord parted) and progressively took possession of the land. Then Joshua oversaw the allotment of the land to the tribes and the establishment of important cities. Finally, Israel had rest in the land. "None of the good promises the LORD had made to the house of Israel failed. Everything was fulfilled" (Joshua 21:45). After bidding the nation farewell and reviewing its history, Joshua exhorted the people to remain faithful to the Lord and then died.

Where is weakness?

It's tempting to believe that weakness isn't a major theme in the book of Joshua, as the central command to Joshua is *be strong* (not *be weak*):

Be strong and courageous, for you will distribute the land
I swore to their ancestors to give them as an inheritance.
Above all, **be strong** and very courageous to observe carefully
the whole instruction my servant Moses commanded you.
Do not turn from it to the right or the left, so that you
will have success wherever you go. This book of instruction
must not depart from your mouth; you are to meditate on it
day and night so that you may carefully observe everything
written in it. For then you will prosper and succeed in
whatever you do. Haven't I commanded you: **be strong**
and courageous? Do not be afraid or discouraged, for the
Lord your God is with you wherever you go (Joshua 1:6-
9, emphasis added).

We're helped by noting what it means to *be strong* and what cer-
tainties motivate it.

The motivating certainty undergirding the command is the Lord's
presence to give Joshua victory and the Israelites the land. Notice
how the passage quoted above is bookended by the Lord's promise
and presence. It opens: "Be strong and courageous, for you will distribute the land I swore to their ancestors to give them as an inheritance." Joshua could be courageous in taking the land because the
Lord swore it would happen. Likewise, Joshua did not need to be
afraid of failure, because the Lord would be with him. The section
closes: "Do not be afraid or discouraged, for the Lord your God is
with you wherever you go." These same ideas appear in the Lord's
opening words, preceding these commands:

Moses my servant is dead. Now you and all the people
prepare to cross over the Jordan to **the land I am giving
the Israelites**. **I have given** you every place where the sole

of your foot treads, **just as I promised** Moses. Your territory
will be from the wilderness and Lebanon to the great river,
the Euphrates River—all the land of the Hittites—and west
to the Mediterranean Sea. No one will be able to stand
against you as long as you live. **I will be with you**, just as
I was with Moses. **I will not leave you or abandon you**
(verses 2-5, emphasis added).

The Israelites would succeed in possessing the land because the
Lord was giving it to them. His promise and his presence guaranteed
that no enemy could stand against them.

It's one thing for a coach to exhort a wrestler to be strong and
courageous because the athlete has disciplined himself in practice,
followed a strength-training regimen, possesses mental toughness,
and has mastered the art of wrestling. The athlete himself is strong;
therefore, the coach commands him to be what he is. But the Lord's
command to Joshua (and to Israel) was another thing altogether.
The Lord did not exhort Joshua to be strong and courageous because
Joshua was a strong man (or because Israel was a strong nation). No,
the Lord commanded Joshua to be strong because the Lord (who is
strong) was with him and would give him success. Strength wasn't
Joshua's inherently. Strength belongs to the Lord alone, and Joshua
could be strong only by knowing and trusting that the Lord was
present to do the work.

We should also notice the manner in which Joshua was to be
strong. The Lord did not tell him to be strong and courageous in
waging war or when fighting as a soldier. No, he said, "Above all, be
strong and very courageous to observe carefully the whole instruction my servant Moses commanded you" (1:7). *Above all*—the most
important way in which this command is to be obeyed is that Joshua
was to be strong and courageous to obey the Lord. As we've seen,

obedience is the fruit of faith. To obey God's commands is to confess one's own weakness: "In and of myself, I do not possess either the wisdom to know what is best or the power to make it happen. Wisdom and power belong to the Lord alone. Therefore, because I trust his wisdom and strength, I will keep his commands even when the external circumstances suggest doing so will lead to failure." As in the wilderness, so in the Promised Land, it would often be the case that following God's commands looked like weakness in the eyes of human counselors. The Lord would ask his people to adopt a weak approach—and, in that context, the Lord's power would be showcased in their weakness.

God's power perfected in weakness is illustrated immediately in the conquest of Jericho. Jericho was a strongly fortified city (6:1). That suggests overtaking the city would require strategical prowess and military might. But man's strongest fortifications are no match for the Lord, who told Joshua, "Look, I have handed Jericho, its king, and its best soldiers over to you" (verse 2). Jericho's best soldiers are no more than toy soldiers in the Lord's hand. How will Joshua triumph—by siegeworks at the walls and a battering ram at the gate? Think again. The Lord gave Joshua what must have seemed the most bizarre military strategy he'd ever encountered:

> March around the city with all the men of war, circling the city one time. Do this for six days. Have seven priests carry seven ram's-horn trumpets in front of the ark. But on the seventh day, march around the city seven times, while the priests blow the rams' horns. When there is a prolonged blast of the horn and you hear its sound, have all the troops give a mighty shout. Then the city wall will collapse, and the troops will advance, each man straight ahead (6:3-5).

What would any other military general think of this strategy? Seven priests marching around a city blowing shofars is no basis for a system of conquest. Supreme military power derives from a military that is massive, not from some farcical ark-bearing ceremony. You can't expect to wield supreme military power over a city just because some walking troops shout at it. I mean, if I went around saying I could conquer cities just by having meandering bishops blow a shofar at it, they'd put me away!

Why would the Lord ordain an approach to conquest that appears so weak? Yes, the plan looked weak. But when executed, God's power was on full display. The wall collapsed, and the soldiers advanced into the city and captured it without a hitch. Contrary to the popular spiritual, Joshua did not fight the battle of Jericho. The Lord did—that's the point of the story, a point Israel failed to grasp.

The Lord commanded the Israelites to destroy the entire city. They weren't to take anything from the city; it was all set apart for the Lord. This, too, seemed a weak strategy in human terms. Jericho would have contained much in terms of wealth, food, clothing, weaponry, animals, and people for slaves. Plundering the city offered the opportunity to materially strengthen Israel. Leaving it behind required the Israelites to believe that their strength didn't lie in material wealth but in the Lord alone.

Unfortunately, a man named Achan failed to trust the Lord and took some of the spoils—a beautiful cloak, five pounds of silver, and a bar of gold (7:21). His sin provoked the Lord's anger, resulting in Israel's defeat at the city of Ai. Ai was significantly smaller than Jericho, so scouts advised, "Don't send all the people, but send about two thousand or three thousand men to attack Ai. Since the people of Ai are so few, don't wear out all our people there" (verse 3). Notice the scouts' perspective: They judged their prospects by human standards of strength. But instead of winning, the Israelite soldiers fled the battlefield. Thus, human measurements of strength and weakness mean nothing if the Lord isn't on your side. But once Israel repented, the Lord sent Joshua back, saying, "Look, I have handed over to you the king of Ai, his people, city, and land" (8:1). They would destroy Ai as they had Jericho—not because Ai was weak and they were strong, but because the Lord gave it to them.

When Joshua bade farewell to the people, he drove home the necessity of living by faith in God's strength. "I am old, advanced in age, and you have seen for yourselves everything the LORD your God did to all these nations on your account, because it was the LORD your God who was fighting for you" (23:2-3). All those military victories? God did it—the Lord was fighting for them. Notice in chapter 24 the emphases in the Lord's recounting of Israel's history from Abraham to the present (emphasis added):

- "**I took** your father Abraham...and **[I] multiplied** his descendants" (verse 3).

- "**I gave** him Isaac, and to Isaac **I gave** Jacob and Esau" (verse 3-4).

- "**I sent** Moses and Aaron, and **I defeated** Egypt by **what I did** within it, and afterward **I brought** you out" (verse 5).

- "Your own eyes saw **what I did** to Egypt" (verse 7).

- "**I brought** you to the land of the Amorites...They fought against you, but **I handed them over** to you. You possessed their land, and **I annihilated** them" (verse 8).

- "Jericho's citizens—as well as the Amorites, Perizzites, Canaanites, Hethites, Girgashites, Hivites, and Jebusites—fought against you, but **I handed them over**" (verse 11).

- "**I sent** hornets ahead of you, and they drove out the two Amorite kings before you" (verse 12).

The Lord repeatedly emphasized that he did all of it; it wasn't by their own strength: "It was **not** by your sword or bow" (verse 12). "**I gave** you a land **you did not labor** for, and cities **you did not build**, though you live in them; you are eating from vineyards and olive groves **you did not plant**" (verse 13).

Joshua wanted Israel to understand that point, because if they forgot the Lord, the Lord would abandon, harm, and completely destroy them (verse 20). In doing so, he drew attention to Israel's spiritual weakness: "You will not be able to worship the LORD" (verse 19). Israel's future would demonstrate that reality. Israel lacked the spiritual strength to remain faithful to the Lord. To be saved, they would need someone to reign over their hearts, remove their sin, and transform them entirely.

LIFE IN THE PROMISED LAND

After Joshua, Israel's life in the land can be divided into two parts—before and after the establishment of Israel's monarchy. We'll consider each in turn.

THE TIME OF JUDGES

The book of Judges recounts the time between Joshua's death and the anointing of King Saul. It pictures a spiraling descent into sin and faithlessness until Israel was essentially indistinguishable from the Canaanite nations.

The Israelites faithfully worshipped the Lord during Joshua's lifetime and until his generation died out. But after that arose a generation "who did not know the LORD or the works he had done for Israel"

(Judges 2:10).[13] Consequently, they "abandoned the LORD" and worshipped other gods (verses 11-13). This angered the Lord, and he "was against them and brought disaster on them, just as he had promised" (verses 14-15). In his compassion, the Lord raised up judges (governors) to save them from their enemies. Unfortunately, these judges could not save the people of Israel from themselves:

> The LORD raised up judges, who saved them from the power of their marauders, but they did not listen to their judges. Instead, they prostituted themselves with other gods, bowing down to them. They quickly turned from the way of their ancestors, who had walked in obedience to the LORD's commands. They did not do as their ancestors did. Whenever the LORD raised up a judge for the Israelites, the LORD was with him and saved the people from the power of their enemies while the judge was still alive. The LORD was moved to pity whenever they groaned because of those who were oppressing and afflicting them. Whenever the judge died, the Israelites would act even more corruptly than their ancestors, following other gods to serve them and bow in worship to them. They did not turn from their evil practices or their obstinate ways (2:16-19).

This cycle plays out until Judges ends with a tragic summary statement: "In those days there was no king in Israel; everyone did whatever seemed right to him" (21:25).

The book of Ruth takes place during the time of the judges, though it does not feature or mention any judge. It tells the story of an Israelite

---

13. Notice the similarity in that statement to Exodus 1:8: "A new king, who did not know about Joseph, came to power in Egypt." Israel in the land became like Pharaoh was in Egypt—forgetful and idolatrous.

woman, Naomi, who traveled with her husband and sons to Moab to escape a famine. While there, her husband died, and her sons married Moabite women. After a decade in Moab, her sons died, leaving her no grandchildren. She was left with two barren Moabite daughters-in-law, Orpah and Ruth. Upon hearing that the Lord provided food for Israel, Naomi set out to return to her hometown of Bethlehem. She urged her daughters-in-law to return to their families and their former gods. The Lord was against her, she argued, and her life was too bitter for them to bear. Orpah returned, but Ruth insisted on being faithful to Naomi and her God.

When they arrived in Bethlehem, Ruth took the initiative to provide food by gleaning after the harvesters. In God's providence, she ended up in the field of Boaz, a relative of Naomi, who showed kindness to Ruth and Naomi. Hearing about Boaz, Naomi remembered that he was a relative qualified to marry Ruth. So Naomi engaged in a bit of crafty matchmaking, which resulted in the marriage of Boaz and Ruth. The newlyweds soon had a child, Obed, who fathered Jesse, the father of King David.

Where is weakness?

The theme of weakness stands out in two areas: moral weakness and inability to save themselves. Joshua spoke prophetically about Israel's moral weakness when he said, "You will not be able to worship the LORD" (Joshua 24:19). He learned this from his predecessor, Moses. Before his death, Moses instructed Levites to keep a copy of the Law in the ark of the covenant to serve as a witness against Israel, saying, "For I know how rebellious and stiff-necked you are. If you are rebelling against the LORD now, while I am still alive, how much more will you rebel after I am dead!" (Deuteronomy 31:27).

The book of Judges puts Israel's moral weakness on full display as the nation repeatedly refuses to keep covenant with the Lord. "In those days there was no king in Israel; everyone did whatever seemed right to him" (Judges 21:25). That summary statement reminds future Israel that their fault lies not in their kings but in themselves, that they are sinners. "Israel did not need a king to lead them into sin; they could fall into immorality all on their own."[14]

While Israel could plunge itself into sin, it lacked the strength to pull itself out. Each time Israel forgot the Lord, acted corruptly, and received punishment, the Lord raised up a judge to save them. Only then would they temporarily (if superficially) return to the Lord. The judges are tragically flawed leaders, but their personal weaknesses aren't the main point. Rather, the judges highlight the weakness of Israel, its inability to save itself. Salvation depends on a God-appointed, Spirit-empowered king to save them—just as God promised in the offspring of the woman.

The judges themselves are often pictures of human weakness through which God's strength is displayed. Deborah was the only female judge mentioned in Judges, and her leadership brought Israel military victory. The female body is typically weaker than the male body, so women weren't ideal for the physical combat and heavy weaponry of that day. Yet the final, lethal blow was dealt by the hand of a woman, Jael, wielding a hammer and tent peg.[15] Salvation came through the "weaker vessel" in order to display the Lord's sovereign power.

Gideon was a rather chicken-hearted man, in hiding when the Lord appeared to him and, in irony, called him a "valiant warrior" (Judges 6:11-12). He repeatedly forestalled obedience by asking for multiple signs. Like Moses, Gideon objected to the Lord's call on the basis of his weakness. "Please, Lord, how can I deliver Israel? Look, my family is the weakest in Manasseh, and I am the youngest in my father's family"

---

14. Iain M. Duguid, "Judges," in *CSB Study Bible: Notes*, eds. Edwin A. Blum and Trevin Wax (Nashville: Holman Bible Publishers, 2017), 360.

15. See Judges 4.

(verse 15). The Lord agreed that Gideon was weak and unable to deliver Israel on his own, and so he added, "But I will be with you" (verse 16). The Lord put his strength on display by intentionally weakening Gideon's army, reducing it from 32,000 to 300 to defeat the Midianites.[16]

The story of Naomi, Ruth, and Boaz highlights the weakness from which redemption springs. Back in Bethlehem, Naomi insisted on being called *bitter* because "I went away full, but the LORD has brought me back empty" (Ruth 1:20-21). The narrator immediately follows Naomi's words with this commentary: "So Naomi came back from the territory of Moab with her daughter-in-law Ruth the Moabitess" (verse 22). Naomi insisted she was brought back *empty*; the narrator notes she came back with Ruth. Naomi counted Ruth as *emptiness*—a worthless, barren, embarrassing Moabite daughter-in-law that no self-respecting Hebrew man would ever marry. Naomi judged her life (and her daughter-in-law's) by a human metric and concluded she was empty—weak.

Ruth was weak, and she knew it. But she also knew that the Lord was strong and able to protect her. So she sought refuge under the Lord's wings (2:12). While the nation descended into apostasy, a Moabite woman stood out as the model Israelite. The unlikely foreigner is a picture of covenant faithfulness, loving the Lord with all that she is and loving her neighbor as herself.

During the period of judges, the Lord empowered leaders with his Spirit to lead and conquer in externally "strong" ways. Yet the salvation brought through such external strength was neither permanent nor the path through which the promised Redeemer would arrive. While the judges saved Israel in loud, dramatic fashion, the Lord was working to bring the true Savior through a quiet, domestic setting in the little town of Bethlehem. Some judges, such as Ehud and Samson, were known for their feats of cunning and strength. But the seed of

---

16. See Judges 7.

the woman would arrive through the unlikeliest of women—a barren, widowed Moabitess picking up random stalks of barley in a stranger's field. Through her weakness, God brought his strength to completion. Ruth foreshadows her distant grandson, born in Bethlehem, considered weak and unwanted by the world, through whom God would save his people forever.

THE TIME OF KINGS

After the judges, Israel's monarchy was established during the ministry of the prophet Samuel, beginning with King Saul and then King David.[17] At the end of Samuel's ministry, the people of Israel called for a king, a desire both Samuel and the Lord condemned due to its impure motives. Nevertheless, the Lord granted their request, and Israel received Saul as its first king. Though Saul saw some military success as king, he ultimately failed via disobedience to God and harmed Israel. The Lord replaced Saul with David, the youngest son of Jesse.[18]

David led Israel to defeat the Philistines and brought the ark of the covenant home to Jerusalem. His reign established peace in the land and blessed the nation, finally allowing Israel to enjoy the abundance of the Promised Land, further fulfilling God's promises to Abraham, Isaac, and Jacob. David requested to build a temple, a house for the Lord, in Jerusalem. Though the Lord rejected David's request, he made a covenant with David that one of his descendants would reign over God's kingdom forever.[19]

Sadly, David's reign ended little better than Saul's. David significantly abused his kingly authority in sinning against Uriah and

---

17. For what follows, see P.E. Satterthwaite, "Samuel," in *New Dictionary of Biblical Theology*, eds. T. Desmond Alexander and Brian S. Rosner, electronic ed. (Downers Grove, IL: InterVarsity Press, 2000).

18. This is recorded in 1 Samuel 1 through 2 Samuel 4.

19. See 2 Samuel 5–10.

Bathsheba, resulting in severe condemnation and the promise that the sword would never leave his house. [20] The king's wickedness unleashed a rapid and expansive descent into sin—rape, murder, and civil war—that spread first through his own household and then the nation. [21] As David raped Bathsheba, David's son Amnon raped his sister Tamar. As David arranged the death of Uriah, David's son Absalom commanded his men to murder Amnon. Such evil would characterize Israel's history during David's reign and under the kings who followed him. [22]

The book of Judges ended with Israel steeped in rape, murder, and civil war because "there was no king in Israel." [23] David's decline illustrates how the problem wasn't that they lacked a king; an unrighteous king lands them in the same situation.

The books of Kings and Chronicles recount the Israelite monarchy following David through the destruction of Jerusalem and Cyrus's decree to rebuild it. The history of Israel's kings followed the pattern of David. It began with faithfulness to the Lord, especially seen in the early days of Solomon. But Solomon's reign and the succession of kings after him quickly spiraled into increasing wickedness until the nation was torn in two, Jerusalem was destroyed, and the people were carried into exile. The narrative leaves the reader questioning whether the monarchy is a blessing or a curse. Moreover, it makes one wonder if the promised offspring of the woman will ever arrive.

Where is weakness?

Israel's motive in requesting a king was a rejection of God's good gift of weakness. Monarchy was the Lord's plan for Israel, not a concession to their demands. Moses commanded Israel to appoint a king

---

20. See 2 Samuel 11–12.
21. See 2 Samuel 13.
22. See 2 Samuel 14–20.
23. See Judges 19–20.

in the Promised Land: "When you enter the land the LORD your God is giving you, take possession of it, live in it, and say, 'I will set a king over me like all the nations around me,' you are to appoint over you the king the LORD your God chooses" (Deuteronomy 17:14-15). Moses followed this with instructions for what kind of king to appoint. He forbade the king from acquiring many horses, many wives, and very large amounts of silver and gold (verses 16-17), which represent military strength, foreign alliances (through intermarriage), and economic strength. We'll revisit this in the next chapter. For now, we notice the thrust of the command—Israel's king would be utterly unlike other kings, making Israel unlike other nations. The distinction is the gift of weakness, as the Lord forbade the pursuit of worldly strength. What, then, should the king pursue?

> When he is seated on his royal throne, he is to write a copy of this instruction for himself on a scroll in the presence of the Levitical priests. It is to remain with him, and he is to read from it all the days of his life, so that he may learn to fear the LORD his God, to observe all the words of this instruction, and to do these statutes. Then his heart will not be exalted above his countrymen, he will not turn from this command to the right or the left, and he and his sons will continue reigning many years in Israel (17:18-20).

In short, the king was to pursue the Lord through the study of and obedience to God's Word. This would result in a humble king who didn't see himself as greater than his people (a contrast to the nations in which the king was revered as a god!).

Israel's king was to be weak in worldly terms in order to show God's strength. The Lord himself would defend, establish, and provide for both the king and the nation. Therefore, Israel's kings didn't need to build up defenses, alliances, and wealth. Though they had the rights of a king, they could make themselves nothing and humble themselves in obedience to God and service to his people. They could walk by faith in God's promise, not by the world's power. A voluntarily humble monarchy, one that loved God and neighbor, would continue indefinitely.[24]

Israel didn't want a "weak" king who forsook worldly strength to rule by faith in the Lord. In rejecting a king who embraced weakness out of faith in the Lord, they were rejecting the Lord himself:

> Listen to the people and everything they say to you. They have not rejected you; they have rejected me as their king. They are doing the same thing to you that they have done to me, since the day I brought them out of Egypt until this day, abandoning me and worshiping other gods (1 Samuel 8:7-8).

The Lord said Israel was abandoning him and worshipping other gods. But what gods were they worshipping? There's no mention of idols or foreign religions in the account. The people of Israel identified the god they worshipped when they said to Samuel, "We must have a king over us. Then we'll be like all the other nations: our king will judge us, go out before us, and fight our battles" (verses 19-20). Israel wanted to be like all the other nations, which meant having a king like the other nations' kings—a strong king. The false god they worshipped was worldly strength, particularly in the form of a king who could provide military strength. To reject God's good gift of a weak king is to bow to the false god named *Strength*. The fear of the Lord requires embracing weakness through faith in the Lord.

Would there ever be a king who embraced such weakness? Yes—absolutely, yes! The Lord made a covenant with David, promising

---

24. See Philippians 2:5-11.

that one of his offspring would reign forever over an eternal king-dom.[25] This son is clearly the longed-for "offspring of the woman" who would bring final and lasting relief from the curse and life to God's people. The fact that he springs from David's lineage is significant. David was initially overlooked, despised, and rejected. When the Lord sent Samuel to anoint one of Jesse's sons as king, he commanded him not to look at their appearance or stature. King Saul was known for his stature; he stood "a head taller than anyone else," and there was "no one like him among the entire population" (10:23-24). He was a picture of human strength, the type of king the nations had, and the kind of king Israel desired. But the Lord warned, "Humans do not see what the LORD sees, for humans see what is visible, but the LORD sees the heart" (16:7). The Lord chose David, the youngest of Jesse's sons, initially rejected by Saul as too young to fight and despised by Goliath as a youth too young to be a military threat. Yet it was this overlooked, rejected, and despised king who delivered Israel from the Philistines.[26] And David's son would be the same.

EXILE AND THE MESSAGE OF THE PROPHETS

In the Old Testament, Israel's story ended no differently than Adam and Eve's—in exile. "Exile, in theological terms, is the experience of pain and suffering that results from the knowledge that there is a home where one belongs, yet for the present one is unable to return there."[27] Like Adam and Eve, the Israelites were sent away from the place God prepared for them. The northern kingdom was exiled to Assyria, while the southern kingdom endured captivity in Babylon. Exile, however, was more than displacement from a homeland. Through their disobedience, they forfeited the Lord's presence.

---

25. See 2 Samuel 7:11-16.
26. See 1 Samuel 17.
27. I.M. Duguid, "Exile," in *New Dictionary of Biblical Theology*, 475.

But despite external appearances, all was not lost. God's grace remained and was proclaimed by God's prophets. The prophets denounced Israel's wickedness, particularly their worship of false gods and their obsession with worldly strength (often seen in how they used power, sex, and wealth). They also offered hope of redemption to be found in humility, repentance, and faith. They spoke of a future day in which "God will restore his favour to the people by renewing his covenant with them (Jer. 31:31–34), by raising up a new, righteous King in the line of David (Is. 9:2–7; 11; Ezek. 34), and by re-establishing the people in their own land."[28]

Where is weakness?

Weakness is found in the promise of salvation, particularly in the promised King. Israel demanded a military conqueror.[29] Yet when the Messiah arrives, he won't be riding a warhorse.

> Rejoice greatly, Daughter Zion!
> Shout in triumph, Daughter Jerusalem!
> Look, your King is coming to you;
> he is righteous and victorious,
> humble and riding on a donkey,
> on a colt, the foal of a donkey (Zechariah 9:9).

In Isaiah 40–55, the prophet comforted God's people with the announcement of this King, God's servant. He won't be a king obsessed with worldly strength, collecting armies, wives, and wealth like so many stamps. What then will this King be like?

- Quiet and peaceful: "He will not cry out or shout or make his voice heard in the streets" (42:2).

---

28. I.H. Marshall, "Jesus Christ," in *New Dictionary of Biblical Theology*, 593.
29. See 1 Samuel 8:19-20.

- Gentle and just: "He will not break a bruised reed, and he will not put out a smoldering wick; he will faithfully bring justice" (verse 3).

- Righteous: "The Lord GOD has opened my ear, and I was not rebellious; I did not turn back" (50:5).

- Patient in suffering because he trusts in God to vindicate him: "I gave my back to those who beat me, and my cheeks to those who tore out my beard...The one who vindicates me is near; who will contend with me?" (verses 6-8).

- Appalling and unattractive: "Just as many were appalled at you—his appearance was so disfigured that he did not look like a man, and his form did not resemble a human being" (52:14).

- Unimpressive, unmajestic, undesirable: "He grew up before him like a young plant and like a root out of dry ground. He didn't have an impressive form or majesty that we should look at him, no appearance that we should desire him" (53:2).

- Despised and rejected: "He was despised and rejected by men...He was like someone people turned away from; he was despised, and we didn't value him" (verse 3).

- Characterized by suffering and sickness: "He was...a man of suffering who knew what sickness was" (verse 3).

- Misunderstood and wrongly condemned: "Yet he himself bore our sicknesses, and he carried our pains; but we in turn regarded him stricken, struck down by God, and afflicted" (verse 4).

- Oppressed and afflicted, offering no defense: "He was

oppressed and afflicted, yet he did not open his mouth" (verse 7).

- Dead and buried: "For he was cut off from the land of the living…He was assigned a grave with the wicked" (verses 8-9).

In sum, he'll be the opposite of a strong king. By the world's metrics, he will be a weak king.

Weakness is also seen in the response expected of God's people. They were to turn away from their sins and their false gods to trust the Lord's promise. Again, in the eyes of the world, this appears weak. After all, Jerusalem had been destroyed, and the people were carried into exile by foreign nations that worshipped other gods. It would appear these were the gods that were powerful and strong—not Yahweh, whose temple lay in ruins. Could the Lord be trusted when the external circumstances seemed to suggest otherwise?

Saving faith required God's people to embrace weakness through faith. The Lord condemned Israel for seeking their well-being through earthly strength.

> For the Lord GOD, the Holy One of Israel, has said:
> "You will be delivered by returning and resting;
> your strength will lie in quiet confidence.
> But you are not willing."
> You say, "No!
> We will escape on horses"—
> therefore you will escape!—
> and, "We will ride on fast horses"—
> but those who pursue you will be faster" (Isaiah 30:15-16).

Israel's true strength wasn't to be found in earthly might. Worldly strength would become a fatal weakness, for when they trusted horses, stronger horses overtook them. Deliverance would only be found by returning to the Lord and resting in him. This meant renouncing their dependence on—and faith in—strength. Sitting down to rest doesn't win earthly battles, but it is the way of salvation. "Your strength will lie in quiet confidence." True strength is found in trusting the Lord to keep his promise, acknowledging that it's God who carries his people from birth to old age, from beginning to end:

> Listen to me, house of Jacob,
> all the remnant of the house of Israel,
> who have been sustained from the womb,
> carried along since birth.
> I will be the same until your old age,
> and I will bear you up when you turn gray.
> I have made you, and I will carry you;
> I will bear and rescue you (Isaiah 46:3-4).

CHAPTER 5

WEAKNESS IN ISRAEL'S LAW

So the previous command is annulled because it was weak
and unprofitable (for the law perfected nothing), but a better
hope is introduced, through which we draw near to God.

HEBREWS 7:18-19

S wear words weren't used in our home. Even mildly bad words
weren't tolerated. I can still taste the soap that scrubbed out my
mouth after I told my mother to "shut up." I definitely still remember—I can feel—the scene in the A&W restaurant. Some construction workers, several booths away from our family, filled the air with
expletives. "Excuse me!" my mother growled in fluent mama bear. "I
don't know if you noticed, but there are children in here. Could you
watch your language?" I wanted to disappear under the table. So did
the construction workers, I think, as they sheepishly muttered, "Yes,
ma'am" and "Sorry, ma'am."

But my mom and her hand soap weren't with me in the men's
room at Hardee's. My eyes scanned the graffiti scratched into the
brown paint on the back of the door. Some of the words I knew,
others I didn't. One word, carved in the center of the door in ALL
CAPS, stood out. I didn't recognize it, so I sounded it out: "F-uh-..."
Then it hit me. I'd just learned to spell the baddest bad word of all

bad words—*the f-word*. I repeated the letters in my head until I had them memorized.

The next week at school, the rain kept us inside for recess. A friend and I sat at our desks in the back row of our first-grade classroom. We'd decided to play a word game. I had the perfect word. My friend failed to guess the correct letters in his allotted number of guesses. So, to my delight, I wrote in the remaining characters. He looked at the word with confusion, so I whispered in his ear, "It's the f-word." (I would spell it, but I wouldn't dare say or even whisper it.) We giggled in six-year-old delight over our acquisition of this forbidden knowledge. Then, lest our teacher find it, I shoved it into my backpack.

One afternoon that week, I was at home minding my own business and not dropping f-bombs when my mother called me out to the back porch. She had me sit down and handed me a piece of paper. I looked at the four-letter word in horror.

"I found that in your backpack," she said. "Did you write it?"

I nodded my affirmation.

"I want you to read something," she said, handing me a small plaque that hung on our living room wall. She left, allowing me a few minutes to think about it. The plaque had our family name—SCHUMACHER—printed at the top. Written from the perspective of a parent to a child, it explained that bearing our surname came with responsibility. It represented our family and its values. How we lived told the world what a "Schumacher" was. We could choose to keep it clean or to cover it with black marks.

When my mother returned, she explained why bad words were disrespectful. She urged me to think about how I would represent the name given to me. That charge—to steward the honor of an inherited name—isn't just a good lesson for children. It's a responsibility central to the relationship between God and his people.

GOD'S NAME-BEARING SONS

Humans were created as God's children to bear God's name.

In the chapter on creation, we noted that being made in "God's image" meant representing God. Adam bore God's name as the "son of God" (Luke 3:38). Since we all descend from Adam, we're all made in God's image to bear his name and "image forth" his glory. How we live tells the world what our Father is like. Unfortunately, Adam and Eve failed miserably.

God chose Abraham (and his offspring) to be another Adam.[1]

God blessed the first man and woman, commissioning them to "be fruitful, multiply, fill the earth, and subdue it" (Genesis 1:28). In the same way, God promised to bless Abraham's offspring, to multiply him greatly and make him extremely fruitful (17:2, 6).[2] God placed Adam and Eve in a fruitful garden where he would dwell with them and from which they would carry out their commission to bless the whole earth.[3] Likewise, God promised to place Abraham's offspring in the land of Canaan—a fertile, garden-like home, "a land flowing with milk and honey" (Genesis 17:8; Exodus 3:8). "Thus at key moments…the narrative quietly makes the point that Abraham and his family inherit, in a measure, the role of Adam and Eve…We could sum up this aspect of Genesis by saying: Abraham's children are God's true humanity, and their homeland is the new Eden."[4] Thus, the Lord would speak of Israel as "my son" (Exodus 4:22-23).

---

1. Peter J. Gentry and Stephen J. Wellum, *God's Kingdom Through God's Covenants: A Concise Biblical Theology* (Wheaton, IL: Crossway, 2015), Kindle loc. 1731.

2. See also Genesis 22:16-24; 26:3-4; 26:24; 28:3; 35:11-12; 47:27; 48:3-4.

3. Genesis 2:15; 3:8.

4. N.T. Wright, *The Climax of the Covenant: Christ and the Law in Pauline Theology* (London; New York: T&T Clark, 1991), 22–23.

As with Adam and Eve, God taught Israel how to live as his people in his place.

Adam and Eve were to live as priests to God in the garden sanctuary, learning to be like him to display his glory over all the earth. Likewise, God taught Israel to live in covenant with him as a nation of priests that would show his glory to the world. This instruction came through God's covenant with Israel enacted at Mount Sinai as recorded in Exodus 19–40 (and unpacked by Moses in Deuteronomy). The Law taught the son (Israel) how to be like his father (the Lord) and bear his name before the world. If they would carefully listen to him and keep his covenant, the Lord promised Israel would be "my own possession...my kingdom of priests and my holy nation" (Exodus 19:5-6). The Law was a call to be owned by God, carrying out priestly service as a nation set apart by his holiness. Holiness—unswerving devotion to the Lord—was outlined in the covenant instruction. "Complete devotion to God on the part of Israel would show itself in two ways: (1) identifying with his ethics and morality, and (2) sharing his concern for the broken in the community."[5] That is to say, devotion to the Lord, being the son who bore his name, meant looking out for and loving the weak.

WEAKNESS IN THE LAW

The Law instructed Israel to imitate the Lord's concern for the weak.

Weakness is a relative term. We know we're weak when we see our strength in comparison to God's. Though we're all inherently weak in contrast to God, there are differences among us regarding the extent and nature of our weaknesses. Some are weaker in particular areas than others. I refer to this as *relative weakness*. If my neighbor is weaker than me in a particular area, I'm *stronger* by contrast. Thus,

5. Gentry and Wellum, *God's Kingdom Through God's Covenants*, Kindle loc. 2775–2776.

among weak humans, there exist the *strong* and the *weak* (or, more accurately, the *weak* and the *weaker*). Each nation and society has weak and strong members. Thus, each society must choose how the strong and the weak relate.

> If the Old Testament teaches us anything, it's that the Lord loves the weak. The OT projects a pattern of the God of Israel caring for the weak and the helpless. These are the ones who, pressed to the margins of life and unable to care for themselves, cry out to the Lord in their affliction. We see this in God's choosing Israel from among the nations, in God's dealing with individuals within Israel, and in God's covenantal commands to care for the weak and afflicted, most notably the widows and orphans.[6]

In the Law, the weak were generally represented by four groups— the poor, the widow, the orphan, and the resident alien. Whether physically, financially, or socially, each category lacked the power to provide for or protect themselves (especially in contrast to the strong). That left them vulnerable to oppression, exploitation, affliction, and other injustices.

The Law protected and provided for the weak in many ways. The poor in Israel weren't to be charged interest, denied justice in a lawsuit, or sold food at a profit.[7] Even sin offerings operated on a sliding scale according to what they could afford to ensure access to atonement and worship.[8] Harvest laws limited what the owner of a

---

6. Leland Ryken, James C. Wilhoit, and Tremper Longman III, eds., "Weak, Weakness," in *Dictionary of Biblical Imagery* (Downers Grove, IL: InterVarsity Press, 1998), 932.

7. Exodus 22:25; 23:6; Leviticus 25:37.

8. Leviticus 5:5-13; 12:8; 14:21.

field could reap and glean, guaranteeing the weak had food.[9] Every third year, a tenth of all produce was gathered and stored in the city so that "the resident alien, the fatherless, and the widow within your city gates may come, eat, and be satisfied" (Deuteronomy 14:29).[10]

The Sabbath provision for the weak went beyond a weekly rest. During Sabbath years, the land, fields, vineyards, and olive groves went uncultivated "so that the poor among your people may eat from it" (Exodus 23:11) and debts were canceled.[11] And during the Year of Jubilee (think, *Super Sabbath*), Israelites who had become slaves through poverty were to be set free.[12]

A key example of God's love for the weak appears in Exodus 22:21-24:

> You must not exploit a resident alien or oppress him, since you were resident aliens in the land of Egypt.
>
> You must not mistreat any widow or fatherless child. If you do mistreat them, they will no doubt cry to me, and I will certainly hear their cry. My anger will burn, and I will kill you with the sword; then your wives will be widows and your children fatherless.

Israel was to love the weak because the Lord loved them when they were weak in Egypt. As they stood at Mount Sinai receiving the Law, the memory of Egypt was fresh in their minds. Israel dwelt in Egypt as resident aliens for over 400 years. When Jacob and his sons first arrived, they survived through kind and generous hospitality. In the end, they suffered oppression and affliction as powerless people. Israel

---

9. Leviticus 19:9-10; 23:22; Deuteronomy 24:19-22.
10. See also Leviticus 26:12.
11. See also Leviticus 25:4-6; Deuteronomy 15:1-3.
12. Leviticus 25:39-41, 54.

knew the best and the worst of life as resident aliens; that knowledge needed to inform their conduct. "You must not oppress a resident alien; you yourselves know how it feels to be a resident alien because you were resident aliens in the land of Egypt" (Exodus 23:9).[13] Therefore, when a foreigner resided in their land, they should love their neighbor as they wanted to be loved in Egypt:

> When an alien resides with you in your land, you must not oppress him. You will regard the alien who resides with you as the native-born among you. You are to love him as yourself, for you were aliens in the land of Egypt; I am the LORD your God (Leviticus 19:33-34).

Behind this reminder is the question, "How did the Lord love you?" The Lord's love for Israel in their weakness becomes the reason the Lord commands Israel to love the weak: "Remember that you were a slave in the land of Egypt and the LORD your God redeemed you; that is why I am giving you this command today" (Deuteronomy 15:15).[14] As alien residents in Egypt, the Israelites were enslaved and exploited. But the Lord redeemed them and gave them protection, provision, and rest.[15] Thus they should love their neighbors as the Lord loved them.

Likewise, Israel was to love the weak because the Lord defends the defenseless. Why do the wicked abuse the weak? Because they think they can get away with it. A widow or orphan seems safe to oppress because no husband or father can get in your way. The disabled seem safe to mock because they lack the physical strength or attributes needed to knock your teeth out. The poor seem safe to

---

13. See also Deuteronomy 10:19.

14. See also Leviticus 25:36-38; Deuteronomy 5:12-15; 24:17-18, 19-22.

15. Tim Chester, *Exodus for You* (Epsom, UK: The Good Book Company, 2016), 168.

exploit because they can't afford to take you to court. The resident alien seems safe to exploit because he's a foreigner, and citizens are prone to protect their own. But the "safety" found in such violence is only an illusion, for the Lord himself takes up their cause. "They will no doubt cry to me, and I will certainly hear their cry. My anger will burn, and I will kill you with the sword" (Exodus 22:23-24). If you're looking for an easy target, don't choose the weak—because when you do, you have to deal with the Lord of Armies!

Since the Lord loves the weak, he takes up their cause personally.[16] "He executes justice for the fatherless and the widow, and loves the resident alien, giving him food and clothing" (Deuteronomy 10:18). God identifies with the vulnerable so closely that he counts the way we treat them as how we treat him. Thus, "the one who mocks the poor insults his Maker" (Proverbs 17:5).[17] When asked which command was the greatest, Jesus replied:

> Love the Lord your God with all your heart, with all your soul, and with all your mind. This is the greatest and most important command. The second is like it: Love your neighbor as yourself. All the Law and the Prophets depend on these two commands (Matthew 22:37-40).

The command to love your Lord cannot be separated from the command to love your neighbor. For, as we have seen, how you regard God's image reveals your regard for God.

Loving the weak as the Lord loved us defines us as God's people, distinguishing us from the world. "God hears the voice of those who are broken in body, in economy, and in spirit. If we are in covenant

16. See also Psalms 12:5; 35:10; 68:5; 146:9; Proverbs 22:22-23; 23:10-11.
17. See also Proverbs 14:31.

relationship with him, we must, like him, hear the voice that is too weak to cry out."[18] As we'll see in a future chapter, Jesus Christ embodies God's love for the poor and calls his people to do the same.

The Law called Israel to remember their weakness and live by the Lord's strength.

Loving the weak is good and right, but it comes with the dangerous temptation to forget our weakness. When we're strong enough to be benefactors, it's easy to forget we're first and foremost beneficiaries. When Israel prospered in the land such that many were relatively strong compared to the poor, widows, orphans, and alien residents, they were in danger of becoming proud, forgetting they lived and prospered only by the Lord's strength.

> Be careful that you don't forget the LORD your God by failing to keep his commands, ordinances, and statutes that I am giving you today. When you eat and are full, and build beautiful houses to live in, and your herds and flocks grow large, and your silver and gold multiply, and everything else you have increases, be careful that your heart doesn't become proud and you forget the LORD your God who brought you out of the land of Egypt, out of the place of slavery. He led you through the great and terrible wilderness with its poisonous snakes and scorpions, a thirsty land where there was no water. He brought water out of the flint rock for you. He fed you in the wilderness with manna, which your ancestors had not known, in order to humble and test you, so that in the end he might cause you to prosper. You may say to yourself, "My power

---

18. Gentry and Wellum, *God's Kingdom Through God's Covenants*, Kindle loc. 2781–2782.

and my own ability have gained this wealth for me," but remember that the LORD your God gives you the power to gain wealth, in order to confirm his covenant he swore to your ancestors, as it is today. If you ever forget the LORD your God and follow other gods to serve them and bow in worship to them, I testify against you today that you will certainly perish. Like the nations the LORD is about to destroy before you, you will perish if you do not obey the LORD your God (Deuteronomy 8:11-20).

Moses cautioned against the temptation to believe that they were strong: "You may say to yourself, 'My power and my own ability have gained this wealth for me.'" That's another way of saying, "I'm not weak." Faithfully stewarding the Lord's name meant saying, "I am weak, but he is strong."

Remembered weakness is a gift.

To counter Israel's pride, Moses commanded them to recall their dependent state. "Remember that the LORD your God gives you power to gain wealth." Reread Moses's words and notice his emphasis on what the Lord did: The Lord brought you out. He led you. He brought water. He fed you. He did it all. The Lord. The Lord. The Lord. The Lord did it all in saving them—and the Lord does it all in sustaining them. They must never forget they depend on the Lord for strength from start to finish. (Dependence on another for strength is inseparable from weakness. You aren't dependent on another for power unless you are weak.) They would undoubtedly perish if they ever forgot their weakness and believed themselves strong in their own might. The nation's life depended on their faith in the Lord, which necessitated continually acknowledging their weakness and total dependence upon the Lord.

God designed Israel's calendar to remind them of their weakness and total dependence on his strength.[19] The Law called Israel to obey a weekly Sabbath, during which everyone and everything in the land rested. Likewise, the Law prescribed a sabbatical year in which the land rested as they neither sowed their fields nor pruned vineyards or groves. The Sabbaths signified the relationship between the Lord and Israel: The Lord's people didn't have to work incessantly, because the Lord provided them rest. The Sabbaths also provided food for the weak. They gave rest to the land that the Lord cared for.

The Sabbath reminded the Israelites that they didn't live by human strength but by the Lord's provision. In an agrarian society, choosing to stop farming is a weak food production strategy! To cease work is to stop providing for yourself. If resting from work one day a week produced concern, then giving the land rest for an entire year would certainly cause anxiety. The natural question is, "If we don't farm, what will we eat?" The Law anticipated and answered that concern:

> If you wonder, "What will we eat in the seventh year if we don't sow or gather our produce?" I will appoint my blessing for you in the sixth year, so that it will produce a crop sufficient for three years. When you sow in the eighth year, you will be eating from the previous harvest. You will be eating this until the ninth year when its harvest comes in (Leviticus 25:20-22).

The Lord promised to provide a crop that would feed them for three years. Observing the Sabbath year required the Israelites to believe that their food came not from their labor but from the Lord. If they trusted in their strength, the Sabbath year would be a terror.

---

19. For what follows, see Exodus 20:8-11; 23:10-12; Leviticus 25:1-7; Deuteronomy 5:12-14; 11:12.

But if they trusted in the Lord's promise, the Sabbath rest would be a delight. They could genuinely rest because the Lord promised to feed them by grace apart from their work.

A similar crisis of faith surrounds Israel's three annual weeklong festivals: the Feast of Unleavened Bread (or Passover), the Feast of Harvest (or Pentecost), and the Feast of Ingathering (or Tabernacles).[20] "Three times a year all your males are to appear before the Lord GOD, the God of Israel" (Exodus 34:23). Sending all the males (and sometimes the whole family) to Jerusalem left the land exposed and unprotected. Three times a year, cities, villages, and farms stood unprotected and vulnerable to attack during the festival (and travel time). This raised the question, "What will happen if we're not there to protect our land with our strength?" The Law also anticipated and answered this question: "No one will covet your land when you go up three times a year to appear before the LORD your God" (verse 24). Walking away from home to attend a festival was a physical confession of faith: "I do not trust in my strength to protect my possession. God's power gave me my inheritance, and God's strength shall keep it."

A weak king is a gift.

The laws governing the selection of Israel's king highlight Israel's dependence on the Lord's strength. In the previous chapter, we surveyed Deuteronomy 17:14-20, which forbids the king from acquiring horses (military strength), wives (diplomatic strength via treaties), and gold (economic strength).

> Moses directs the king to renounce his own power by limiting the number of his warhorses, his treasury, and his political alliances through marriage. All nations strengthen themselves by increasing their armories, their defense budget,

---

20. Exodus 23:13-17.

and their international alliances. But Israel's king limits these well-known sources of national strength.[21]

What's happening here? "Structurally, this section on the king comes at the centre of Israel's constitution. This is all the more surprising, since the office of king...appears to be divested of any real powers and authority within Israelite society."[22] Instead of trusting in worldly sources of strength, "the future ruler of Israel must adhere to certain standards to assure the success of his reign, placing his confidence in the Lord."[23] A king that embodies weakness and trusts in the Lord is a gift to Israel because, standing at the center of the nation, he reminds Israel that "in the economy of God's kingdom, one must be weak to be strong."[24]

Rejecting a weak king would be a symptom of rejecting weakness with faith in God to choose confidence in the world's strength. That's why future Israel would reject Jesus:

> Israel misses seeing the Messiah because they are looking in the wrong direction. They expect a Messiah that will rival Rome in pomp and power, not a crucified Messiah hanging on a Roman cross. They want human wealth and power for their security and significance, not the heavenly wealth and power that come from martyrdom and that alone endures and ultimately triumphs over evil.[25]

---

21. Bruce K. Waltke, *An Old Testament Theology: An Exegetical, Canonical, and Thematic Approach* (Grand Rapids: Zondervan, 2007), 397.

22. Edward J. Woods, *Deuteronomy: An Introduction and Commentary*, ed. David G. Firth, Tyndale Old Testament Commentaries, vol. 5 (Nottingham, UK: InterVarsity Press, 2011), 218.

23. Eugene H. Merrill, "Deuteronomy," in *CSB Study Bible: Notes*, eds. Edwin A. Blum and Trevin Wax (Nashville: Holman Bible Publishers, 2017), 290.

24. Waltke, *An Old Testament Theology*, 397.

25. Waltke, 397.

When we see the conquering Lion of Judah, the true Davidic King, he appears as a "slaughtered lamb" (Revelation 5:5-6). The King conquered through the weakness of the cross.[26] May God give us the grace to see and receive King Jesus today!

A weak army is a gift.

The Law limited the king's acquiring of military might (horses, in particular, and chariots by implication). When Israel defeated armies with horses and chariots, they hamstrung the horses and burned the chariots—they didn't keep them for their armament.[27] So, assuming Israel had a king who feared the Lord, its armament would be "no more than that of foot soldiers."[28] Nothing in the Law called for (or permitted) a standing army in Israel, and no taxes went to support a military. Israel wasn't to have professional soldiers. They came from their homes and vocations without training in battle or maneuvers. Then the Law whittled down their number by dismissing from service any man who had recently built a new house, planted a vineyard, gotten engaged (but not married), or was simply scared.[29] Israel's military was an exercise in divesting superior weaponry and rejecting might. Israel's army, by every human measurement, was weak.

The armies they went out against would have followed an opposite path of preparation. They would have a sizeable standing army of trained soldiers with superior weaponry, horses, and chariots. The sight of a professional, well-equipped war machine would naturally strike fear into the hearts of an untrained band of volunteer foot soldiers. But it was not to be so in Israel!

---

26. See 2 Corinthians 13:4.

27. Joshua 11:6, 9.

28. J.A. Thompson, *Deuteronomy: An Introduction and Commentary,* Tyndale Old Testament Commentaries, vol. 5 (Downers Grove, IL: InterVarsity Press, 1974), 241.

29. Deuteronomy 20:5-8.

The Law included rules for war, delivered by Moses in Deuteronomy 20. The first rule was to be fearless in the face of a sizable, well-equipped military. "When you go out to war against your enemies and see horses, chariots, and an army larger than yours, do not be afraid of them, for the LORD your God, who brought you out of the land of Egypt, is with you" (verse 1). They were not to be afraid, because the Lord, the God who brought them out of Egypt, was with them. Recall what happened at the Red Sea: "He has thrown the horse and its rider into the sea…He threw Pharaoh's chariots and his army into the sea" (Exodus 15:1, 4). The sight of horses and chariots should remind them of the Lord's victory. Rather than stir fear and cowardice, "the presence of hostile chariots and horses might serve to arouse a greater faith."[30] Therefore, when a larger army approached, the priest was to address the Israelite army and say:

> Listen, Israel: Today you are about to engage in battle with your enemies. Do not be cowardly. Do not be afraid, alarmed, or terrified because of them. For the LORD your God is the one who goes with you to fight for you against your enemies to give you victory (Deuteronomy 20:3-4).

The reason they weren't to be afraid is because the Lord would fight their enemies. That was the lesson of the Red Sea: "The LORD is a warrior; the LORD is his name" (Exodus 15:3).

That's why the Law so freely dismissed so many from military service. The Lord didn't need anyone to fight for him. He gave Israel their land to inherit and enjoy it. Therefore, those who hadn't yet enjoyed their house, vineyard, or wife were free to go and do so—the Lord didn't need them. Instead, he wanted them to enjoy

---

30. Thompson, *Deuteronomy*, 241.

the inheritance he'd given them. That's an amazing stance when a nation faces war!

> Such an idealistic view of life, in which the value of community and personal well-being take precedence over that of war (revealing a somewhat subdued and ambivalent stance on warfare), was also possible only because of the profound conviction that military strength and victory lay, in the last resort, not in the army, but in God.[31]

The Lord didn't need a big army, but the army needed the Lord. Since the battle would be won through faith, the army must be composed solely of those who believed.

It may seem that these procedures would reduce the army to too small a size. But then Yahweh could save by many or by few. The size of the army was less important than the faith of those who composed it.[32] The fear-filled soldier judged the war in terms of human strength. He trusted in horses, not in the Lord. Because unbelief is contagious, frightened soldiers were sent home lest they infect the rest. The fearless were unfazed by their relative weakness because they rested in God's power.

Israel's weak army shouldn't have been a source of shame but a cause for boasting. They could afford to be weak because Yahweh the Warrior fought their battles! As Jesus's people, we should not fear our weaknesses. Instead, we should hear the Lord Jesus say, "My grace is sufficient for you, for my power is perfected in weakness," and then respond with Paul, "I will most gladly boast all the more about my weaknesses, so that Christ's power may reside in me" (2 Corinthians 12:9).

---

31. Woods, *Deuteronomy*, 230.
32. Thompson, *Deuteronomy*, 243.

THE MOSAIC LAW IS WEAK

Perhaps the most shocking aspect of weakness in Israel's Law is the weakness of the Law itself. That would sound heretical if it weren't biblical. The apostle Paul wrote, "For what the law could not do since it was weakened by the flesh, God did" (Romans 8:3). There was nothing wrong with the Law: "The law is holy, and the commandment is holy and just and good" (7:12). The Law was not imperfect but impotent. It lacked the power to deal with sin. It couldn't produce in its subjects what it demanded. The Law could instruct sinners in the Lord's way but couldn't make them walk in it. It couldn't put away sin and transform the sinner. To be clear, the Law wasn't the problem; the flesh was. But the Law, "weakened by the flesh," was powerless against the problem.

Moses knew about that weakness. He spoke of it as he bade the Israelites farewell in Deuteronomy 30. Moses knew they were unable to keep the Law. The covenant curses would fall on them, and they would go into exile. But because the Lord is merciful, he would supply a solution. The Lord would gather his people and transform their hearts: "The LORD your God will circumcise your heart and the hearts of your descendants, and you will love him with all your heart and all your soul so that you will live" (Deuteronomy 30:6). But the fulfillment of the Law would require the end of the Old Covenant (the Law) and the introduction of the New Covenant.

God solved the problem through Jesus, crucified as a sacrifice for our sins. "He condemned sin in the flesh by sending his own Son in the likeness of sinful flesh as a sin offering, in order that the law's requirement would be fulfilled in us who do not walk according to the flesh but according to the Spirit" (Romans 8:3-4). Christ fulfilled the Law's demands in his righteous living and substitutionary death, as proved by his resurrection. Then, ascending into heaven, he poured his Spirit into the hearts of his people so that, having been forgiven and reborn, we might begin to walk in righteousness. In this way, Jesus fulfilled the Mosaic Law, bringing it to its proper end, and established the New Covenant in his blood.

The author of Hebrews writes about the weakness and the end of the Mosaic Law: "So the previous command is annulled because it was weak and unprofitable (for the law perfected nothing)" (7:18-19). The specific command referenced is the Levitical priesthood in the Law of Moses. These priests had to offer sacrifices daily, "first for their own sins, then for those of the people" (verse 27). They could not effectively deal with sin, because "the law appoints as high priests men who are weak" (verse 28). The end of sin required a better priest, one who was "holy, innocent, undefiled, separated from sinners, and exalted above the heavens" (verse 26). That priest is Jesus. But Jesus isn't from the tribe of Levi—and, therefore, not qualified to be a priest of the Old Covenant (the Mosaic Law).[33] Thus, through Jesus, the Law was annulled and "a better hope is introduced, through which we draw near to God" (verse 19). "Jesus has also become the guarantee of a better covenant" (verse 22).

THE NEW COVENANT IS NOT WEAK

The *better covenant* is the New Covenant made in Christ's blood.[34] It is better because it doesn't share the weakness of the Mosaic Covenant. "For if that first covenant had been faultless, there would have been no occasion for a second one" (Hebrews 8:7). The Law's "fault," as we've seen, was the sinful flesh of God's people, which it couldn't change. Therefore, the Lord promised a New Covenant:

> See, the days are coming, says the Lord,
> when I will make a new covenant

---

33. See Numbers 18; Hebrews 7:11-12.
34. See Luke 22:20.

with the house of Israel
and with the house of Judah—
not like the covenant
that I made with their ancestors
on the day I took them by the hand
to lead them out of the land of Egypt.
I showed no concern for them, says the Lord,
because they did not continue in my covenant.
For this is the covenant
that I will make with the house of Israel
after those days, says the Lord:
I will put my laws into their minds
and write them on their hearts.
I will be their God,
and they will be my people.
And each person will not teach his fellow citizen,
and each his brother or sister, saying, "Know the Lord,"
because they will all know me,
from the least to the greatest of them.
For I will forgive their wrongdoing,
and I will never again remember their sins (Hebrews 8:8-12).

This New Covenant is not like the covenant made at Sinai. "By saying a new covenant, he has declared that the first is obsolete" (verse 13). Under the Old Covenant, some members knew the Lord (they were converted) and some didn't. But under the New Covenant, every member of the covenant community knows the Lord personally and is forgiven fully.

The Old Covenant could not circumcise the heart—but God could. The Law was a "ministry that brought death, chiseled in letters on stones" (2 Corinthians 3:7). But in the New Covenant, God writes his law on minds and hearts (not tablets of stone). The New Covenant truly transforms people through God's Spirit. "The letter kills, but the Spirit gives life" (verse 6).

When Moses spoke with the Lord, his face glowed with the glory of the Old Covenant—a glory that slowly faded until he met with the Lord again. He veiled his face "to prevent the Israelites from gazing steadily until the end of the glory of what was being set aside" (verse 13). Had they continued gazing at it, they would have seen that the Old Covenant was temporary, fading until it was set aside for a new covenant (verses 7, 13). The New Covenant does not share that weakness—its glory never fades.

The glory of the New Covenant is "the light of the gospel of the glory of Christ" (4:4)—the message of Christ crucified for sins and raised from the dead. God "has shone in our hearts to give the light of the knowledge of God's glory in the face of Jesus Christ" (verse 6). The gospel does what the Law could not—it transforms sinners. By looking at the "glory of the Lord" in the gospel of Christ, believers are "being transformed into the same image from glory to glory" (3:18). The New Covenant accomplishes what the Law only commanded: It makes us a people characterized by God's love such that we "fulfill the law of Christ" as the true and final "Israel of God" (Galatians 6:2, 16).

———

The plaque my mom had me read convicted me, but it didn't change me. Only the gospel of Jesus Christ can change us. So let's put our hope in Jesus Christ, our great high priest, who put an end to sin through his death and resurrection. Let's glory in our New Covenant relationship with God in Christ as a forgiven people with new hearts! Let's gaze always on God's glory in the light of Christ so that it might continually transform us into his image. By grace through faith in Jesus, we can live as a people who bear his name and give him glory.

CHAPTER 6

WEAKNESS IN ISRAEL'S WORSHIP

I love you, LORD, my strength.

PSALM 18:1

My family attended church almost every Sunday. If I spent the night at the house of a friend who didn't attend church, my parents picked me up on their way. Nothing felt as embarrassing as being woken up by a friend's mom so I could get ready for church and wait by the front door while my friend slept in. That may have been the occasion one Sunday morning as I sat in worship dwelling on how annoyed I was with my friend. He was bigger, stronger, taller, and won almost every competition—and he didn't have to go to church! As I stewed in bitterness, I found a way to win. If there were a scoreboard in heaven keeping track of our godliness, then I would win by a landslide. While he slept, I was in church racking up points. Working for God, worshipping the Lord—that was where I triumphed in my strength. If only he could see the scoreboard. I still remember which pew I was sitting in as I thought up that competition. I still cringe at little boy Eric's awful theology. While I knew that worshipping God was right, I had no clue what worship was.

(RE)MADE TO WORSHIP

God made human beings to be worshippers. God created humans in his image to fill and rule the earth, displaying his glory throughout creation in how they lived. That gets at the heart of worship: Worship gladly displays and declares God's worth to him and all creation. We also noted that God created humans for priestly service. We worship God by serving in his presence, dwelling with him in a relationship of grace. The creation story reminds us that God made us worshippers in our lives as rulers on earth and in our service as priests before him.

The Lord remakes his people into worshippers. God's purpose for humans didn't end when sin entered the picture. The Lord is redeeming people and restoring them to their original purpose. In the end, God's people will be kings and priests who worship him and reign with him forever: "The throne of God and of the Lamb will be in the city, and his servants will worship him...They will reign forever and ever" (Revelation 22:3, 5). God's relationship with Israel illustrates his purpose for all his people. He rescued Israel from Egyptian slavery so that they could "sacrifice to the LORD" (Exodus 3:18; see also 5:3; 8:26). He saved Israel so that they could worship him: "You will be my kingdom of priests and my holy nation" (19:6). Israel's worship has much to teach us about weakness.

WE DEPEND ENTIRELY UPON GOD TO BE WORSHIPPERS

In chapter 1, we noted this weakness: *We depend entirely upon God for our purpose.* We didn't get to choose our purpose. The Lord made us to be worshippers. We wouldn't be worshippers unless he gave us that purpose. That weakness is emphasized in God's acts of redemption.

We depend entirely upon God to be restored as worshippers.

After the fall into sin, humans remained worshippers—unfortunately, in their depraved state, they worship anything and everything but God. "They exchanged the truth of God for a lie, and worshiped and served what has been created instead of the Creator, who is praised forever" (Romans 1:25). Since humans are too weak to save themselves, they're too weak to restore themselves to acceptable worship. So long as we're out of fellowship with God, we can't worship him rightly.

We cannot return to the state of true worshippers unless the Lord redeems us and transforms us. We should "take seriously the extraordinary biblical perspective that acceptable worship is something made possible for us by God."[1] Before God's worth can be declared by his people, they must first experience it in redemption. That principle is illustrated in Israel's worship—before they could worship the Lord as he desired, they had to be redeemed out of slavery. Scripture emphasizes that it's "only possible to serve the LORD acceptably because of his gracious initiative, rescuing his people from bondage to other masters, and revealing his will to them."[2]

We depend entirely upon God to know how to worship.

After rescuing the Israelites, God brought them to Mount Sinai, where he entered a covenant with them, giving them his Law to teach them how to be a "kingdom of priests" (Exodus 19:6). In a real sense, the entire Mosaic Law dealt with worship. In Exodus 20–23, the Law instructed Israel to display the Lord's worth to the nations (how to worship). Israel would not know how to worship the Lord unless he taught them.

---

1. David Peterson, *Engaging with God: A Biblical Theology of Worship* (Downers Grove, IL: InterVarsity Press, 1992), 19.

2. Peterson, 73.

Likewise, in Exodus 25–40, the Lord explained in considerable detail how to build the tabernacle and its furnishings. Following Exodus, Leviticus details how sacrifices were to be offered in the temple along with instructions for the priesthood. The tabernacle functioned as God's dwelling place among his people in the wilderness. It was there that atonement was made for sin, the people brought their offerings, and priestly service was rendered. Thus, the tabernacle became central to Israel's national, corporate, and personal worship of the Lord. The tabernacle and its extensive instructions remind us that worship is always a response to God's revelatory and redeeming acts.

There is a danger to be noted in the exhaustive rules for worship in the tabernacle (and, later, the temple). The Israelites would be tempted to think that they were offering acceptable worship if they simply followed the directions. Nothing, of course, could be further from the truth. Acceptable worship begins in the heart, acknowledging one's weakness and coming to the Lord, whose strength supplies every need.

TRUE WORSHIP IS AN ACKNOWLEDGMENT OF WEAKNESS

Psalm 50 opens with a courtroom scene. Heaven and earth are summoned to witness the judgment of God's people (verses 1-4). The defendant is Israel: "Gather my faithful ones to me, those who made a covenant with me by sacrifice" (verse 5). The mention of sacrifice brings worship to the forefront. "God is the Judge" (verse 6). The court is gathered to hear his verdict on the question "Is Israel's worship acceptable?"

The Lord is the key witness against the defendant (verse 7). The crime, he says, is not that Israel failed to keep the rules for sacrifices and offerings. "I do not rebuke you for your sacrifices or for your burnt offerings, which are continually before me" (verse 8). So, what is the issue? Verses 9 to 13 get at the crime.

The Lord explains that he doesn't need any of the animals they sacrifice (verses 9-10). Every creature on earth is already his (verse 11). If the Lord were hungry, he wouldn't tell Israel—he owns everything in the world (verse 12)! That idea is ridiculous anyway, as he obviously does not "eat the flesh of bulls or drink the blood of goats" (verse 13). These statements hint at the mindset of the worshippers: They believed their offerings were something God needed from them. They fail to see that worshippers are incapable of bringing to God anything that isn't his already. Worship involves offering back to God what he has graciously given.

Next, the Lord exhorts Israel, "Offer a thanksgiving sacrifice to God, and pay your vows to the Most High" (verse 14). A *thanksgiving sacrifice* (also called a fellowship sacrifice), like a *freewill offering* (payment of a vow), is "a sacrifice in which lay worshippers are allowed to share in the sacred meal, normally a priestly privilege."[3] Both priests and worshippers shared the meal with the Lord, eating meat, bread, and wine directly from the Lord's table, "declaring publicly that God had met their needs."[4] That's the heart of worship: "Look! The Lord met my needs!" "If they praised God this way, then their sacrifices would be offered for the proper reasons—to express their dependence on God and their gratitude for their deliverance."[5]

The Israelites had worship backward. They approached the Lord as though he were weak and they were strong. A god that needs something is a weak god. If worshippers supply what the god lacks, they are the stronger party. Worship then becomes about using their strength to compensate for the god's weakness. The Lord called Israel

---

3. R.T. Beckwith, "Sacrifice," in *New Dictionary of Biblical Theology*, eds. T. Desmond Alexander and Brian S. Rosner, electronic ed. (Downers Grove, IL: InterVarsity Press, 2000), 757.

4. Allen P. Ross, *Recalling the Hope of Glory: Biblical Worship from the Garden to the New Creation* (Grand Rapids: Kregel, 2006), 338.

5. Ross, 338.

to reverse the equation—to acknowledge that they were weak and he was strong.

True worship is the glad declaration of our weakness—our utter inability to give ourselves what we need—and the all-satisfying sufficiency of God's strength, which has abundantly supplied all we need. That truth has immediate application for Christians because true worship happens only through faith in Jesus Christ. Peter tells us that "his divine power has given us everything required for life and godliness" (2 Peter 1:3). Where and how does God provide us with everything? "Through the knowledge of him who called us by his own glory and goodness" (verse 3). "Knowledge of him" is knowledge of Jesus, "the encounter with Jesus Christ that began in conversion and continues thereafter."[6] God gives us everything—our forgiveness, sanctification, and future glorification—in Christ by grace through faith. We bring nothing. We add nothing. God supplies it all—everything. "The church must not conclude that godliness comes from their own inherent abilities since the gifts given to believers are rooted in the knowledge of Christ."[7]

When we gather for Christian worship, we must guard against the error of the Israelites. Debates about the externals of Christian worship often divide between the *regulative principle* and the *normative principle*. The former states that corporate worship may only use elements distinctly affirmed or commanded by Scripture. The latter holds that corporate worship may include any element not prohibited by Scripture. Those debates are important—we want to honor God in our worship! But both camps can easily fall into the error of Psalm 50. One worshipper may look at the worship service and say, "How wonderful we are to order our service exactly as God

---

6. Thomas R. Schreiner, *1, 2 Peter, Jude*, The New American Commentary, vol. 37 (Nashville: Broadman & Holman Publishers, 2003), 292.

7. Schreiner, 292.

commands!" The other may say, "How glorious is our freedom to worship in these ways!" Both turn the focus on themselves and what they bring to God. They make worship itself the focus of worship—and God hates it. External forms of biblical worship that are devoid of sincere dependence upon and satisfaction in Christ are no better than pagan sacrifices.[8]

TRUE WORSHIP OVERFLOWS
IN LOVE FOR THE WEAK

The trial in Psalm 50 continues with a rhetorical question: "What right do you have to recite my statutes and to take my covenant on your lips?" (verse 16). That likely refers to the recitation of the Law accompanying a covenant renewal ceremony. The implied answer is that they have no right to recite these things. Why? Because they weren't living these things: "You hate instruction and fling my words behind you" (verse 17). The Lord then unleashes a litany of charges, all of which reveal their treatment of others: They keep friendly company with thieves and adulterers, speak evil and deceit, and malign and slander their own family members (verses 18-20). The Law, as we've seen, connects love for God with love for neighbor. "If the worshippers do not love the Lord as they should, then they will not love other people righteously."[9] "You have done these things, and I kept silent; you thought I was just like you" (verse 21). Because the Lord hadn't rebuked them immediately, they assumed he approved of their evil. But, he says, "I will rebuke you and lay out the case before you" (verse 21).

The prophets repeatedly denounced Israel's worship due to their treatment of the weak. Amos confronted an Israel that loved to boast about bringing numerous offerings.[10] But the Lord said, "I hate, I

---

8. See Isaiah 66:3.

9. Ross, *Recalling the Hope*, 338.

10. See Amos 4:4-5.

despise, your feasts! I can't stand the stench of your solemn assemblies"
(Amos 5:21). He rejected their offerings and refused their songs (verses
22-23). And why was their worship unacceptable? They abused the
weak. "Amos highlights taking advantage of the poor (2:6), oppress-
ing the poor and the needy (4:1), extortion of the poor (5:11), taking bribes to pervert justice for the poor in the gates (i.e., the courts
[5:12]), immorality (2:7), abuse of rights (2:8), desecration of vows and
obstruction of prophets (2:11-12), and violence and robbery (3:10)."[11]

Isaiah opens with a condemnation of Judah's worship as a tram-
pling of courts, useless offerings, and detestable incense, which the
Lord could not stand and hated (see Isaiah 1:11-13). Their worship
burdened him. He was tired of putting up with them, so he refused
to look at them or hear their prayers (verses 14-15). They followed all
the external forms, keeping festivals and offering sacrifices, but their
hands were "covered with blood" (verse 15). How was their worship
defiled? The once-faithful town was void of justice and filled with
evil, as wicked rulers perverted justice and abused the weak (verses
21-23). "They do not defend the rights of the fatherless, and the widow's case never comes before them" (verse 23). They wrote oppressive laws "to keep the poor from getting a fair trial and to deprive
the needy among my people of justice, so that widows can be their
spoil and they can plunder the fatherless" (10:1-2).

Jeremiah stood in the temple and chastised Judah's deceitful chant-
ing: "This is the temple of the LORD, the temple of the LORD, the temple of the LORD" (Jeremiah 7:4). The people believed that because the
Lord chose Zion as his dwelling place, then no harm could befall it
or them as inhabitants. They turned the location of worship into the
object of worship, trusting in the temple instead of the Lord. But they
were not safe in the temple. What invalidated their worship? They

11. Ross, *Recalling the Hope*, 334.

"oppress the resident alien, the fatherless, and the widow," "shed innocent blood," and "follow other gods," in addition to stealing, mur-
dering, committing adultery, and swearing falsely (verses 5-10). They
made the Lord's house a "den of robbers" where unrepentant thieves
could hide safely (verse 11). True worship of the Lord meant love for
neighbor, particularly the weak: "Administer justice and righteousness. Rescue the victim of robbery from his oppressor. Don't exploit
or brutalize the resident alien, the fatherless, or the widow. Don't
shed innocent blood in this place" (22:3).

Ezekiel brought a full slate of sin against Jerusalem's inhabitants:
contempt of parents, exploitation of resident aliens, oppression of the
fatherless and widow, slander for bloodshed, sexual immorality, the
violation of women, bribery for bloodshed, usury, extortion (Ezekiel
22:4-12). "Once again the prevailing sins were social injustices borne by
a spirit of self-gratification and characterized by an indifference to the
needs of others. Not only did this nullify worship, but it also brought
God's judgment on the nation."[12] Because the Israelites abused the
weak, God's glory left the temple and the city altogether (Ezekiel 10–11).

Each prophet announced the same solution—repent and seek
the Lord. Repentance meant amending their ways regarding their
neighbors, especially the weak. "But let justice flow like water, and
righteousness, like an unfailing stream" (Amos 5:24). "Pursue justice.
Correct the oppressor. Defend the rights of the fatherless. Plead the
widow's cause" (Isaiah 1:16-18).

> Mankind, he has told each of you what is good
> and what it is the LORD requires of you:
> to act justly,
> to love faithfulness,
> and to walk humbly with your God (Micah 6:8).

---

12. Ross, *Recalling the Hope*, 337.

Act justly—with particular attention to upholding the rights of the weak. Love faithfulness—practice covenant faithfulness (*hesed*) as characterized by Yahweh-like concern for the least of these. Walk humbly with your God—live with God in a way that declares your dependence upon him, honoring him as the giver of all good things.

Asaph concluded Psalm 50 with this same warning (verses 22-23):

> Understand this, you who forget God,
> or I will tear you apart,
> and there will be no one to rescue you.
> Whoever offers a thanksgiving sacrifice honors me,
> and whoever orders his conduct,
> I will show him the salvation of God.

Honor the Lord with a true "thanksgiving sacrifice," a humble declaration of total dependence on the Lord. Order your conduct by reversing the mistreatment of others described in verses 18-20—do justice and embody the Lord's neighborly kindness. In true worship, confessing our weakness and loving the weak are inseparable.

We find a fitting illustration in Paul's instructions for the Lord's Supper found in 1 Corinthians 11. Like the prophets before him, Paul denounced the Corinthian church's worship in no uncertain terms: "When you come together, then, it is not to eat the Lord's Supper" (verse 20). "Should I praise you? I do not praise you in this matter!" (verse 22). What could he mean? They were at church. They recited Jesus's words of institution. They received the bread and wine, just as Jesus commanded. How was that not the Lord's Supper? To understand Paul's condemnation of their worship, we must grasp Paul's understanding of the Lord's Supper, found in verses 23-26:

> For I received from the Lord what I also passed on to you:
> On the night when he was betrayed, the Lord Jesus took
> bread, and when he had given thanks, broke it, and said,
> "This is my body, which is for you. Do this in remembrance
> of me." In the same way also he took the cup, after supper,
> and said, "This cup is the new covenant in my blood. Do
> this, as often as you drink it, in remembrance of me." For as
> often as you eat this bread and drink the cup, you proclaim
> the Lord's death until he comes.

In some Christian traditions, the meal is called the *eucharist*, which is taken from the Greek word translated *give thanks*.[13] Other traditions refer to the meal as *communion* because it is a communal meal in which we fellowship with God and other believers. Both correctly grasp the nature of the Lord's Supper as a thanksgiving sacrifice.

As discussed earlier, a thanksgiving sacrifice was a communal meal that all worshippers shared with the Lord. They ate the sacrifices— meat, bread, and wine—directly from the Lord's table as a public declaration that God had supplied all their needs. The Lord's Supper is all these things. It is a repurposing of the Passover meal—a covenant renewal ceremony between the Lord and his people. The Lord Jesus is the host, inviting every member of the covenant community to commune at his table. They receive the bread and the wine as a symbolic consumption of the sacrifice ("this is my body…this is my blood"), a sacrifice that enacts the New Covenant through the forgiveness of sins.[14] They do this as a proclamation of total dependence on Christ, the living sacrifice through which God supplied their every need.

A thanksgiving sacrifice required communion with God and

---

13. The Greek word for "give thanks" is *eucharisteō*, from which we get the word *eucharist*.
14. See Matthew 23:26-29; Mark 14:22-25; Luke 22:15-20; John 6:51-53.

fellowship with other covenant community members. When the Israelites mistreated the weak among them, they failed to love one another and, consequentially, forfeited communion with God. It was the same in Corinth when social divisions appeared, especially as they ate this communal meal. "Each one eats his own supper" indicates that while they all ate at the same time, they didn't all eat the same meal, with the result that "one person is hungry while another gets drunk!" (verse 21). Those with status, power, and wealth enjoyed a lush banquet, while the lower classes went home unsatisfied. Rather than being a "love feast," they "despise the church of God and humiliate those who have nothing" (verse 22). The humiliation of the weak goes hand in hand with hating the body of Christ.

Paul stresses that the Lord's Supper proclaims the Lord's death. The cross is the culmination of Jesus's voluntary humiliation, in which he offered his life to save his people. The Lord's Supper is a public reenactment—a proclamation—of that love. The church gathers as one to say, "God has abundantly provided us with all we need in the death and resurrection of our Lord!" Therefore, the Corinthian church's discrimination against its weakest members contradicted the meaning of "the Lord's Supper." They weren't proclaiming Christ. Thus, Paul spoke his judgment: "When you come together, then, it is not to eat the Lord's Supper" (verse 20). Their act of worship was unacceptable.

In a similar vein, James condemned favoritism in corporate worship:

> My brothers and sisters, do not show favoritism as you hold on to the faith in our glorious Lord Jesus Christ. For if someone comes into your meeting wearing a gold ring and dressed in fine clothes, and a poor person dressed in filthy clothes also comes in, if you look with favor on the one wearing the fine clothes and say, "Sit here in a good place," and yet you say to the poor person, "Stand over

there," or "Sit here on the floor by my footstool," haven't
you made distinctions among yourselves and become judges
with evil thoughts? (James 2:1-4).

Their worship gathering was invalid because they favored the
wealthy and discriminated against the poor in their seating arrange-
ments. Instead of humble worshippers, they'd become evil judges.
James inquired, "Didn't God choose the poor in this world to be
rich in faith and heirs of the kingdom that he has promised to those
who love him?" (verse 5). By dishonoring the weak, they failed to
fulfill "the royal law" (the law of King Jesus): "Love your neighbor as
yourself" (verses 6-8). Instead, when they showed partiality to garner favor with the strong, that law convicted them as sinners. Their
idolatry of the strong betrayed their belief that they required the rich
to get what they needed (or wanted). They didn't depend entirely on
the Lord. Instead of being an assembly to worship God, their gathering became a courtroom in which they were judged as lawbreakers.
Their mistreatment of the weak was disregard for the gospel, render-
ing their worship unacceptable.

WORSHIP IN SONG: CELEBRATING GOD'S STRENGTH DISPLAYED IN OUR WEAKNESS

Any chapter on worship would be incomplete without discussing
singing, which has always played a vital role in the worship of God's
people. Israel's first act of worship after the Lord rescued them from
Egypt was a song of praise, recorded in Exodus 15:1-21. The theme
of the song is summarized in verse 2: "The LORD is my strength and
my song; he has become my salvation." It wasn't sufficient to say that
the Lord strengthened them. No, the Lord himself was their strength.
They had no power in and of themselves; they were inherently weak.
Without the Lord, they had no strength.

That message is the theme of Israel's songbook. The main point of the book of Psalms is that the Lord God reigns as King, and his people are entirely dependent upon him for life and salvation. The book opens with that message. Psalm 1 asserts that those who delight in the Lord have life and strength, like a tree that takes constant nourishment from a stream. But those who won't live by drinking God's Word will perish. Psalm 2 reminds us that the Lord's goodness comes through the promised King, his Son. Those who love him have life, while those who rebel against him will be crushed into lifeless dust. The book closes with the same message. The final psalms (145–150) declare that God our Maker is the Lord enthroned in Zion. Everyone and everything owe their existence to God the King—apart from his will, they do not exist. Therefore, everyone and everything—weak and dependent creatures—should acknowledge, proclaim, and celebrate who God is for them in all his strength.

Every song in the Psalter speaks to the Lord's strength—and, by implication, our corresponding weakness. The psalms of petition bring requests to God because the singer understands he cannot provide for himself. Even the psalms of lament, complaining about the Lord's apparent indifference or inaction, are confessions of our weakness and God's strength. The lamenter confesses his inability to change the situation, acknowledging that the all-powerful Lord must intervene. The psalms of thanksgiving recognize that provision and answered prayers owe entirely to God's strength (and, therefore, not ours). Consider a few ways the Psalms celebrate the Lord's strength in our weakness:

Weakness is a reason for the Lord to act.

- "Be gracious to me, LORD, for I am weak" (6:2).

- "As my strength fails, do not abandon me" (71:9).

- "Listen to my cry, for I am very weak" (142:6).

Weakness is the reason the Lord responds.

- "'Because of the devastation of the needy and the groaning of the poor, I will now rise up,' says the LORD" (12:5).

- "As a father has compassion on his children, so the LORD has compassion on those who fear him. For he knows what we are made of, remembering that we are dust" (103:13-14).

God rescues the weak.

- "LORD, who is like you, rescuing the poor from one too strong for him, the poor or the needy from one who robs him?" (35:10).

- "God in his holy dwelling is a father of the fatherless and a champion of widows" (68:5).

- "He will have pity on the poor and helpless and save the lives of the poor" (72:13).

God strengthens those who acknowledge their weakness.

- "LORD, you have heard the desire of the humble; you will strengthen their hearts. You will listen carefully, doing justice for the fatherless and the oppressed so that mere humans from the earth may terrify them no more" (10:17-18).

- "God—he clothes me with strength and makes my way perfect" (18:32-36).

- "Who is like the LORD our God—the one enthroned on high, who stoops down to look on the heavens and the earth? He raises the poor from the dust and lifts the needy from the trash heap in order to seat them with nobles—with the nobles of his people. He gives the childless woman a household, making her the joyful mother of children. Hallelujah!" (113:5-9).

- "Happy is the one whose help is the God of Jacob, whose hope is in the LORD his God, the Maker of heaven and earth, the sea and everything in them. He remains faithful forever, executing justice for the exploited and giving food to the hungry. The LORD frees prisoners. The LORD opens the eyes of the blind. The LORD raises up those who are oppressed. The LORD loves the righteous. The LORD protects resident aliens and helps the fatherless and the widow, but he frustrates the ways of the wicked" (146:5-9).

God is his people's strength.

- "I love you, LORD, my strength" (18:1).

- "LORD, the king finds joy in your strength" (21:1).

- "My strength, come quickly to help me" (22:19).

- "The LORD is my strength and my shield" (28:7).

- "The LORD is the strength of his people" (28:8).

- "The course of my life is in your power" (31:15).

- "I will keep watch for you, my strength" (59:9).

- "To you, my strength, I sing praises" (59:17).

- "God is the strength of my heart, my portion forever" (73:26).

- "Happy are the people whose strength is in you" (84:5).

- "You are their magnificent strength" (89:17).

- "My hand will always be with him, and my arm will strengthen him" (89:21).

- "The LORD is my strength and my song; he has become my salvation" (118:14).

Being strong means confessing you are weak by waiting on the Lord's strength.

- "Wait for the LORD; be strong, and let your heart be courageous. Wait for the LORD" (27:14).

- "Be strong, and let your heart be courageous, all you who put your hope in the LORD" (31:24).

True faith knows that earthly strength is weakness when compared to God's might, so it seeks and boasts only in the Lord's strength.

- "Some take pride in chariots, and others in horses, but we take pride in the name of the LORD our God. They collapse and fall, but we rise and stand firm" (20:7-8).

- "A king is not saved by a large army; a warrior will not be rescued by great strength. The horse is a false hope for safety; it provides no escape by its great power. But look, the LORD keeps his eye on those who fear him—those who depend on his faithful love to rescue them from death and to keep them alive in famine. We wait for the LORD; he is our help and shield" (33:16-20).

- "Seek the LORD and his strength; seek his face always" (105:4).

- "In vain you get up early and stay up late, working hard to have enough food—yes, he gives sleep to the one he loves" (127:2).

- "He is not impressed by the strength of a horse; he does not value the power of a warrior. The LORD values those who fear him, those who put their hope in his faithful love" (147:10-11).

———

May we never shrink from declaring that, in saving us, "God has chosen what is weak in the world" and saved us through Christ, "the power of God" (1 Corinthians 1:24, 27). May we gladly sing:

> *Jesus loves me—this I know,*
> *For the Bible tells me so:*
> *Little ones to him belong—*
> *They are weak, but he is strong.*[15]

---

15. Anna Bartlett Warner, "Jesus Loves Me," originally published as a song in *Bradbury's Golden Shower of S.S. Melodies: A New Collection of Hymns and Tunes for the Sabbath School*, ed. William B. Bradbury (New York, 1862).

CHAPTER 7

WEAKNESS IN ISRAEL'S WISDOM

The fear of the LORD is the beginning of wisdom,
and the knowledge of the Holy One is understanding.

PROVERBS 9:10

As a kid, I loved Easter. (Still do!) Dying hard-boiled eggs. Getting new "church clothes." Waking up to a basket filled with jelly beans, malted milk eggs, and a chocolate rabbit. Heading to church for worship and breakfast. Then we'd hit the road to gather with my grandparents, aunts, uncles, and cousins for a meal and a fun afternoon. That fun always included an Easter egg hunt. Each family brought dyed Easter eggs, which we hid around the yard and found, and eventually peeled and ate. Almost every childhood recollection of Easter is good. Almost.

One year, we hosted the family gathering at our house. A few weeks later, on a warm spring afternoon, a friend and I were playing in our oversized sandbox when she made a discovery. "Look what I found," she exclaimed.

"That's one of the Easter eggs we couldn't find," I replied. Then, taking the egg from her, I peeled the shell and took a bite.

It didn't take me long to realize that it isn't wise to eat a hard-boiled egg that's been hidden in a sandbox for several weeks. I regurgitated it—and whatever else I'd eaten that day—as I ran crying back to the house.

That was the day I learned the difference between knowledge and wisdom. Intellectual knowledge discerns it's an Easter egg your cousin buried in the sandbox weeks ago. Wisdom understands not to eat it.

WISDOM IN THE OLD TESTAMENT

Wisdom literature occupies a significant portion of the Old Testament, most notably in the books of Job, Proverbs, and Ecclesiastes.[1] Generally, "wisdom in the Old Testament describes the practical skills associated with living a successful life. These range from the ability to create highly skilled works to the intellectual capability required to make choices that result in favorable outcomes and avoid troubles."[2] Wisdom "refers to practical knowledge, the ability to understand reality from God's perspective and to act on that understanding."[3]

To understand wisdom, we must grapple with its place in the storyline of the Bible. So far, our study of weakness has followed the plot points of redemptive history, the grand story of how God is redeeming his people and establishing his kingdom in the world. We began at creation, then looked at the Fall and the subsequent promise of redemption. Then we examined how that promise unfolded in Israel's history, after which we've been considering three aspects of Israel's national life: the Law, worship, and now wisdom. That order is intentional. The Lord redeemed the Israelites from slavery and gave them the Law at Sinai, making them his kingdom through covenant

---

1. Some scholars consider Song of Songs or portions of it to be wisdom literature.

2. Martin A. Shields, "Wisdom," in *The Lexham Bible Dictionary*, ed. John D. Barry et al. (Bellingham, WA: Lexham Press, 2016), Logos Bible Software edition.

3. Douglas J. Moo, *The Letters to the Colossians and to Philemon*, Pillar New Testament Commentary (Grand Rapids: Eerdmans, 2008), 170.

and giving them instructions for living. Through that revelation, Israel knew how to honor the Lord and live as his people in the world—worship and wisdom, respectively.

Worship and wisdom follow redemption as the culmination of a restored relationship with the Lord. Worship and wisdom are the capstones of living as God's people in God's place under the rule of God's King. The height of Old Testament worship appears in the Psalms (primarily written by David, Israel's greatest king) and the temple (built by Solomon, David's son). Old Covenant wisdom culminates in the books of Proverbs and Ecclesiastes, both written by David's son Solomon, to whom the Lord gave "wisdom, very great insight, and understanding as vast as the sand on the seashore" (1 Kings 4:29). The place of wisdom in the unfolding story of salvation presses home the point that we cannot be wise apart from a relationship with God as Creator and Redeemer. Thus, "wisdom begins with a holy reverence for the One who has rescued Israel and brought her to himself. Wisdom in this sense is not separate from Yahweh's redemptive acts but a response to them."[4]

WHAT WISDOM UNDERSTANDS ABOUT WEAKNESS

Wisdom understands that only the weak can become wise.

Only God is inherently wise.

> Who has directed the Spirit of the LORD,
> or who gave him counsel?
> Who did he consult?
> Who gave him understanding
> and taught him the paths of justice?

---

4. C.G. Bartholomew, "Wisdom Books," in *New Dictionary of Biblical Theology*, eds. T. Desmond Alexander and Brian S. Rosner, electronic ed. (Downers Grove, IL: InterVarsity Press, 2000), 120.

Who taught him knowledge
and showed him the way of understanding? (Isaiah 40:13-14).

The answer to those questions is *no one*. God is eternally wise. He didn't become wise; he always was. No one has ever taught God anything. He can't grow in wisdom. He possesses all wisdom in himself. He never needs counsel or instruction. He's the source of all wisdom.

Regarding wisdom, humans are weak. We have no inherent wisdom. Thus, to be wise, we must confess our weakness and go to the Lord for instruction. We must renounce our own interpretation of the world and live by faith in what God has revealed. Wisdom is always the result of a proper relationship with the Lord, our Creator and Redeemer.

Wisdom was revealed in Creation.

"The LORD founded the earth by wisdom and established the heavens by understanding" (Proverbs 3:19). God ordered creation according to the principles of wisdom. In creation, some of that wisdom was revealed. The Lord revealed instructions on how to live in the garden, giving the first humans their purpose and mandate. Thus, "human beings were always dependent upon God's giving them the interpretation of the universe and of their relationship to it."[5]

Humans were tasked with growing in wisdom as they walked with the Lord. "Finding wisdom means discovering how to follow the order that God has built into his world."[6] Humans were to use their God-given rational faculties to explore the world and discover how it works as they dwelt in harmony with their Creator. Life would have gone according to design had the first humans lived according to God's wisdom.

---

5. G. Goldsworthy, "Proverbs," in *New Dictionary of Biblical Theology*, 210.
6. C.G. Bartholomew, "Wisdom Books," 121.

Wisdom was lost in the Fall.

Adam and Eve rejected the Lord's wisdom to live according to their own. That rebellion is called *sin*. It continues today whenever humans attempt to interpret reality apart from God's revelation. "Human rationality and intelligence are misused when humans interpret the world of experience apart from the revelation of God. The result is a different and erroneous view which may work well at the mundane and pragmatic level of human wisdom but which is ultimately self-destructive."[7] So long as humans live with a hostile attitude toward God, their independent wisdom will always bring death. Through the Fall, "creation was subjected to futility" (Romans 8:20). Until creation is restored, wise living remains a frustrating and sometimes bewildering quest.

Wisdom is restored in redemption.

For humans to be wise again, they must be restored to a proper relationship with the Lord. Only through faith in God's promises and submission to his instruction may human wisdom flourish. Therefore, Old Testament wisdom literature is clear: To be wise, you must know Yahweh.

- "The fear of the LORD is the beginning of knowledge; fools despise wisdom and discipline" (Proverbs 1:7).

- "For the LORD gives wisdom; from his mouth come knowledge and understanding" (2:6).

- "Don't be wise in your own eyes; fear the LORD and turn away from evil" (3:7).

- "The fear of the LORD is the beginning of wisdom, and the knowledge of the Holy One is understanding" (9:10).

---

7. Goldsworthy, "Proverbs," 211.

- "The fear of the LORD is what wisdom teaches, and humility comes before honor" (15:33).

Note the repeated occurrence of "the LORD." "The LORD" (in small caps) appears in many English-language Bibles to translate the Hebrew word *Yahweh*. Yahweh is the personal name of the Lord, which he graciously revealed to his covenant people. When "the LORD" is used, it points to a covenant relationship with Yahweh as Redeemer and God.

Wisdom does not result from a generic fear of a generic God. "The framework of the fear of the Lord indicates that the empirical data cannot be rightly understood or interpreted without the wisdom of God given in his covenant of redemptive revelation."[8] Wisdom begins in a saving, covenantal relationship with a personal God, Yahweh—a relationship that exists only by grace through faith.

"The fear of the LORD" is reverential trust in him. This fear is saving faith that recognizes the Lord's all-surpassing strength and wisdom, acknowledging total dependence upon it. Faith means confessing one's lack of strength and wisdom (weakness) and the need for the Lord's. We see both aspects of faith (renouncing our strength and receiving God's) in Proverbs 3:5-7:

> Trust in the LORD with all your heart,
> and do not rely on your own understanding;
> in all your ways know him,
> and he will make your paths straight.
> Don't be wise in your own eyes;
> fear the LORD and turn away from evil.

Here "trust in the LORD" (verse 5) and "fear the LORD" (verse 7) are synonymous. Both involve confessing our own weakness—"do

---

8. Goldsworthy, "Proverbs," 210.

not rely on your own understanding" and "don't be wise in your own eyes." Both involve total dependence on the Lord's strength: "Trust in the LORD with all your heart." Old Testament wisdom "firmly rejects human autonomy as the path to truth."[9]

"The fear of the LORD is the beginning of wisdom" (9:10). Consider the implications of this truth. A six-year-old who trusts in Jesus is further along the road to wisdom than an atheist entrepreneur who studies a chapter of Proverbs daily for business acumen while renouncing the Lord. Those principles may prove temporarily helpful in a limited capacity, but he's not wise. He believes that he has the power to comprehend wisdom and the strength to live it out apart from the grace and presence of the Lord. He's proud, and his existence will end in destruction. There is no wisdom apart from knowing the Lord:

> I am more stupid than any other person,
> and I lack a human's ability to understand.
> I have not gained wisdom,
> and I have no knowledge of the Holy One (30:2-3).

But the six-year-old understands and trusts that her present and future are in the loving hands of her Creator and Redeemer, Jesus Christ. She knows where life is, and she is on the path to flourishing.

Wisdom understands the weakness of worldly strength.

Proverbs opens with a father-to-son appeal to live wisely. Fearing the Lord involves resisting temptation: "If sinners entice you, don't be persuaded" (Proverbs 1:10). This enticement consists in using one's strength to take advantage of the weak (verses 11-14):

---

9. Bartholomew, "Wisdom Books," 120.

Come with us!
Let's set an ambush and kill someone.
Let's attack some innocent person just for fun!
Let's swallow them alive, like Sheol,
whole, like those who go down to the Pit.
We'll find all kinds of valuable property
and fill our houses with plunder.
Throw in your lot with us,
and we'll all share the loot.

That temptation appears throughout Proverbs. From the world's perspective, the abuse of strength is a sure path to gain. Solomon, however, reveals the delusion: "But they set an ambush to kill themselves; they attack their own lives. Such are the paths of all who make profit dishonestly; it takes the lives of those who receive it" (verses 18-19). Thus, "there is a way that seems right to a person, but its end is the way to death" (14:12; 16:25). Wisdom trusts that the Lord is just and won't allow the wicked to prosper forever. The "strong" may be more robust than their neighbors, but they're not stronger than Yahweh. It's better—wiser—to fear him.

From a worldly perspective, using strength to take advantage of the weak seems like a sure win. You can take their stuff, and they cannot oppose you. But wisdom understands that the outcome isn't ultimately a matter of which person is stronger. There are more than two parties involved. The Lord loves the weak and defends them. Therefore, to use your strength to oppress the weak is to challenge the Lord, who takes up their cause:

- "The one who oppresses the poor person insults his Maker, but one who is kind to the needy honors him" (14:31).

- "The LORD tears apart the house of the proud, but he protects the widow's territory" (15:25).

- "The one who mocks the poor insults his Maker" (17:5).

- "Kindness to the poor is a loan to the LORD, and he will give a reward to the lender" (19:17).

- "Don't rob a poor person because he is poor, and don't crush the oppressed at the city gate, for the LORD will champion their cause and will plunder those who plunder them" (22:22-23).

- "Don't move an ancient boundary marker, and don't encroach on the fields of the fatherless, for their Redeemer is strong, and he will champion their cause against you" (23:10-11).

Wisdom knows that human strength and ingenuity are no match for the Lord. Better to use your strength generously, giving it away to serve others while trusting the Lord, than to hoard it for yourself while exploiting your neighbor.

Wisdom often looks weak. Hoarding wealth seems to be the path of strength, a sure protection against poverty. Yet wisdom knows:

> One person gives freely,
> yet gains more;
> another withholds what is right,
> only to become poor.
> A generous person will be enriched,
> and the one who gives a drink of water
> will receive water.
> People will curse anyone who hoards grain,

but a blessing will come to the one who sells it
(Proverbs 11:24-26).

What looks like the path to weakness—generous giving—is actually the path to life and flourishing. But that path can only be followed by faith in the Lord. "The reason is that wisdom means something more than simply knowing certain precepts; it is about moral character and a settled lifestyle that are impervious to the seductions of evil men and women."[10]

In the same vein, the weak of the world can accomplish as much as (or more than) the strong if they're wise. In Proverbs 30:24, Agur points out that "four things on earth are small, yet they are extremely wise." "The Hebrew word carries the idea of not only 'small' in size, but also weak in strength or insignificant in comparative contribution."[11] What weak things does he have in mind?

Ants are not a strong people,
yet they store up their food in the summer;
hyraxes are not a mighty people,
yet they make their homes in the cliffs;
locusts have no king,
yet all of them march in ranks;
a lizard can be caught in your hands,
yet it lives in kings' palaces (verses 25-28).

These examples remind us that "size does not always win the prize! Girth does not equal greatness! Through industrious preplanning

10. Andreas J. Köstenberger and Gregory Goswell, *Biblical Theology: A Canonical, Thematic, and Ethical Approach* (Wheaton, IL: Crossway, 2023), 291.

11. John A. Kitchen, *Proverbs: A Mentor Commentary*, Mentor Commentaries (Fearn, Ross-shire, UK: Mentor, 2006), 697.

(verse 25), cautious defense (verse 26), organized cooperation (verse 27), and courageous boldness (verse 28), victory may be gained by those lacking the might and fight of the world."[12] Yes, "a wise warrior is better than a strong one, and a man of knowledge than one of strength" (24:5).

Wisdom understands the weakness of human wisdom.

Much of the wisdom found in Proverbs operates on the principle of consequence. "Wisdom does teach that wise acts generally lead to success and blessing."[13] But what is true *generally* isn't true universally. There are exceptions to the rule. Depending on who you are, the exceptions may feel like the norm.

The book of Job wrestles with a notable exception. Job was the father of seven sons and three daughters and a wealthy man: "His estate included seven thousand sheep and goats, three thousand camels, five hundred yoke of oxen, five hundred female donkeys, and a very large number of servants" (Job 1:2-3). He was "the greatest man among all the people of the east" (verse 3). What should we expect to happen to "a man of complete integrity, who feared God and turned away from evil?" (verse 1).

Proverbs 3:7-8 says, "Fear the Lord and turn away from evil. This will be healing for your body and strengthening for your bones." But that's not what happened to Job. Instead, the pleasures of his life were painfully stripped away. Invaders stole his work animals and murdered his farmhands (Job 1:13-15). Fire from heaven devoured his sheep and shepherds (verse 16). Raiders stole his camels and killed the servants who kept them (verse 17). A strong wind collapsed his son's house, killing all his sons and daughters (verses 18-19). Finally,

---

Satan "infected Job with terrible boils from the soles of his feet to the top of his head" (2:7). That is a far cry from "healing for your body and strengthening for your bones."

How can we make sense of Job's suffering? Job's wife called on him to "curse God and die" (2:9). The bulk of the book involves his friends making extended arguments, calling on Job to confess and repent of whatever sin brought about this suffering. But both Job's wife and his friends misapplied wisdom. They understood wisdom principles as rigid rules operating like a vending machine. If you put in the coins of righteousness, out comes blessing. But put in the spare change of folly, and out comes suffering. Job's wife understood God to be breaking the rules: Job was just, but God didn't keep his end of the bargain. Therefore, he was to be cursed. Job's friends reasoned the other way: If Job suffered, he must have sinned since (they thought) suffering is always the result of personal iniquity.

Job, however, insisted on his righteousness, calling down curse after curse on himself should his integrity have been compromised. In doing so, he challenged God to appear and explain himself: "Here is my signature; let the Almighty answer me. Let my Opponent compose his indictment" (31:35-37). Eventually, the Lord answered Job from a whirlwind. But his answer wasn't what Job expected. The Lord demanded that Job answer him: "Who is this who obscures my counsel with ignorant words? Get ready to answer me like a man; when I question you, you will inform me" (38:2-3).

The Lord took Job back to creation. "Where were you when I established the earth? Tell me, if you have understanding" (verse 4). "The LORD founded the earth by wisdom and established the heavens by understanding" (Proverbs 3:19). Therefore, if Job is wise enough to challenge the Lord, he should be able to explain the wisdom of creation. Then, in a litany of questions, the Lord called Job to explain the earth's measurements and foundation (Job 38:5-7), the sea's birthplace and boundaries (verses 8-11). Had Job commanded the sun to rise, walked on the bottom of the ocean, seen the gates of death, or grasped the extent of the earth (verses 12-18)? Did he know the home of light and darkness, where snow and hail are stored, or the source of the wind (verses 19-24)? Did Job control floods, lightning, rain, ice, frost, constellations, and clouds (verses 31-35)? Did he feed the lions and ravens or know the intricacies of wildlife childbirth (38:39–39:4)? Did Job reign over the wild donkey, ox, ostrich, horse, hawk, or eagle (verses 5-30)? All these questions ultimately ask one thing: Does Job have the perspective of the Lord? Did he order everything by his wisdom? The Lord demands, "Will the one who contends with the Almighty correct him? Let him who argues with God give an answer" (40:2).

> Job answered the LORD:
> I am so insignificant. How can I answer you?
> I place my hand over my mouth.
> I have spoken once, and I will not reply;
> twice, but now I can add nothing (verses 4-5).

He could only confess his ignorance and then shut his mouth. But the Lord wasn't satisfied. He challenged Job again:

> Get ready to answer me like a man;
> when I question you, you will inform me.
> Would you really challenge my justice?
> Would you declare me guilty to justify yourself?
> Do you have an arm like God's?
> Can you thunder with a voice like his? (verses 7-9).

The Lord told Job to put on his big boy pants, which would certainly be soiled by the time they were done. The Lord demanded that

Job become like him—to show himself his equal—and then he'd submit to Job's arrogant assertions.

> Adorn yourself with majesty and splendor,
> and clothe yourself with honor and glory.
> Pour out your raging anger;
> look on every proud person and humiliate him.
> Look on every proud person and humble him;
> trample the wicked where they stand.
> Hide them together in the dust;
> imprison them in the grave.
> Then I will confess to you
> that your own right hand can deliver you (verses 10-14).

The Lord capped his survey of creation with the unrivaled creatures Behemoth and Leviathan (40:15–41:34). Did Job know and control these giants?

Finally, Job confessed the unparalleled sovereignty of the Lord: "I know that you can do anything and no plan of yours can be thwarted" (42:2). He confessed his limited perspective and his foolish attempt to speak beyond it: "Surely I spoke about things I did not understand, things too wondrous for me to know" (verse 3). He renounced his small view of the Lord: "I had heard reports about you, but now my eyes have seen you. Therefore, I reject my words and am sorry for them; I am dust and ashes" (verses 5-6).

Job foolishly believed his wisdom equaled the Lord's. He thought he could see and understand what unfolded in the world from God's perspective if only God would show him. From that perspective, Job believed that he could judge the Lord's work just as well as God did. The lesson he learned (and we should too) is that we cannot comprehend the ways of the Lord. "God cannot reveal to Job, with his limited perspective, what can be understood only from the standpoint of the creator. Job isn't wrong to seek truth and justice, but as a mortal, he simply cannot understand."[14]

Wisdom is possible because there is a Creator. But exhaustive understanding is impossible for humans because of the distinction between Creator and creature. We're not the Lord. We're not capable of possessing the Lord's limitless wisdom. We're weak; he's strong. Our wisdom is weak in comparison to his. Because we're not the Lord, we cannot see and understand from his perspective. We can only fear the Lord and put our hope in him.

Wisdom understands the weakness of life in this world.

In Ecclesiastes, an aged King Solomon reflects on what he's learned after a long life as the wisest man on earth. The lesson is shocking: "'Absolute futility,' says the Teacher. 'Absolute futility. Everything is futile'" (Ecclesiastes 1:2). That's his answer to the question "What does a person gain for all his efforts that he labors at under the sun?" (verse 3). Everything is futile.

Solomon explains that as "king over Israel in Jerusalem," he made a concerted effort to "examine and explore through wisdom all that is done under heaven" (verses 12-13). He did this as the wisest man ever to live: "I have amassed wisdom far beyond all those who were over Jerusalem before me, and my mind has thoroughly grasped wisdom and knowledge" (verse 16). Using his superior wisdom to examine what lasting gain is to be found in this life, he concludes, "I have seen all the things that are done under the sun and have found everything to be futile, a pursuit of the wind" (verse 14). "I applied my mind to know wisdom and knowledge, madness and folly; I learned that this too is a pursuit of the wind" (verse 17). His efforts

---

14. Å. Viberg, "Job," in *New Dictionary of Biblical Theology*, 202.

only worsened things: "For with much wisdom is much sorrow; as knowledge increases, grief increases" (verse 18).

Solomon's search for gain in this life was exhaustive. He used his wisdom to examine pleasure and enjoy what is good (2:1). He explored the limits of laughter and pleasure, wine, achievements, houses, vineyards, gardens, parks, and orchards so large they required reservoirs to water them, servants, slaves, livestock, treasures of silver and gold, musicians, concubines, and greatness.[15] He didn't limit himself: "All that my eyes desired, I did not deny them. I did not refuse myself any pleasure" (verse 10). And what did he find? "When I considered all that I had accomplished and what I had labored to achieve, I found everything to be futile and a pursuit of the wind. There was nothing to be gained under the sun" (verse 11).

Under the sun is Solomon's term for life in this world, the realm where humans live. It's all futile—a vapor, something impossible to be caught and kept. It's there, and then it's gone. That's the weakness of life in this world—it can't provide any lasting joy.

How, then, should we live "under the sun"? We should enjoy life as God makes it possible. "There is nothing better for a person than to eat, drink, and enjoy his work. I have seen that even this is from God's hand, because who can eat and who can enjoy life apart from him?" (2:24). Some have more enjoyment; some have less. None can keep it. Under the sun, gain is futile, and we cannot make sense of it. Therefore, we must live by faith in the Lord and not our own understanding. Our understanding and power are too weak to gain God's perspective. We must fear and trust God, leaving the judgment of everything to him.

> When all has been heard, the conclusion of the matter is
> this: fear God and keep his commands, because this is for

---

15. See Ecclesiastes 2:2-9.

all humanity. For God will bring every act to judgment, including every hidden thing, whether good or evil (12:13-14).

WISDOM IN THE FLESH

The story of redemption is the quest for restored wisdom. The Lord established the earth on the principles of wisdom and instructed the first man. Through "the most cunning of all the wild animals that the LORD God had made," twisted wisdom slithered into the garden (Genesis 3:1). The first humans then cast aside God's wisdom to follow their own interpretation of reality and, "claiming to be wise, they became fools" (Romans 1:22). But the Lord promised a Redeemer, "the seed of the woman," who would appear to crush the head of the serpent.

We've followed the storyline of the Old Testament, looking for the promised offspring. The Lord promised to make Abraham's offspring great, which he did through the nation of Israel. He redeemed Israel, gave them his Law, and placed them in his land. Eventually, he gave them King David, a man after God's own heart. David would not reign forever. But the Lord promised that his son would sit on his throne as the Forever King.

After David's death, his son Solomon took the throne. After Solomon's kingdom was established, the Lord appeared in a dream and told him to ask for whatever he'd like. Solomon asked for wisdom and knowledge to lead God's people (2 Chronicles 1:10). This pleased the Lord, who gave him wisdom and knowledge, "so that there has never been anyone like you before and never will be again" (1 Kings 3:12).

The greatness of Solomon's wisdom is illustrated in the visit of the Queen of Sheba, who "heard about Solomon's fame connected with the name of the LORD and came to test him with difficult questions" (10:1). When she observed Solomon's wisdom, "it took her breath away" (verse 5). She told Solomon:

The report I heard in my own country about your words
and about your wisdom is true. But I didn't believe their
reports until I came and saw with my own eyes. Indeed, I
was not even told half of your great wisdom! You far exceed
the report I heard (2 Chronicles 9:5-6).

Solomon was the pinnacle of Israel's wisdom. Insofar as he was
wise, he blessed the nation. Everything seemed complete under his
reign. Wisdom flourished in the king, and worship flourished in the
temple. God's people were in God's place under God's rule.

But Solomon followed the path of David, Israel, and Adam. He
did everything the Law forbade Israel's king from doing—he acquired
many horses (even from Egypt), many wives, and excessive silver and
gold.[16] Tragedy followed:

When Solomon was old, his wives turned his heart away to
follow other gods. He was not wholeheartedly devoted to
the LORD his God, as his father David had been. Solomon
followed Ashtoreth, the goddess of the Sidonians, and
Milcom, the abhorrent idol of the Ammonites. Solomon
did what was evil in the LORD's sight, and unlike his father
David, he did not remain loyal to the LORD (1 Kings 11:4-6).

Following his sin, Israel's story ran in reverse. After his death, the
kingdom was divided. King after king led the divided kingdom into
further foolishness, unrighteousness, and idolatry. Jerusalem and the
temple were destroyed as God's people were carried off in captivity in
foreign lands. In exile, they were no better off than Israel in Egypt and
no further along than Adam and Eve trembling outside the garden.

---

16. See Deuteronomy 17:14-20; 2 Chronicles 9:13-28; 1 Kings 11:1-3.

Even Solomon's wisdom couldn't maintain Israel's blessing forever. For Solomon was weak and finite—a mortal sinner who would die. His wisdom followed him to the grave, and Israel disintegrated.

Solomon's tragic tale teaches us that we need wisdom greater than Solomon's. We need a king who thoroughly embodies wisdom and never ceases to reign. We need a wise king who isn't subject to sin and whose heart remains faithful to the Lord. We need a king who can impart such transforming wisdom to us so that we flourish as God's people forever. That king is Jesus Christ.

In the incarnation, the second person of the Trinity (the eternal Son of God) "became wisdom from God for us" (1 Corinthians 1:30). It's not just that Jesus is wise. It's more than that. "Christ is… the wisdom of God" (verse 24). "In him are hidden all the treasures of wisdom and knowledge" (Colossians 2:3). Jesus perfectly embodies how to live as God's people in God's world under God's reign. To know him is to know wisdom. Jesus is the comprehensive display of God's wisdom.

When John the Baptist doubted whether Jesus was the Messiah, he sent messengers to ask him. Jesus answered, "Wisdom is vindicated by her deeds" (Matthew 11:19). Later, he condemned the scribes and Pharisees for failing to repent and believe after seeing him. Jesus promised that the Queen of Sheba would rise at the judgment to condemn them "because she came from the ends of the earth to hear the wisdom of Solomon; and look—something greater than Solomon is here" (12:42). If a pagan woman from the other side of the world could recognize Solomon's wisdom, Israel's teachers were without excuse for failing to recognize Wisdom Incarnate when he spoke to them.

Solomon encourages us to seek wisdom "like silver and search for it like hidden treasure" (Proverbs 2:4). We own that treasure when we receive Christ, for "in him are hidden all the treasures of wisdom and knowledge" (Colossians 2:3). "Christ is the only source required for wisdom and knowledge."[17] "Everything we might want to ask about God and his purposes can and must now be answered...with reference to the crucified and risen Jesus, the Messiah."[18]

The gospel is "foolishness to those who are perishing" (1 Corinthians 1:18). Foolishness rejects the good news that Jesus is God in the flesh, the King who conquers sin through his crucifixion and resurrection. When we believe the gospel, we see that "Christ is the power of God and the wisdom of God" (verse 24). Now that Christ has come, "God's wisdom is inseparable from the cross."[19]

The only way to be wise is by being united to Jesus through faith. "We are perfect in wisdom if we truly know Christ, so that it is madness to wish to know anything besides Him."[20] Therefore, we ought not to seek any wisdom outside him. For when the gospel comes to you, "bearing fruit and growing," then "you may be filled with the knowledge of his will in all wisdom and spiritual understanding, so that you may walk worthy of the Lord, fully pleasing to him" (Colossians 1:5-6, 9-10). By faith in Jesus, God has "given us everything required for life and godliness through the knowledge of him" (2 Peter 1:3). "Christ is the one in whom is to be found all that one needs in order to understand spiritual reality and to lead a life pleasing to God."[21]

We don't possess the wisdom embodied in Christ by our own strength. We're too weak for that. God chose us and united us with Christ by his power and wisdom so that he would receive all the glory.

17. Andreas J. Köstenberger, "Colossians," in *CSB Study Bible: Notes*, eds. Edwin A. Blum and Trevin Wax (Nashville: Holman Bible Publishers, 2017), 1896.

18. N.T. Wright, *Colossians and Philemon: An Introduction and Commentary*, Tyndale New Testament Commentaries, vol. 12 (Downers Grove, IL: InterVarsity Press, 1986), 99.

19. Alan F. Johnson, *1 Corinthians*, IVP New Testament Commentary Series, vol. 7 (Westmont, IL: IVP Academic, 2004), 59.

20. John Calvin and John Pringle, *Commentaries on the Epistles of Paul the Apostle to the Philippians, Colossians, and Thessalonians* (Bellingham, WA: Logos Bible Software, 2010), 175.

21. Moo, *The Letters to the Colossians and to Philemon*, 169.

"It is from him that you are in Christ Jesus, who became wisdom from God for us—our righteousness, sanctification, and redemption—in order that, as it is written: Let the one who boasts, boast in the Lord" (1 Corinthians 1:30-31).

So, what should we do if we want to be wise? We should turn our eyes to the person and work of Jesus. Come to him, learn from him, receive him, trust in him, and ask him to shape and fashion us into his image. And, as God gives us Christ, boast in him:

> I offer thanks and praise to you, God of my ancestors, because you have given me wisdom and power (Daniel 2:23).
>
> Christ is the power of God and the wisdom of God (1 Corinthians 1:24).

CHAPTER 8

WEAKNESS IN JESUS'S INCARNATION

The Word became flesh and dwelt among us.

JOHN 1:14

A re you claustrophobic?" It was the first question in my job interview at the farmers' cooperative. I sensed it was the only question that mattered. I'd never had an issue with confined spaces, so I answered in the negative. The foreman explained that they had two horizontal, cylindrical diesel fuel tanks. Grain dust from the millions of bushels of soybeans they handled each year worked its way inside the tanks. The dust mixed with the diesel, forming sludge the color, consistency, and smell of peanut butter. They hired me to clean it out.

He outfitted me with a pair of coveralls and rubber boots (two left boots, as he couldn't find a right boot). Then we walked to the worksite. A circle, little more in diameter than the span of my shoulders, had been cut at the end of each tank. A skid loader sat in front of one of the tanks, its bucket lifted to the hole. We climbed into the bucket.

I stuck my head into the hole and let my eyes adjust to the darkness. A shovel stood upright in a sea of "peanut butter" three feet deep in the center. Near the entry point, the sludge had been cleared to provide a place for me to stand. My task was to scoop shovelful after shovelful of the sludge through the hole into the skid loader bucket. As the bucket filled, the foreman would return to dump it.

The temperatures averaged in the high eighties, with near 100 percent humidity. The only ventilation the tank offered was the hole I'd climbed in through and a four-inch hole in the top of the tank where a hose once connected. It didn't take long to drench my coveralls in sweat each day. Since it was a horizontal cylinder, I had no flat surface on which to stand. So I balanced on the curved floor, slick with red rivulets of residual diesel, walking in my two left boots from the edge of the soy-and-diesel concoction to the hole. The full-time co-op workers had a good time teasing the college kid that got stuck with the job they'd all avoided. On occasion, one of them had a laugh banging on the side of the tank with an iron rod. And the foreman regularly made sure I understood that I wasn't shoveling fast enough to please him.

The morning after my first day of work, I woke up hurting everywhere. My hands were curled in the position they'd gripped the shovel, tendons popping as I tried to straighten my fingers. Every muscle protested every move. No matter what I did—whether I sneezed, belched, or passed gas—everything smelled like peanut butter. I'd never been so ready for school to start again as I was after those last two weeks of summer break.

I hated that job. I hated crawling into the hot, humid, disgusting confines of that tank. I hated putting on the unwashed coveralls, crusty with the potent accumulation of evaporated sweat, soy dust, and diesel fuel. But I did it. I needed the paycheck. Had I the choice to do it over again, I probably wouldn't.

As I think of that job, I can't help but ponder what Jesus did for us. Compared to his humiliation, my job was a cakewalk. Jesus descended from his Father's side in glory into the sin-tainted, corrupted, and disgusting confines of our fallen world. He willingly put on human nature, living as a fully human person, experiencing all the pain and suffering our decaying bodies endure. What's more, he died beneath the Father's wrath for sins he didn't commit. He did it. He didn't need to do it. He chose to do it for the joy set before him and his love for us. Had he to do it over again, he would.

JESUS IS FULLY GOD AND FULLY MAN

Jesus is the centerpiece of history. Everything in Scripture is about him.[1] Everything we've seen in the past seven chapters is meant to bring us to Jesus. So it would be a shame if you closed this book without knowing who he is. That's the aim of this book—to leave you impressed with and in love with Jesus Christ, the eternal Son of God who made himself weak to save us.

Jesus is fully God.

To understand who Jesus is, we must return to the beginning.

> In the beginning was the Word, and the Word was with God, and the Word was God. He was with God in the beginning. All things were created through him, and apart from him not one thing was created that has been created (John 1:1-3).

John takes us back to Genesis 1:1: "In the beginning God created the heavens and the earth." Before anything was created, the Word was. *The Word* refers to the eternal Son of God who would assume human nature as Jesus of Nazareth. (John likely uses *the Word* to refer to Jesus because Jesus "communicates" God to us—we see who God is when we see Jesus.[2]) The Word existed "in the beginning"—he's eternal.

---

1. See Luke 24:27; John 5:46.
2. See John 1:18.

"The Word was with God." The Word is distinct from God in some sense. If that's all that John said, we might believe that the Word isn't God but some eternal being that's always been with God. But John adds, "And the Word was God." The Word was with God, and he was God. "All things were created through him, and apart from him not one thing was created that has been created." The Word is the God who created the heavens and the earth in the beginning. Jesus—the Word—is fully God.

What does it mean that *the Word was with God* and *the Word was God*? John offers a glimpse into the eternal nature of the Triune God. Christians understand that God eternally exists in three persons: the Father, the Son, and the Holy Spirit. Each of the persons in the Trinity is fully God. The Father is God.[3] The Son is God.[4] The Spirit is God.[5] Yet each is a distinct person not to be confused with the other. The Father is neither the Son nor the Spirit. The Son is neither the Father nor the Spirit. The Spirit is neither the Father nor the Son. And yet, there is only one God.[6] We worship one God who eternally exists in three persons. How this is so is a mystery too great for us to understand fully.

Jesus is fully God. In his pre-incarnate state, he eternally existed in the "form of God," equal to God (Philippians 2:6). "God was pleased to have all his fullness dwell in him" (Colossians 1:19). In his divine nature, Jesus possesses all the attributes of God. He's all God is because he is God—eternal and independent, all-knowing and all-wise and all-powerful. In his divine nature, the Son has no weaknesses. That's what makes the next bit so astonishing.

---

3. Philippians 1:2.

4. Titus 2:13.

5. Acts 5:3-4.

6. Isaiah 44:6-8; 45:21-22; Deuteronomy 4:35; 6:4-5; 32:39; 1 Kings 8:60.

Jesus is fully human.

"The Word became flesh and dwelt among us" (John 1:14). That's the doctrine of the incarnation—the eternal Son of God becoming flesh. Without relinquishing his divine nature, he acquired a human nature such that he's now (and always will be) fully God and fully man. The all-powerful Son of God took on the weakness of human nature.

Just how human was Jesus? For starters, Jesus called himself a man, and Jesus never lied.[7] So, if he says he's a man, he's a man. The author of Hebrews says that because those he came to save "have flesh and blood in common, Jesus also shared in these" (Hebrews 2:14). He "had to be like his brothers and sisters in every way" (verse 17). So Jesus didn't merely appear human—he shared our flesh-and-blood human nature in every way, including our weakness.

Jesus lived with limited human strength.

Jesus entered the world as a weak and helpless baby, dependent upon others for his needs. He had to be fed, carried, and changed. Like other children, "the boy grew up and became strong" (Luke 2:40). (The very fact that he *became* strong implies that he was weak.) He grew from infancy into childhood, progressing into adolescence and, ultimately, into adulthood's (limited) strength. But even as an adult, Jesus didn't outgrow normal human weakness. He was susceptible to sickness, harm, injury, and death.

When Herod set out to kill the child Jesus, the Lord instructed Joseph to "take the child and his mother, flee to Egypt, and stay there until I tell you" (Matthew 2:13). Had they stayed, Jesus really could have been killed by a soldier; the flight to Egypt was necessary protection. As an adult, Jesus was tempted by the devil to throw himself off the temple to prove God would protect him from all harm

---

7. John 8:40; 1 Peter 2:22; see also Acts 2:22.

(4:6). Jesus did not reply, "Nice try, but my body isn't susceptible to harm!" but "It is also written: Do not test the Lord your God" (verse 7). On another occasion, the congregation at the synagogue "got up, drove him out of town, and brought him to the edge of the hill that their town was built on, intending to hurl him over the cliff. But he passed right through the crowd and went on his way" (Luke 4:29-30). Had they thrown him off the cliff, barring miraculous intervention, Jesus would have died. But, without any indication of a miraculous event, "he escaped their grasp" to avoid actual harm (John 10:39).

Isaiah prophesied that the Messiah would be "a man of suffering who knew what sickness was" (Isaiah 53:3). While we have no recorded instance, there's no reason to think he never got sick. The fact that he was sinless didn't exempt his body from the effects of the curse. His was a body of decaying dust, just like ours. He lived the whole human experience—sickness included. Mary may have applied ointment to baby Jesus's diaper rash. Perhaps Joseph held a cold compress to Jesus's forehead while he suffered through a fever. Maybe he cried after falling and scraping his knee. Jesus could have caught a stomach bug or gotten food poisoning from a nasty piece of fish and spent the night vomiting. He "bore our sicknesses, and he carried our pains" (verse 4).

Jesus lived a genuine human life.[8] He got hungry, thirsty, and worn out. He slept, perspired, and breathed. Jesus grew troubled and deeply moved; he wept. He became deeply distressed, sorrowful, and grieved to the point of death, entering into such anguish that he had to be strengthened by an angel. Another man had to carry his cross. Ultimately, his body bled, and he died. Before the resurrection,

---

8. For the following points, see Matthew 4:2 and Luke 4:2; John 19:28; John 4:6; Mark 4:38; Luke 22:43-44; Mark 15:37 and Luke 23:46; John 11:33, 35, 38 and Luke 19:41-44; Matthew 26:37-38, Mark 14:32-34, and Luke 22:43-44; Luke 23:26; Matthew 27:50, Mark 15:37, Luke 23:46, and John 19:30, 34.

Jesus's earthly body was no more powerful than yours or mine. He was as dependent upon food, drink, rest, and oxygen as you and me. His body was weak.

"Jesus' solidarity with human beings is not superficial but profound and genuine...He is fully and truly human, beset by the physical weaknesses and mortality that characterize human existence."[9] In other words, Jesus was weak.

Jesus lived with limited human knowledge.

Baby Jesus didn't know all things. "Jesus increased in wisdom" (Luke 2:52). His mother and father (and others) taught him things he didn't know: how to walk, talk, feed himself, read, and tie his sandals. He grew in wisdom by living life in this world and understanding through experience how it works. He sat in the temple, listening to the teachers and asking them questions.[10]

Even in adulthood, Jesus learned things. "He learned obedience from what he suffered" (Hebrews 5:8). How can it be that the Son "learned obedience"? Though in his omniscience, he knew obedience conceptually, the Son didn't *know* obedience experientially.[11] In the incarnation, Jesus assumed "the form of a servant, taking on

9. Thomas R. Schreiner, *Hebrews*, Evangelical Biblical Theology Commentary, edited by T. Desmond Alexander, Thomas R. Schreiner, and Andreas J. Köstenberger, (Bellingham, WA: Lexham Press, 2021), 103.

10. Luke 2:46.

11. Each person of the Trinity—the Father, the Son, and the Holy Spirit—is coeternal and coequal in every way. The Athanasian Creed puts it this way: "And in this Trinity none is afore or after another; none is greater or less than another. But the whole three persons are coeternal, and coequal. So that in all things, as aforesaid, the Unity in Trinity and the Trinity in Unity is to be worshipped. He therefore that will be saved must thus think of the Trinity." *Historic Creeds and Confessions*, electronic ed. (Oak Harbor: Lexham Press, 1997). *Coeternal* and *coequal* include authority. The Father does not have eternal authority over the Son or the Spirit. The Son does not have eternal authority over the Father or the Spirit. The Spirit does not have eternal authority over the Father or the Son. Thus no member of the Trinity eternally submits to or obeys any other member of the Trinity. Therefore, before the incarnation, the Son had never obeyed anyone—nor had the Father nor the Spirit. God obeys no one—that is central to the glory of God!

the likeness of humanity. And when he had come as a man, he humbled himself by becoming obedient to the point of death—even to death on a cross" (Philippians 2:7-8). In this way, "although he was the Son, he learned obedience from what he suffered" (Hebrews 5:8). Jesus gained an experiential knowledge of obedience by submitting to God even when it was painful.

Jesus gained information by asking questions. When the hemorrhaging woman touched his robe, Jesus asked, "Who touched me?" (Luke 8:45). Nothing indicates this is a rhetorical question, asked only to draw attention to the woman. Jesus stated that he knew power went out from him, but he didn't know the recipient—only that "someone did touch me" (verse 46). When Jesus visited Martha and Mary after the death of Lazarus, he asked, "Where have you put him?" (John 11:34). The passage does not indicate his question was insincere, posed only to bring the sisters along. His question was as genuine as him being deeply moved, troubled, and weeping, despite knowing he would raise Lazarus from the dead.[12]

Jesus experienced amazement.[13] That's significant because astonishment is "a very human trait."[14] Calvin writes, "Wonder cannot apply to God, for it arises out of what is new and unexpected: but it might exist in Christ, for he had clothed himself with our flesh, and with human affections."[15]

Jesus didn't know when he would return. "Now concerning that day and hour no one knows—neither the angels of heaven nor the Son—except the Father alone" (Matthew 24:36).

---

12. John 11:11, 33, 35, 38.

13. Matthew 8:10; Luke 7:9; Mark 6:6.

14. Leon Morris, *The Gospel According to Matthew*, Pillar New Testament Commentary (Grand Rapids: Eerdmans, 1992), 194.

15. John Calvin and William Pringle, *Commentary on a Harmony of the Evangelists Matthew, Mark, and Luke*, vol. 1 (Bellingham, WA: Logos Bible Software, 2010), 382.

How could Jesus be limited in strength and knowledge if he's God?

As Christians, we confess that the Son is fully God, all-powerful and all-knowing. At no point does Jesus cease to be God; he never surrenders a single aspect of his deity. So how can we say that Jesus lived with limited human strength and knowledge? In Philippians 2:5-8, we read,

> Christ Jesus, who, existing in the form of God, did not consider equality with God as something to be exploited. Instead he emptied himself by assuming the form of a servant, taking on the likeness of humanity. And when he had come as a man, he humbled himself by becoming obedient to the point of death—even to death on a cross.

In eternity, the Son existed "in the form of God" and possessed "equality with God." In his decision to become incarnate, he "did not consider equality with God as something to be exploited." He refused to clutch his divine prerogatives. He could not become an obedient slave if he used his divine rights and privileges to his advantage. These (though not his deity) had to be set aside; he had to "[empty] himself by assuming the form of a servant, taking on the likeness of humanity." Steve Wellum explains:

> As Jesus lived a fully human life, he had the ability to exercise his divine power and authority, but he chose to obey his Father's will for us and for our salvation. As the Son, he continued to live and act in Trinitarian relation to his Father and the Spirit as he had always done from eternity, but now as the *incarnate* Son he is able to live a fully human life in order to redeem us. During his life, acting as the last Adam, in filial obedience to his Father,

sometimes Jesus denied himself the exercise of his divine might and energies for the sake of the mission…Never once, though, did our Lord act in his own interest, because he always acted in light of who he is as the eternal Son. Even as he faced the cross, he willingly and gladly bore our sin and deployed no resources beyond those which his Father allowed *and* in relation to the Spirit.[16]

Jesus lived a life of human weakness depending on the Father and the Spirit by faith.

Jesus depended on his Father.

He made it quite clear that he didn't operate independently. "I do nothing on my own" (John 8:28-29). Indeed, the Son of Man is incapable of independent action. "I can do nothing on my own" (5:30).[17] Just as humans depend on God for their mandate at creation, so Jesus received his commission from the Father: "If God were your Father, you would love me, because I came from God and I am here. For I didn't come on my own, but he sent me" (8:42). Jesus sent his disciples into the world the same way the Father sent him.[18] Jesus spoke and did only the words and works given to him by the Father.[19] Praying for his disciples, he said, "Now they know that everything you have given me is from you" (17:7). "The strange way of putting the last point—that everything you have given me comes from you…carefully emphasizes Jesus' dependence upon his Father."[20]

---

16. Stephen J. Wellum, *God the Son Incarnate: The Doctrine of Christ*. Foundations of Evangelical Theology, ed. John S. Feinberg (Wheaton, IL: Crossway, 2016), 414–415.

17. See also John 5:19.

18. John 17:18.

19. John 8:28-29; 12:49-50; 14:10, 24, 31; 17:7-8.

20. D.A. Carson, *The Gospel According to John*, Pillar New Testament Commentary (Grand Rapids: Eerdmans, 1991), 559–560.

Jesus depended on the Spirit.

In Acts 10:38, Peter describes "how God anointed Jesus of Nazareth with the Holy Spirit and with power, and how he went about doing good and healing all who were under the tyranny of the devil, because God was with him." Notice the beginning and the end of this statement. God anointed Jesus with the Spirit and with power (together meaning the power of the Holy Spirit). Peter adds "because God was with him" to emphasize the source of Jesus's ministerial power. "The power wherein Christ exceeded proceeded from the Spirit alone."[21]

God gave Jesus "the Spirit without measure" (John 3:34). The Spirit led Jesus into the wilderness, and Jesus returned from the wilderness in the Spirit's power.[22] "The Lord's power to heal was in him" (Luke 5:17). He drove out demons "by the Spirit of God" (Matthew 12:28), exorcisms "performed not by his own power but by the power of God, i.e., by the Spirit of God."[23] Jesus rejoiced in the Spirit.[24] In his crucifixion, Jesus offered himself to God "through the eternal Spirit" (Hebrews 9:14), which "implies that he had been divinely empowered and sustained in his office."[25]

The night before his crucifixion, Jesus retreated with his disciples to Gethsemane. He encouraged them to sit while he prayed. He took Peter, James, and John with him and, expressing his deep grief, told them, "Remain here and stay awake with me" (Matthew 26:38). Then he went further to pray fervently, being strengthened by an

---

21. John Calvin and Henry Beveridge, *Commentary upon the Acts of the Apostles*, vol. 1 (Bellingham, WA: Logos Bible Software, 2010), 443.

22. Matthew 4:1; Mark 1:12; Luke 4:1, 14.

23. G.R. Beasley-Murray, "Jesus and the Spirit," in *Melanges Bibliques en Homage au R. P. Beda Rigaux*, eds. A. Deschamps and A. de Hallelaneux (Gembloux: Duculot, 1970), 471. As quoted in Issler, "Learning from Jesus."

24. Luke 10:21.

25. William L. Lane, *Hebrews 9-13*, Word Biblical Commentary, vol. 47B (Dallas: Word, 1991), 240.

angel while in anguish.[26] Returning, Jesus found his friends asleep. He asked Peter, "So, couldn't you stay awake with me one hour? Stay awake and pray, so that you won't enter into temptation. The spirit is willing, but the flesh is weak" (verses 40-41). A willing spirit is insufficient to overcome the weakness of the flesh; God's power is needed. "Jesus's acknowledgment that the flesh is weak may have applied to himself also that night, given his suffering. Natural human weaknesses (hunger, fatigue, etc.) can pose great spiritual danger."[27] Therefore, Jesus's disciples must find the strength to resist temptation like Jesus did through prayer.[28] Jesus's prayers weren't insincere, offered only as an example, but were genuine expressions of faith requesting or acknowledging the Father's help and provision. Jesus genuinely sought help and strength from God in prayer—just as we should.

Jesus lived by faith in God.

If Jesus lived a human life of dependence on God through the power of the Spirit, it follows that he lived a life of faith. God had made the Messiah promises, which Jesus trusted him to keep. He lived by faith: "During his earthly life, he offered prayers and appeals with loud cries and tears to the one who was able to save him from death, and he was heard because of his reverence" (Hebrews 5:7). Jesus prayed fervently "during his life on earth, for he, like any other human being, was completely dependent on God. He looked to God to meet his needs and to answer his pleas."[29]

The author of Hebrews goes on to present faith as "the assurance of things hoped for, the conviction of things not seen" (Hebrews 11:1 ESV). Tom Schreiner explains:

---

26. Luke 22:43-44.

27. Ross H. McLaren, "Mark," in *CSB Study Bible: Notes*, eds. Edwin A. Blum and Trevin Wax (Nashville: Holman Bible Publishers, 2017), 1588.

28. See Matthew 6:13; 1 Corinthians 10:13.

29. Schreiner, *Hebrews*, 162.

Faith is assured that what is hoped for will become a reality. It is convinced that the unseen promises of God will be fulfilled... Faith relies on God's promises, believing what he says even if it can't see how they will be fulfilled. Faith looks to the future, banking on the word of God instead of taking its cue from present circumstances. Faith trusts God in danger and distress, knowing he will reward his own.[30]

The remainder of Hebrews 11 illustrates this in the lives of Old Testament forerunners who believed God would keep his promises despite it seeming impossible from a human perspective. These form a "large cloud of witnesses surrounding us," encouraging us to endure until the end (Hebrews 12:1). Yet, while they're great examples, "the supreme example is Jesus himself."[31] The "Hall of Faith" culminates in Jesus's example—"the author and perfecter of faith" (12:2 NASB95).[32] The context leads us to conclude that "Jesus is understood as being himself a believer."[33] In the Old Testament, the Lord made promises to the coming Messiah, which Christ was called to believe despite seeing no evidence of their fulfillment.

What promises did the Lord make to the Messiah? "Ask of me, and I will make the nations your inheritance and the ends of the earth your possession" (Psalm 2:8). "Sit at my right hand until I make your enemies your footstool" (110:1). "I will establish the throne of his kingdom forever" (2 Samuel 7:13). The Lord promised the Messiah that he would destroy his enemies and give him the nations as

---

30. Schreiner, *Hebrews*, 376.

31. Schreiner, *Hebrews*, 376.

32. Despite many English translations reading "of our faith," the word *our* does not appear in the Greek manuscripts.

33. Paul Ellingworth, *The Epistle to the Hebrews: A Commentary on the Greek Text*, New International Greek Testament Commentary (Grand Rapids: Eerdmans, 1993), 640.

an eternal kingdom. But the prophet Isaiah makes plain that death stands between the promise and its fulfillment:

> Yet the LORD was pleased to crush him severely.
> When you make him a guilt offering,
> he will see his seed, he will prolong his days,
> and by his hand, the LORD's pleasure will be accomplished.
> After his anguish,
> he will see light and be satisfied.
> By his knowledge,
> my righteous servant will justify many,
> and he will carry their iniquities.
> Therefore I will give him the many as a portion,
> and he will receive the mighty as spoil,
> because he willingly submitted to death,
> and was counted among the rebels;
> yet he bore the sin of many
> and interceded for the rebels (Isaiah 53:10-12).

The Messiah's days would be lengthened only after the Lord crushed him as a sacrifice for sin. Only after his anguish would he see light. He would be given the multitudes as an inheritance only after carrying the rebels' sins in death. The Messiah would willingly submit to death through faith: "For you will not abandon me to Sheol; you will not allow your faithful one to see decay. You reveal the path of life to me; in your presence is abundant joy; at your right hand are eternal pleasures" (Psalm 16:10-11).

The Old Testament predicted a Messiah who knew the Lord promised the overthrow of his enemies and an eternal kingdom comprised of people from every nation, which he would enjoy at God's right hand in glory after he submitted to death under God's wrath as a sacrifice for the sins of those people. That Messiah is "Jesus, the pioneer and perfecter of our faith. For the joy that lay before him, he endured the cross, despising the shame, and sat down at the right hand of the throne of God" (Hebrews 12:2). When Jesus looked at the cross, his human eyes saw only the cold finality of death. But by faith, he believed God would raise him from the dead, crush his enemies, exalt him to his right hand, and gather in the nations as his inheritance—an eternal kingdom of joy. In that way, Jesus truly is our "champion in the exercise of faith and the one who brought faith to complete expression."[34]

Yet Hebrews 12:2 isn't written merely to celebrate Jesus's faith. He's also our "model of faith," demonstrating what it means to persevere as a human believer.[35]

> Still, the main point here is Jesus' example to believers. The believers are to run the race to the end, just as Jesus completed his course. He endured the suffering and shame of the cross. The shame of the cross was proverbial in the ancient world. He was fortified to bear up under the agony of such a death on account of "the joy that lay before him." Hence he could scorn and despise the temporary shame, acting bravely since he knew something far better was coming.[36]

We "run with endurance the race that lies before us" by "keeping our eyes on Jesus" (12:1-2). When we read that Jesus "offered prayers and appeals with loud cries and tears to the one who was able to save

---

34. Lane, *Hebrews 9–13*, 411.

35. David L. Allen, *Hebrews*, The New American Commentary (Nashville: B&H Publishing, 2010), 574–575.

36. Schreiner, *Hebrews*, 378–379.

him from death" (5:7), we learn what it means to trust God's promises through the power of the Holy Spirit. Our confidence grows when we read that "he was heard because of his reverence" (verse 7). When we see his resurrection from the dead and ascension to God's right hand in power, our conviction of God's faithfulness to keep his promises is solidified.

The weakness of Jesus is a good gift to us.

"The entire Gospel story can be viewed as Jesus taking on weakness for the sake of Israel and of the world."[37] In the incarnation, Jesus voluntarily assumed a genuine human nature, sharing our weaknesses, except without sin. He lived a life of real faith, depending entirely upon his Father and the Spirit in every aspect of life and ministry. A weak Messiah doesn't sound like good news. That's why so many rejected him. "He didn't have an impressive form or majesty that we should look at him, no appearance that we should desire him" (Isaiah 53:2). Walking by sight, the world could only see a crucified man whose mission failed. But those with faith have eyes to see that he's the perfection of God's power and the fulfillment of God's promises.

Jesus made himself weak to be our merciful high priest.

Here is comfort for weak humans:

> Now since the children have flesh and blood in common, Jesus also shared in these, so that through his death he might destroy the one holding the power of death—that is, the devil—and free those who were held in slavery all their lives by the fear of death. For it is clear that he does not reach out to help angels, but to help Abraham's offspring. Therefore,

---

37. Leland Ryken, James C. Wilhoit, and Tremper Longman III, eds., *Dictionary of Biblical Imagery* (Downers Grove, IL: InterVarsity Press, 1998), 933.

he had to be like his brothers and sisters in every way, so that he could become a merciful and faithful high priest in matters pertaining to God, to make atonement for the sins of the people. For since he himself has suffered when he was tempted, he is able to help those who are tempted (Hebrews 2:14-18).

Jesus shared our flesh-and-blood nature and experience; he "is fully and truly human, beset by the physical weaknesses and mortality that characterize human existence."[38] To be a "merciful and faithful high priest in matters pertaining to God," Jesus "had to be like his brothers and sisters in every way," which includes every human weakness except our "moral weakness."[39] Why is this?

First, Jesus shared our weakness "to make atonement for the sins of the people." By sharing our human nature, Jesus had flesh and blood to offer as a sacrifice. Since he was sinless, his body was an acceptable sacrifice. "By his own blood," he "obtained eternal redemption" (Hebrews 9:12), removing sin "by the sacrifice of himself" (verse 26). Apart from succumbing to death, he could not atone for sin. The Law had weak men for priests, who had to offer sacrifices for their own sins and were "prevented by death from remaining in office" (7:23). But sinless Jesus, after dying for our sin and rising from the dead, "has been perfected forever" (verse 28).

Second, Jesus shared our weaknesses "to sympathize with our weaknesses." Human nature allowed Jesus to experience temptation.

---

38. Schreiner, *Hebrews*, 103.

39. Note: moral weakness—sinful depravity—is not inherent to human nature. Before the Fall, Adam and Eve were fully human but not sinfully depraved. Likewise, in the resurrection, God's redeemed shall be fully human but not depraved. So the fact that Jesus lacks a sinful nature does not detract from his humanity.

Because our high priest "has been tempted in every way as we are, yet without sin," he's able "to sympathize with our weaknesses" (4:15). Jesus knows what it's like to be weak like us because he was weak like us. Therefore, "he is able to deal gently with those who are ignorant and are going astray, since he is also clothed with weakness" (5:2).

Finally, Jesus shared our weakness to help those who are tempted. "For since he himself has suffered when he was tempted, he is able to help those who are tempted" (2:18). Jesus is able to help us when we're tempted because he knows what it's like to be tempted. He knows from experience what help is needed to face temptation successfully. Furthermore, because he has removed our sins, no obstacle prevents his helping us! "Therefore, let us approach the throne of grace with boldness, so that we may receive mercy and find grace to help us in time of need" (4:16). Don't let your weakness keep you from his throne! This is our great hope: *Little ones to him belong—he was weak to make us strong!*

CHAPTER 9

WEAKNESS IN JESUS'S LIFE AND MINISTRY

He drove out the spirits with a word and healed
all who were sick, so that what was spoken through
the prophet Isaiah might be fulfilled: He himself
took our weaknesses and carried our diseases.

MATTHEW 8:16-17

In kindergarten, *South Pacific* set the course of my life. I sat in a folding chair, fixated on the hole-in-the-wall stage at one end of our community school's dark gymnasium. Honestly, I can't recall the musical's storyline and know only a few lines from a few songs. But I remember scenes from that high school production. Most of all, I remember the lead actor. (I still remember his name, though not the character's name!) He talked the most. He sang the most. At the end, people clapped for him the most. Right then and there, I knew that when I grew up, I would be him—the guy who got the most applause.

After the curtain fell on my first high school play, I told a friend we should go out into the audience. When he asked why, I said, "So people can tell us how good we did!" He replied, "Why would we want to do that?" Inwardly, I wondered why he *wouldn't* want to do that but realized that seeking applause wasn't something you could admit to. It would have to be done secretly, under a veil of humility. The desire for applause—for glory—followed me (and drove me) through high school, college, seminary, and into the pastorate.

One of the many means God's used to chip away at my pride is my friend Kendall, one of the most faithful and humble pastors I've known. We connected just as I began my first pastorate out of seminary. We met halfway between our respective towns for breakfast each week, traveled to pastors' conferences, and even tag-teamed teaching systematic theology to pastors in Ukraine. On one occasion, we attended a men's event at a local church. As the men socialized, I did what I always did at any event—I tried to engage those I deemed most important and influential. At some point, I noticed Kendall wasn't with me. I scanned the room from one cluster of men to the next, unable to find him. Finally, my eyes landed on an old man with a long, scraggly beard and tattered overalls. He stood in the corner of the room, and next to him stood Kendall, engaging him in conversation with genuine interest.

I realized that's where Kendall always was wherever we went—seeking out those on the fringe, the nobodies, the down-and-outs, the losers (that's probably why he befriended me!). He didn't see himself as too important for anyone and didn't care for anyone's applause. In that moment, the Holy Spirit pierced my heart. Kendall's humility and self-effacing love for others were qualities I didn't understand and didn't have—but I knew I should! Nearly twenty years later, the Lord has used Kendell's example to convict, correct, and instruct me more times than I can count. I still want to be more like Kendall because he's so much like the Jesus we see in Scripture—a friend to the weak.

JESUS IDENTIFIED WITH THE WEAK

In Jesus's earthly life, his identification with the weak began with those waiting for him and those who first heard the news of his arrival.

The stories of Jesus' birth provide vivid profiles of the pious weak of Israel, such as Anna, a widow of great age, who is "looking for the redemption of Jerusalem" (Lk 2:38). The song of Mary (Lk 1:46-55) dwells on the theme of God's overthrow of the mighty and his care for the lowly ones in Israel. Mary considers herself a lowly servant who is now exalted (Lk 1:48). The prophecy of Zechariah (Lk 1:68-79) pictures Israel as languishing in bondage and awaiting God's rescue, his dawning light to illumine "those who sit in darkness and in the shadow of death" (Lk 1:79 NIV).[1]

Jesus was "born king of the Jews" (Matthew 2:2). Yet the infant monarch wasn't born in a palace. His mother "laid him in a manger, because there was no guest room available for them" (Luke 2:7). Nor was he born in the capital city of Jerusalem, where the wise men expected to find the king.[2] He was born in Bethlehem, which was so "small among the clans of Judah" (Micah 5:2) that it was "omitted from the extensive lists of Judah's towns in Joshua 15:33–60."[3] The little Lord was born to weak (scandalous) parents in a weak village to sleep in a weak cradle.

Jesus's birth established the pattern of his life. He "associated with the underdogs of his society—tax collectors, prostitutes and the poor—more than with the rich and prestigious... The Gospels are populated by the weak, the little people of Israel who are powerless in the face of Roman, Herodian and Sadducean politics and the demands of wealthy landlords."[4] So complete was his identification with weakness that people had trouble believing he could be the Messiah. "Isn't

---

1. Leland Ryken, James C. Wilhoit, and Tremper Longman III, eds., *Dictionary of Biblical Imagery* (Downers Grove, IL: InterVarsity Press, 1998), 933.

2. Matthew 2:1-2.

3. Bruce K. Waltke, "Micah," in *New Bible Commentary: 21st Century Edition*, ed. D.A. Carson et al., 4th ed. (Leicester, UK; Downers Grove, IL: InterVarsity Press, 1994), 828.

4. Ryken, Wilhoit, and Longman, *Dictionary of Biblical Imagery*, 907, 933.

this Jesus the son of Joseph, whose father and mother we know? How can he now say, 'I have come down from heaven'?" (John 6:42). John the Baptist had announced Jesus as the one "who is more powerful than I" (Matthew 3:11). Yet, sitting in prison, John doubted whether Jesus was the Messiah.[5] Evidently, he hadn't expected the weakness of persecution and a Messiah who didn't prevent it. In reply, Jesus pointed to his ministry to the weak as evidence of his messiahship: "Go and report to John what you hear and see: The blind receive their sight, the lame walk, those with leprosy are cleansed, the deaf hear, the dead are raised, and the poor are told the good news, and blessed is the one who isn't offended by me" (Matthew 11:4-6).

Jesus was weak in public.

Jesus didn't shrink from allowing others to see his weakness and humiliation. Before eating his last meal with his friends (and his betrayer!), Jesus stooped and washed their feet, "a task normally reserved for the lowliest of menial servants."[6] In fact, "some Jews insisted that Jewish slaves should not be required to wash the feet of others; this job should be reserved for Gentile slaves, or for women and children and pupils."[7] Nevertheless, Jesus wrapped a towel around himself (the dress of a lowly slave) and assumed the weakest status in the room, foreshadowing his ultimate identification with weakness on the cross.[8] From birth to death, Jesus put his weakness on full public display.

My friend Christine Chappell pointed out that "Jesus was willing to be weak while his friends were watching."[9] She elaborates:

5. Matthew 11:1-3.

6. D.A. Carson, *The Gospel According to John*, Pillar New Testament Commentary (Grand Rapids: Eerdmans, 1991), 462.

7. Carson, *The Gospel According to John*, 462.

8. Philippians 2:5-8.

9. Christine M. Chappell (@christinemchappell), "Jesus was willing to be weak while his friends were watching," Instagram, June 14, 2023, www.instagram.com/p/CtedDj-u-ZW.

But consider Christ in the garden of Gethsemane. Though he was weakened by his agony, he didn't stop praying (Luke 22:43). Though he was "overwhelmed with sorrow to the point of death," he made no attempt to disguise his distress (Matt. 26:38). Though he sweat "great drops of blood" from his brow, ("fear and intense mental contemplation are the most frequent causes," National Library of Medicine) he didn't tell Peter, John, and James to look away (Luke 22:44). Instead, he told them to "Remain here and watch" (Mark 14:34). To behold him as he entered his hour—as he engaged the Father in trembling and weakness (Heb. 4:15). That Jesus was willing to be weak while his friends were watching is an incredible—and perhaps even unexpected—encouragement for us. He suffered his sorrow neither stoically nor secretly. Surely in Christ we are free to do the same.[10]

What an encouraging example he is to us! Jesus didn't hide his weakness from enemy or follower, mother or brother, friend or betrayer. We should not be ashamed of public weakness, whether our own or that of fellow Christians.[11] In our humiliations, we're following in the footsteps of Christ—and he's not ashamed of us![12]

Jesus came for the weak.

Jesus's earliest recorded sermon consists of one sentence. After his wilderness temptation, Jesus returned to Galilee and taught in their synagogues. In Nazareth, his hometown, he was invited to read the Scripture and give the sermon. When they handed him the scroll of Isaiah, Jesus unrolled it to the passage we know as Isaiah 61:1-2 and stood up to read it.

---

10. Chappell, "Jesus was willing."
11. 2 Timothy 1:8-18; 1 Peter 4:18.
12. Hebrews 2:10-11; 11:16; Mark 8:38.

The Spirit of the Lord is on me,
because he has anointed me
to preach good news to the poor.
He has sent me
to proclaim release to the captives
and recovery of sight to the blind,
to set free the oppressed,
to proclaim the year of the Lord's favor (Luke 4:18-19).

Then he sat down (as was the custom) to deliver his one-line sermon: "Today as you listen, this Scripture has been fulfilled" (verse 21). In other words, "That's me. I'm the one the Spirit anointed and sent to preach good news to the poor." Jesus came to declare good news to the weak—"the people who are most in need of divine help and who wait upon God to hear his word."[13] The good news was that God's grace had arrived and their condition would be reversed. Captives would be released. The blind would see. The oppressed would be set free. Jesus came to deliver God's favor to those too weak to help themselves. We must never underestimate God's genuine concern for those who are materially poor, enslaved, blind, or oppressed. Yet we must see that Jesus came to deliver us from an even more significant and urgent need—our moral weakness, sin.[14]

A short time later, as Jesus called his first disciples, he stopped by the tax office and told Levi, the tax collector, "Follow me." Levi (also known as Matthew) left everything behind and followed Jesus. Levi hosted a large banquet for Jesus, which many tax collectors attended. It scandalized the Pharisees and scribes, who challenged the disciples,

---

13. I. Howard Marshall, *The Gospel of Luke: A Commentary on the Greek Text*, New International Greek Testament Commentary (Exeter: Paternoster Press, 1978), 183.

14. That's why Jesus forgave the sins of the paralytic before he healed him. He emphasized the priority of spiritual weakness over physical or social weakness.

"Why do you eat and drink with tax collectors and sinners?" (Luke 5:30). We should ask the same question. Why *did* Jesus associate with tax collectors? Did they fit the description of those Jesus said he was sent to? They weren't poor, oppressed captives. Instead, they worked for the wealthy, oppressive captors—the Romans! Far from being poor, tax collectors "fleeced their fellow-Jews and filled their own pockets very successfully."[15] They were considered to be gangsters, traitors, and beyond redemption "because of their constant contact with Gentiles, their collaboration with those who charged the people with extortionate tax rates, and their notorious dishonesty."[16] It would seem they were the people from whom the poor, the captives, and the oppressed needed to be delivered. But here was Jesus, eating and drinking with them!

Jesus answered them (and us), "It is not those who are healthy who need a doctor, but those who are sick. I have not come to call the righteous, but sinners to repentance" (Luke 5:31-32). Notice the parallels in those two sentences. Doctors aren't for the healthy but for the sick. Jesus didn't come to call the righteous but sinners. In this way, Jesus points us beyond external human conditions to the ultimate form of weakness—our depravity. Ungodliness is the ultimate weakness: "For while we were still **helpless**, at the right time, Christ died for the **ungodly**" (Romans 5:6, emphasis added). Being a sinner is the ultimate poverty, captivity, blindness, oppression, and sickness. In our depravity, we're spiritually impoverished, slaves to sin, blind to God's glory, trapped by the devil, and dead in our sins.[17] Sinners are the weak to whom the Christ was sent with good news "to proclaim the year of the Lord's favor." For through Jesus's ministry, we inherit the riches of Christ's glory, are set free from sin, see

---

15. I. Howard Marshall, "Luke," in *New Bible Commentary*, 990.

16. David E. Garland, *Luke*, Zondervan Exegetical Commentary on the New Testament (Grand Rapids: Zondervan, 2012), 251.

17. Matthew 5:5; Romans 6:20; 2 Corinthians 4:4; Ephesians 2:1-2; 1 Timothy 3:7; 2 Timothy 2:22.

the glory of the Lord, and are made alive in Christ.[18] As we observe how Christ sought and served the weak, let his every compassionate act point us to the cross where he sought and served sinners like us.

Jesus served the weak.

Jesus served the socially weak by showing them honor or defending them from mistreatment. When his disciples rebuked people for bringing infants and little children to Jesus, he rebuked his disciples and welcomed the little ones.[19] Jesus honored the impoverished widow's offering and rebuked those who took advantage of widows.[20] He defended women who loved and served him.[21] Jesus reproved a synagogue leader for valuing a woman, "a daughter of Abraham," less than his ox or donkey (Luke 13:10-17). He used terms of endearment, such as "my son" and "daughter," when speaking to outcasts.[22] Jesus loved the unclean and touched the untouchables.[23] He loved foreigners, dignified racial enemies, and showed compassion to political oppressors.[24] Jesus was a friend of sinners.[25]

Jesus's service to the weak is seen most clearly in his interaction with the sick. The Greek word group that means *weak*, *weakness*, or *to be weak* is used most often in the New Testament for *sickness*.[26] The reason for this is apparent: When our bodies are sick, we become physically weak. In Jesus's day, there was no more readily available

---

18. Romans 6:18; 2 Corinthians 3:13; Ephesians 1:17; 2:4-5; 3:16; Colossians 1:27; 1 Peter 1:4.

19. Matthew 19:13-15; Mark 10:13-16; Luke 18:15-17.

20. Mark 12:38-44; Luke 20:45–21:4.

21. Mark 14:3-9; Luke 7:36-50; John 12:1-8.

22. Matthew 9:2, 22; Mark 5:34; Luke 8:48.

23. Mark 1:40-44.

24. Matthew 8:5-13; 15:21-28; Mark 2:14-17; Luke 7:1-10; 10:25-37; John 4:4-42.

25. Matthew 9:9-13; 11:19; Mark 2:14-17; Luke 5:27-31; 15:2.

26. Gustav Stählin, "Ἀσθενής, Ἀσθένεια, Ἀσθενέω, Ἀσθένημα," in *Theological Dictionary of the New Testament*, eds. Gerhard Kittel, Geoffrey W. Bromiley, and Gerhard Friedrich (Grand Rapids: Eerdmans, 1964), 491.

means of demonstrating his concern for the weak than serving those afflicted by sickness or demons.[27] As Jesus preached the gospel, he healed "every disease and sickness among the people" (Matthew 4:23).[28] These included life-threatening illnesses, fever, paralysis, various skin diseases, intense pains, epilepsy, chronic bleeding, blindness, hearing loss, mutism, debilitating deformities, edema, and death.[29] He also freed people from demonic affliction.[30]

Why did Jesus do this? Matthew writes, "He drove out the spirits with a word and healed all who were sick, so that what was spoken through the prophet Isaiah might be fulfilled: He himself took our weaknesses and carried our diseases" (8:16-17). Jesus's extensive healing ministry verified that he was the Suffering Servant in Isaiah 53 who took our weaknesses. As Isaiah 53 unfolds, it becomes apparent that our sicknesses (consequences of the Fall) point toward their cause—our sin and the punishment it deserves.

> He was despised and rejected by men,
> a man of suffering who knew what sickness was.
> He was like someone people turned away from;
> he was despised, and we didn't value him.
> Yet he himself bore our sicknesses,
> and he carried our pains;
> but we in turn regarded him stricken,
> struck down by God, and afflicted.

27. Demonic affliction often caused physical distress, but the Gospel writers distinguish between natural disease and demonic oppression causing sickness. See Matthew 8:16-17; Mark 1:34; Luke 4:40-41; Acts 19:12.

28. See also Mark 1:32-34; Luke 4:31-41; Matthew 8:15.

29. Matthew 4:24; 8:1-15; 9:1-8, 18-26, 32-34; 12:22-24; 15:29-31; 17:14-21; 21:14; Mark 1:29-31, 39-45; 2:1-12; 5:21-43; 7:31-37; 8:22-26; 9:14-29; Luke 4:38-39; 5:12-15, 17-26; 7:1-17; 8:40-56; 9:37-43; 11:14; 13:10-17; 14:1-4; John 4:46-54; 9:1-41; 11:1-44.

30. Matthew 4:24; 8:16-17, 28-34; 9:32-34; 12:22-24; Mark 1:23-28, 32-34, 39; 5:1-20; Luke 4:31-37, 40-41; 8:1-3, 26-39; 11:14.

> But he was pierced because of our rebellion,
> crushed because of our iniquities;
> punishment for our peace was on him,
> and we are healed by his wounds.
> We all went astray like sheep;
> we all have turned to our own way;
> and the LORD has punished him
> for the iniquity of us all (Isaiah 53:3-6).

Jesus's service to the socially and physically weak should call to mind his greater service to our greatest weakness: "For while we were still weak, at the right time Christ died for the ungodly" (Romans 5:6 ESV).

Jesus loved the weak.

Have you ever had a waiter or waitress that seemed annoyed to serve you? They huffed with impatience while taking your order and made you feel like getting a refill was a form of torture. It can ruin the whole dining experience. You never want to return to that restaurant—and if you do, you definitely don't want to have that server again. When that happens, you certainly don't feel loved! The good news is that our Suffering Servant, Jesus, doesn't serve the weak like that. He not only serves the weak, but he serves them in love.

Compassion drove Jesus's ministry to the weak. "Compassion, a form of love, is aroused within us when we are confronted with those who suffer or are vulnerable," and it "often produces action to alleviate the suffering."[31] When a leper came to Jesus, fell on his knees, and begged to be made clean, Jesus was "moved with compassion" and touched him (Mark 1:40-42). He healed and fed the large crowds that followed him to remote places because he "had compassion on

---

31. David H. Engelhard, "Compassion," in *Evangelical Dictionary of Biblical Theology*, electronic ed., Baker Reference Library (Grand Rapids: Baker Book House, 1996), 109.

them" (Matthew 14:13-21).[32] When Jesus saw a widow going to bury her only son, "he had compassion on her" and raised him from the dead (Luke 7:13). When people cried out for mercy, he was "moved with compassion" and answered their pleas (Matthew 20:29-34).[33]

Jesus taught that loving your neighbor as yourself meant having compassion on those in need.[34] So he rebuked those who paid scrupulous attention to tithing herbs while neglecting mercy.[35] When his opponents used a man with a withered hand as a trap to accuse him, "he was grieved at the hardness of their hearts," at their lack of compassion (Mark 3:1-6).

Jesus's compassion for the weak points us again to his ultimate ministry—the forgiveness of sins. "Salvation through the forgiveness of their sins" arrived in Jesus "because of our God's merciful compassion" (Luke 1:77-78). So when Jesus saw the crowds, "he felt compassion for them, because they were distressed and dejected, like sheep without a shepherd," and urged his disciples to "pray to the Lord of the harvest to send out workers into his harvest" (Matthew 9:36-38).[36] He received sinners because he was like the father who saw his prodigal son a long way off "and was filled with compassion" and "ran, threw his arms around his neck, and kissed him" (Luke 15:20). Never let your sinful weakness keep you from coming back to Jesus.

Jesus blessed the weak.

Because Jesus loved and came to rescue the weak, he blessed them: the poor, the hungry, the spiritually impoverished, those who weep, mourners, the humble, those longing for righteousness, and those

---

32. Matthew 15:32-39; Mark 8:1-9.
33. Mattthew 9:27-31; 15:22-28; 17:14-21; Mark 9:20-27; 10:46-52; Luke 18:35-43.
34. Luke 10:25-37.
35. Matthew 23:23.
36. See also Mark 6:34.

persecuted and hated for his sake.[37] He called them to rejoice and be glad because the kingdom belonged to them, and their reward was great.[38] "Although the Beatitudes do not mention the weak per se, the poor in spirit, the mourners, the meek and the persecuted all share in a weakness that qualifies them for the blessing of the kingdom of God."[39]

That's why Jesus took the little children (exemplars of weakness) in his arms and blessed them. "The kingdom of God belongs to such as these. Truly I tell you, whoever does not receive the kingdom of God like a little child will never enter it" (Mark 10:14-15). We can't be saved unless we're willing to confess our weakness and humbly receive God's strength in Christ.

Jesus revealed the kingdom to the weak.

The kingdom of Christ looks weak on the outside (just like those who inherit it), so many missed it in his day (and still miss it in ours). It begins small, like a mustard seed or a measure of yeast, and later produces a glorious outcome.[40] Human strength (flesh and blood) is entirely incapable of perceiving the truth about the King and his kingdom; it must be revealed to us by God.[41] That's why, when the seventy-two returned from a successful mission trip, Jesus rejoiced and said:

> I praise you, Father, Lord of heaven and earth, because you have hidden these things from the wise and intelligent and revealed them to infants. Yes, Father, because this was your good pleasure. All things have been entrusted to me by my Father. No one knows who the Son is except the

---

37. Luke 6:20-22; Matthew 5:1-10.

38. Luke 6:23; Matthew 5:11-12.

39. Ryken, Wilhoit, and Longman, *Dictionary of Biblical Imagery*, 933.

40. Matthew 13:31-33; Mark 4:30-32; Luke 13:18-21.

41. John 1:12-13; Luke 9:43-45; 18:34.

Father, and who the Father is except the Son, and anyone
to whom the Son desires to reveal him (Luke 10:21-22).

The kingdom is hidden from the strong (the wise and intelligent)
and revealed to the weak (infants). For that reason, Jesus taught the
crowds parables that he only explained to his disciples in private: "The
secrets of the kingdom of God have been given for you to know, but
to the rest it is in parables, so that looking they may not see, and hearing they may not understand" (Luke 8:10).[42] "This is why they were
unable to believe, because Isaiah also said: He has blinded their eyes
and hardened their hearts, so that they would not see with their eyes
or understand with their hearts, and turn, and I would heal them"
(John 12:39-40). And this is why, when Peter correctly identified Jesus
as "the Messiah, the Son of the living God," he replied, "Blessed are
you, Simon son of Jonah, because flesh and blood did not reveal this
to you, but my Father in heaven" (Matthew 16:16-17). If we see the
truth about Jesus, we should not boast about the strength of our per-
ception but rejoice that God has shown us grace in our weakness.

Jesus called his disciples to embrace their weakness.

Jesus regularly reminded his followers of their weakness, refer-
ring to them as *little ones*, the *least*, *little flock*, and *little children*.[43] He
reminded them that they were "not able to do even a little thing," such
as adding one moment to their life span (Luke 12:25-26).[44] They must
embrace being as weak as children to enter the kingdom because it's
impossible for anyone to be saved apart from God's supernatural work.[45]

---

42. Matthew 13:10-17; Mark 4:10-12.
43. Little ones (Matthew 10:42; 18:6, 10, 14; Mark 9:42; Luke 17:2); least (Matthew 11:11; Luke
7:28; 9:48); little flock (Luke 12:32); little children (John 13:33).
44. See also Matthew 6:27.
45. Matthew 19:13-30; Mark 10:13-27; Luke 18:15-30; see also Matthew 21:14-16.

Those who will enjoy God's kingdom confess their spiritual poverty—"Father, I have sinned against heaven and in your sight. I'm no longer worthy to be called your son"—as opposed to those who appeal to their slavish good works (Luke 15:11-32). God does not receive those who trust in themselves for righteousness, but he justifies the one who strikes his chest and cries, "God, have mercy on me, a sinner!" (18:9-14). The faith that characterizes God's people is persistent prayer, illustrated by a powerless widow who persists in pestering the judge until he gives her justice (verses 1-8). To belong to Jesus, we must embrace our weakness and constantly call upon God for strength.

Jesus warned against worldly strength.

Jesus knew the temptation to rely on the things the world sees as strength—he'd faced those temptations himself.[46] But he refused to be the kind of king the crowds wanted.[47] His kingdom does not belong to this world; it's not won or established through the fighting or political maneuverings of earthly kingdoms.[48]

Jesus warned his disciples against clinging to worldly strength. Earthly wealth is easily lost, but heavenly treasure is imperishable.[49] Those who rest in their earnings and wealth-management skills are fools that don't possess the treasure that God is.[50] Worldly strength feels good at the time, but it ends with this life and gains nothing in the next. "Woe to you who are rich, for you have received your comfort. Woe to you who are now full, for you will be hungry" (Luke 6:24-25). Earthly power can kill the body but is powerless beyond that, so we should "fear him who has authority to throw people into hell after death" (12:5).

---

46. Matthew 4:1-11.
47. John 6:15.
48. John 18:36.
49. Matthew 16:19-20; Luke 12:33.
50. Luke 12:16-21.

Better, then, to forsake worrying about this life, sell our possessions, give to the poor, seek the kingdom, and trust that our heavenly
Father will supply our needs.[51] But this isn't accomplished by merely
divesting oneself of worldly possessions—the heart must be resting in God's strength by faith.[52] Those who set their hope on God's
strength don't need to be afraid, for they have great value in God's
eyes.[53] "Don't be afraid, little flock, because your Father delights to
give you the kingdom" (12:32).

Jesus pointed the weak to real strength.

Though Jesus's people were weak in the world, he assured them
they had access to real strength in him. Jesus is the stronger one who
has attacked, overpowered, disarmed, and plundered the "strong man"
Satan (Luke 11:20-22).[54] Jesus's miracles, performed through the
Spirit, signaled that the power of God's kingdom had broken into
the present age.[55] He's a strong foundation for life.

> Therefore, everyone who hears these words of mine and acts
> on them will be like a wise man who built his house on
> the rock. The rain fell, the rivers rose, and the winds blew
> and pounded that house. Yet it didn't collapse, because its
> foundation was on the rock. But everyone who hears these
> words of mine and doesn't act on them will be like a foolish
> man who built his house on the sand. The rain fell, the
> rivers rose, the winds blew and pounded that house, and it
> collapsed. It collapsed with a great crash (Matthew 7:24-27).

---

51. Matthew 6:25-34; Luke 12:22-33.
52. Matthew 6:21, 24; Luke 12:34.
53. Matthew 10:26-33; Luke 12:6-7.
54. Matthew 12:28-29; Mark 3:26-27.
55. Luke 4:36; Acts 10:38.

The difference is found not in the houses but in the strength of their respective foundations. Jesus is the strong rock.

Jesus's followers have no power in themselves unless they remain in him and he in them—therefore, they must abide in him by faith.[56] "For truly I tell you, if you have faith the size of a mustard seed, you will tell this mountain, 'Move from here to there,' and it will move. Nothing will be impossible for you" (Matthew 17:20). "Everything is possible for the one who believes" (Mark 9:23).

Jesus assured his people that their heavenly Father knows their needs before they ask, so they can pray with confidence that he will answer.[57] Through prayer, God will supply daily nourishment, forgiveness of sins, protection from temptation, and deliverance from the evil one.[58] He's not a stingy neighbor who gives reluctantly out of annoyance but a Father who knows how to give good gifts to those who ask him.[59] So Jesus assured them, "Ask, and it will be given to you. Seek, and you will find. Knock, and the door will be opened to you. For everyone who asks receives, and the one who seeks finds, and to the one who knocks, the door will be opened" (Matthew 7:7-8).[60]

Jesus promised to provide his followers with strength, even after he departed. Through the same Spirit that empowered him, they would be "empowered from on high" (Luke 24:49).[61] Though he sends them as (weak) sheep among (strong) wolves, they should not be afraid; the Holy Spirit will help them and speak through them in that hour.[62]

Human bodies require food and drink to sustain their strength. But Jesus reminded his followers that earthly food perishes—and so

---

56. John 15:4.
57. Matthew 6:7-8.
58. Matthew 6:9-13; Luke 11:1-4.
59. Luke 11:5-13.
60. Luke 17:5-6.
61. See also Acts 1:8; John 14:26.
62. Matthew 10:16-20; Mark 13:11; Luke 12:11-12.

do those who work for it. True life and strength aren't found in this world's food. But the Father has given "true bread from heaven" (John 6:32). Jesus is "the bread of God...who comes down from heaven and gives life to the world" (verse 33). To eat this bread is to believe in Jesus, which results in strength and life that never ends.[63]

> "I am the bread of life," Jesus told them. "No one who comes to me will ever be hungry, and no one who believes in me will ever be thirsty again. But as I told you, you've seen me, and yet you do not believe. Everyone the Father gives me will come to me, and the one who comes to me I will never cast out. For I have come down from heaven, not to do my own will, but the will of him who sent me. This is the will of him who sent me: that I should lose none of those he has given me but should raise them up on the last day. For this is the will of my Father: that everyone who sees the Son and believes in him will have eternal life, and I will raise him up on the last day" (verses 35-40).

May the Father give us this bread always.

---

63. John 6:53-58.

WEAKNESS IN JESUS'S DEATH, RESURRECTION, AND ASCENSION

For he was crucified in weakness, but
he lives by the power of God.

2 CORINTHIANS 13:4

I grew up attending weekly worship at a traditional Lutheran church. The long, rectangular sanctuary had two sections of wooden pews, stained-glass windows, and a vaulted ceiling. Its front featured a slightly elevated area with a pulpit and lectern, communion rail, and altar. The wall behind the altar was open on either side, and people (like the pastor or ushers) went in and out of the space behind it. The area behind the wall mystified me as a small child. What was back there?

At some point, I began thinking that God lived behind that wall. After all, the pastor said we couldn't run in the church building because it was "God's house." I hadn't found God in any other part of the church so, I reasoned, he must live back there. It made sense: If the temple had a Holy of Holies, the church would too. So I imagined that behind the wall was the dwelling place of God.

One day, I found myself in the sanctuary (with no pastor in sight) and decided to venture behind the wall. Entering slowly, I first encountered an open space for communion preparation. The space narrowed to a hallway, at the end of which was an exit door and a custodial closet. In the middle (where the Holy of Holies would be!) was a door. There it was! I cautiously put my hand on the doorknob and cracked the door. No bright light melted my face off, so I opened it further and flipped on the light switch. In all its bright white glory, I beheld…a bathroom. Yep. There, where the throne should be, stood a toilet. To say I was disappointed is an understatement.

If someone told you that God's glory was on display behind a closed door, what would you expect to see when you opened it? (Certainly not a bathroom!) You might quote the awesome scenes in Isaiah 6 or Revelation 4. The first thing that comes to mind, however, probably isn't "a crucified king." But it should be, for through the weakness of a crucified Messiah, God displayed his glory more fully than at any other point in history.

THE CROSS: THE EPITOME
OF JESUS'S WEAKNESS

In the past two chapters, we saw how Jesus assumed human nature with all its weakness (except sin) and how Jesus identified with and served the weak. We should not miss how those two realities meet and culminate at the cross. Death is the ultimate form of weakness. Dying in the place of sinners is the ultimate identification with and service to the weak. Jesus's crucifixion is the pinnacle of both his human weakness and his love for the weak.

We must not underestimate Jesus's weakness at the cross.

Indeed, according to Paul, Christ was crucified "out of weakness [*ex astheneias*]," not, as the main English versions

(ESV, NIV, NRSV) have it, "in" weakness. The difference between the two readings is of fundamental importance. For Christ to be crucified "out of" weakness means that weakness was, or had become, inherent to him. Weakness *belongs* to Christ. [1]

Jesus died "because of weakness."[2] That's not to say weakness was the only reason he died or that he was forced to die; he died voluntarily—he could have called on his Father to send an army of angels.[3] "What Paul means is that Christ lay down his life 'out of' the context of weakness, i.e., because weakness was what he had chosen in his determination to do the Father's will."[4] That context of weakness, his human nature, involved genuine weakness that gave way to real death. "It was finally out of this weakness (and not by external forces) that Christ was crucified."[5]

It's nearly impossible for us to grasp the extent of human weakness communicated in the phrase *Christ crucified.* New Testament authors don't spill much ink describing the physical suffering of the cross. We are right to see that the ultimate significance of the cross is what's happening behind the scenes, the spiritual transaction taking place as the Messiah bears God's wrath for sinners. But that does not imply that the physical agony has no significance. The Gospels' authors don't describe the horror of crucifixion, because they didn't have to. Their first-century readers understood it immediately—and recoiled in horror. We should do the same—but we

---

1. Mark A. Seifrid, *The Second Letter to the Corinthians,* The Pillar New Testament Commentary, gen. ed. D.A. Carson (Grand Rapids: Eerdmans, 2014), 478.

2. D.A. Carson, *A Model of Christian Maturity* (Grand Rapids: Baker Publishing, 1984), Kindle ed., 209.

3. John 10:18, Matthew 26:53.

4. Carson, *A Model of Christian Maturity*, 210.

5. Seifrid, *The Second Letter to the Corinthians*, 478.

never will if we see the cross as an accessory and not an instrument of torture.

The process of crucifixion started long before a soldier picked up a hammer and nail.[6] After Jesus was arrested, bound, and questioned, Pilate "had him flogged" (John 19:1). The Romans used three forms of flogging—*fustiagatio*, *flagellatio*, and *verberatio* (listed from least to most severe). The first, which Jesus received here, was a warning for less serious offenses "usually accompanied by a stern warning against any repetition of such an offense."[7] Pilate hoped, to no avail, that this would satisfy the Jews.[8]

Succumbing to the crowd's demands, Pilate had Jesus flogged again before handing him over to be crucified.[9] This second flogging was likely the *verberatio*, a beating so brutal some recipients died, women were exempt from seeing it, and it "even horrified the emperor."[10] One modern scholar comments, "The outcry about Mel Gibson's movie *The Passion of the Christ* and its realism was misguided. In reality, the flogging scene, bloody though it was, was not as terrible as the real event would have been!"[11]

> The victim was stripped and tied to a post, and then beaten
> by several torturers (in the Roman provinces they were
> soldiers) until they were exhausted, or their commanding
> officer called them off. For victims who, like Jesus, were

---

6. The exact order of events can be challenging to synchronize between the four Gospels, but I will do my best (with the guidance of scholars) to describe what likely transpired.

7. Gerald L. Borchert, *John 12–21*, The New American Commentary, vol. 25B (Nashville: B&H Publishers, 2002), 246.

8. Luke 23:22.

9. Matthew 27:26.

10. James R. Edwards, *The Gospel According to Mark*, Pillar New Testament Commentary (Grand Rapids: Eerdmans, 2002), 464–465.

11. Grant R. Osborne, *Matthew*, Zondervan Exegetical Commentary on the New Testament, vol. 1 (Grand Rapids, MI: Zondervan, 2010), 1022.

neither Roman citizens nor soldiers, the favoured instrument was a whip whose leather thongs were fitted with pieces of bone or lead or other metal.[12]

This brutal beating "could leave victims with their bones and entrails exposed," which obviously hastened the death of those that survived.[13] In this instance, an accelerated death mattered. Crucifixion could last for days, but the Sabbath was approaching, and the Jews disapproved of bodies remaining on the cross on the Sabbath.[14]

Then, "the governor's soldiers took Jesus into the governor's residence and gathered the whole company around him" (Matthew 27:27). *Whole company* technically refers to 600 soldiers, though it may refer merely to all the soldiers present. Yet "for such a rare treat" (having a Jewish "king" at their disposal), it "may be no exaggeration."[15] Either way, Jesus was surrounded by many soldiers "recruited from non-Jewish inhabitants of the surrounding areas...who would have no love for the Jews."[16]

The soldiers viciously mocked Jesus's kingship.[17] After stripping him, they covered him with a scarlet garment, "some old cloak or rug grabbed by a soldier and flung around Jesus to give him the comic appearance of being clad with an emperor's robe."[18] They twisted together a crown of thorns, likely the up-to-twelve-inch thorns of the date palm, which are "exceedingly sharp to the touch and can easily puncture thick plastics, to say nothing of flesh."[19] After crowning

---

12. D.A. Carson, *The Gospel According to John*, Pillar New Testament Commentary (Grand Rapids: Eerdmans, 1991), 597.

13. Carson, 597.

14. John 19:31.

15. R.T. France, *Matthew: An Introduction and Commentary*, Tyndale New Testament Commentaries, vol. 1 (Downers Grove, IL: InterVarsity Press, 1985), 399.

16. France, 399.

17. See Matthew 27:28-30.

18. Borchert, *John 12–21*, 249.

19. Borchert, 248.

him, they put a staff in his hand as a scepter, knelt, and mocked him, "Hail, king of the Jews!" They spat on him and struck him on the head. After having their fun, they removed the robe, replaced his clothes, and took him off to crucify him.[20]

The condemned were forced to carry the crossbeam to the execution site.[21] Jesus began by carrying his cross but, being weakened by torture, could not continue, so the soldiers forced Simon of Cyrene to carry it.[22] "When they came to a place called Golgotha (which means Place of the Skull), they gave him wine mixed with gall to drink. But when he tasted it, he refused to drink it" (Matthew 27:33-34). This may refer to a Jewish custom based on Proverbs 31:6-7: "Give beer to one who is dying and wine to one whose life is bitter. Let him drink so that he can forget his poverty and remember his trouble no more." The Talmud records: "When one is led out to execution, he is given a goblet of wine containing a grain of frankincense, in order to benumb his senses... The noble women in Jerusalem used to donate and bring it."[23] After tasting and understanding what was offered, Jesus refused the narcotic and accepted God's will "in a fully conscious state."[24] Jesus would endure his final hour not through dulled senses but through faith in God's promise to give the Messiah life after death.[25] Then came the crucifixion itself.

Crucifixion originates in the ancient Near Eastern practice of displaying corpses on spikes to humiliate defeated enemies.[26] The Carthaginians and Romans transformed the practice "by devising a cruel,

20. Matthew 27:31; John 19:17.

21. Leon Morris, *The Gospel According to Matthew*, Pillar New Testament Commentary (Grand Rapids: Eerdmans, 1992), 713.

22. See Matthew 27:32.

23. Morris, *The Gospel According to Matthew*, 715.

24. Edwards, *The Gospel According to Mark*, 471.

25. See Isaiah 53:10-11.

26. Osborne, *Matthew*, 1028.

inhumane torturous death upon a cross."[27] "Cicero affirmed that 'this most cruel and terrible punishment' was so degrading that it should not even be discussed by Roman citizens. It was reserved for the lowest of the low."[28] To begin, the soldiers would have stripped Jesus naked and laid him across the crossbeam, affixing his arms by driving iron nails through the wrists into the wood before lifting the beam onto the vertical beam. His legs were affixed to the vertical beam with nails driven through the ankles (with the legs twisted) or through the feet with toes pointed down. The arms and legs were not stretched tight, allowing a victim to lift himself to breathe, thereby extending the agony. There was no position of relief, resulting in severe pain to fatigued and cramping muscles.[29]

We tend to picture the crucified Jesus high off the ground. "In reality, most crosses were probably near or slightly above eye-level,"[30] making it possible for those like his mother and John to hear his words. "His naked body would hang there, unprotected from the gaze of onlookers, and from assaults by troublesome insects and predatory animals."[31] Passersby mocked him mercilessly.[32]

Then came the end. Using whatever strength remained, Jesus pushed down on the nails, lifting his chest to fill his lungs, and proclaimed, "It is finished" (John 19:30). He used his final breath to loudly declare his faith: "Father, into your hands I entrust my spirit"

---

27. Osborne, 1028.

28. Michael Green, *The Message of Matthew: The Kingdom of Heaven*, The Bible Speaks Today (Downers Grove, IL: InterVarsity Press, 2001), 295.

29. For a more thorough medical depiction of crucifixion and its effects on the body, see C. Truman Davis, "The Crucifixion of Jesus: The Passion of Christ from a Medical Point of View," *Arizona Medicine* 22, no. 3 (March 1965): 183–187.

30. James R. Edwards, *The Gospel According to Luke*, ed. D.A. Carson, Pillar New Testament Commentary (Grand Rapids: Eerdmans, 2015), 685.

31. J. Knox Chamblin, *Matthew: A Mentor Commentary*, Mentor Commentaries (Ross-shire, UK: Mentor, 2010), 1398.

32. Matthew 27:40-43.

(Luke 23:46). Jesus died as he lived—offering "prayers and appeals with loud cries and tears to the one who was able to save him from death" (Hebrews 5:7).

As sundown approached, the Jews asked Pilate to have the legs of the crucified broken to hasten death so that their bodies would not remain up on the Sabbath. But when the soldiers came to Jesus, they saw he was dead. One of the soldiers plunged his spear into Jesus's side, and blood and water came out. "The Evangelist is emphasizing Jesus' death, his death as a man, his death beyond any shadow of doubt."[33]

After this, Joseph of Arimathea, a member of the Sanhedrin, retrieved Jesus's corpse. Nicodemus accompanied him with seventy-five pounds of embalming spices, which they used when wrapping his body in linen clothes. They laid him in Joseph's tomb and rolled a stone against the entrance. Mary Magdalene and the other Mary witnessed the preparation and burial, seeing and knowing that Jesus was truly dead.[34]

The weakness of Jesus's human life culminated in a corpse. But we would be mistaken if we understood the cross as mere physical weakness. It was not. The physical weakness vividly demonstrates a much darker and more urgent weakness—sin.

THE CROSS: THE EPITOME OF MORAL WEAKNESS

Sin (moral weakness) is an offense to God deserving the curse of death. In describing the weakness of Jesus's humanity, we've repeatedly emphasized that Jesus did not sin.[35] Yet, in 2 Corinthians 5:21, we find words so startling we might think them blasphemous were they not found in Scripture: "He made the one who did not know sin to be sin for us, so that in him we might become the righteousness of God." Jesus

---

33. Carson, *The Gospel According to John*, 623.

34. John 19:31-42; Luke 23:50-56.

35. See Hebrews 4:15; 1 Peter 1:19; 2:22; 1 John 3:5.

is "the one who did not know sin." God made Jesus *to be sin*. We are comfortable reading, "Christ died for our sins" (1 Corinthians 15:3), "he was delivered up for our trespasses" (Romans 4:25), and "he bore the sin of many" (Isaiah 53:12). We tolerate these expressions because they preserve a distinction between Jesus and sin. He carried sins, was delivered up for sins, and died for sins. Those actions correspond to sin and its consequences—yet Christ and sin remain distinct. But here Paul tells us that God made Jesus *to be sin*. That is too much—or is it?

In scandalous language, Paul pulls back the curtain of earthly perspective to make the core spiritual reality plain. Sin is more than something we do, more than a status. Sin lives in and seizes us at the core of who and what we are as fallen rebels.[36] Sin involves the whole person.[37] Therefore, to save us, it wasn't enough for Christ to do the right things and refrain from the wrong things. Nor was it sufficient that he offered to God the works we did not or could not do. To redeem the "whole person," Christ had to take the place of (identify with) the "whole sinner."[38] Therefore, God made Jesus to be our "moral weakness," to be sin.

---

36. See Romans 7:7-25.

37. "Paul does not describe 'sin' as a mere act, or even as mere guilt, but as the guilt and power of evil that have taken up residence in the human being. He speaks not merely of sin as an act of transgression, but as a reality that has *possessed* the human being and has become inseparable from our person, much like the instances of demon possession that we find in the Synoptic Gospels. 'Sin' has to do not merely with our *works*, but with our whole *person* in guilt and rebellion, condemned and enslaved." Seifrid, *The Second Letter to the Corinthians*, 262.

38. "In God's saving action, Christ was put in our place. Yet Christ did not take our place in the sense of becoming merely one more sinner among other sinners. Paul is emphatic: '*the One who knew no sin*, God made to be sin on our behalf.' Christ thus became the 'sinless sinner.' In this sense, Christ's 'place-taking' was exclusive and substitutionary. It is likely, in fact, that Paul's identification of Christ with sin recalls the usage of Leviticus in which the sacrificial offering for sin is identified *with the people* in their sin. The Levitical sacrifice was not merely an action or work, but entailed an identification of 'being.' This thought is clear in Paul's words. He speaks of God making 'the One who knew no sin' *to be sin*. This defining description of Christ makes clear the ontological nature of the saving event. It is not merely Christ's work that God offered in our place, but it is Christ himself: 'God made him to *be* sin.'" Seifrid, *The Second Letter to the Corinthians*, 261–262.

"He made him sin" echoes the equally jarring language of Galatians 3:13: "Christ redeemed us from the curse of the law by becoming a curse for us, because it is written, Cursed is everyone who is hung on a tree."[39] Paul quotes from Deuteronomy 21:22-23:

> If anyone is found guilty of an offense deserving the death penalty and is executed, and you hang his body on a tree, you are not to leave his corpse on the tree overnight but are to bury him that day, for anyone hung on a tree is under God's curse. You must not defile the land the LORD your God is giving you as an inheritance.

When a guilty party's body was impaled on a spike or hanged from a tree limb, it communicated to every observer that God cursed this one. This explains why the Jews wanted Jesus crucified (hung on a tree) but didn't want his body left up on the Sabbath. They wanted to proclaim that he was under God's curse without defiling the land. It also explains why Jesus's manner of death (crucifixion) mattered—he really was being cursed for sin (though not his own).

In Christ crucified, God showed the world the unvarnished severity of sin and the curse. Christ embodied these. When we witness Christ's life, we see the living, breathing embodiment of all that God called his people to be. When we witness Christ's death, we see the lifeless, breathless embodiment of all that we are and deserve. The worst weakness in the universe is a condemned sinner receiving God's curse. In taking their place, Christ became weaker than his people

---

39. Notice that Paul is not content to say that Christ saved us by "being *cursed* for us," but that he saved us "by *becoming* a curse for us." The curse was death—in becoming dead, he embodied the curse.

will ever be. Christ became this weakness for us so that, seeing him cursed in our place, we could live.[40]

THE CROSS: GOD'S POWER TO SAVE

Strength is the opposite of weakness. If death is the epitome of human physical weakness, then the pinnacle of strength is an immortal body. If sin is moral weakness, then moral strength is incorruptible righteousness. On the cross, Christ became the pinnacle of physical and moral weakness so that we might become immortal and incorruptible. Faith means believing that Jesus was made as weak as I am so that in him I might be as strong as he is.

The cross is a glorious exchange wherein Christ becomes what we are and receives what we deserve so that in him we might become as he is and receive what he deserves. That's what Paul gets at in 2 Corinthians 5:21: "He made the one who did not know sin to be sin for us, so that in him we might become the righteousness of God." How does this work?

A few verses earlier, we read, "In Christ, God was reconciling the world to himself" (verse 19). The need for reconciliation recalls what we saw in chapter 3. Our descent into moral weakness (sinful rebellion) makes us God's enemies, deserving of wrath. So extensive is our moral weakness that we are incapable of doing anything to improve our lot. Humans could not become righteous even when

---

40. When the Israelites grumbled against God and Moses in the wilderness, the Lord sent venomous serpents to bite the people, and many died (see Numbers 21:4-9). The deadly snakes were the fitting punishment for their sin. When they confessed their sin, and Moses interceded, the Lord told Moses, "Make a snake image and mount it on a pole. When anyone who is bitten looks at it, he will recover" (Numbers 21:8). The bronze snake was "mounted on a pole"— impaled, hung on wood and, therefore, cursed. The impaled serpent signified the end of their curse. Whenever someone was bitten (that is, cursed to die for their sin), if "he looked at the bronze snake, he recovered" (verse 9). Looking carries the idea of believing. They would be saved if they believed that the Lord had cursed their curse and put death to death. Jesus says his crucifixion functions similarly: "Just as Moses lifted up the snake in the wilderness, so the Son of Man must be lifted up, so that everyone who believes in him may have eternal life" (John 3:14).

God spelled out his righteous requirements in the Law. But "what the law could not do since it was weakened by the flesh, God did. He condemned sin in the flesh by sending his own Son **in the likeness of sinful flesh** as a sin offering" (Romans 8:3, emphasis added).

God sent his Son, Jesus Christ, to the cross as a sin offering. Having no sin, he didn't deserve God's wrath; he merited no curse. But on the cross, God "made him sin" ("in the likeness of sinful flesh") by counting our trespasses against him. He viewed Christ as the guilty sinner and treated him as such, cursing him with death. He cursed him (not us!) for our sin because "in Christ, God was reconciling the world to himself, not counting their trespasses against them" (2 Corinthians 5:19). In this way, God "erased the certificate of debt, with its obligations, that was against us and opposed to us, and has taken it away by nailing it to the cross" (Colossians 2:14).

Nothing about us had yet changed at the time of Christ's death. Notice how Paul describes our state when Christ died: "For **while we were still helpless**, at the right time, Christ died for the ungodly" (Romans 5:6). "But God proves his own love for us in that **while we were still sinners**, Christ died for us… For if, **while we were enemies**, we were reconciled to God through the death of his Son, then how much more, having been reconciled, will we be saved by his life" (verses 8-11, emphasis added). Christ died while we were still helpless (literally, weak), sinners, and enemies of God.[41] That happened "so that in him we might become the righteousness of God" (2 Corinthians 5:21).

How do we move from being weak, sinful enemies to being "the righteousness of God"? We "become the righteousness of God" by

---

41. Note that those three are used interchangeably. Being sinners, helpless, and enemies of God are inseparable realities. To be one is to be all three. That makes the cross all that more mind-boggling. The sinless Son became the "sinless sinner." The Word that spoke everything into existence became "helpless." The beloved Son, in whom God was well pleased, became an enemy of God. God viewed and treated him as such on the cross so that God could view and treat us as righteous friends. *Hallelujah! What a Savior!*

being united with Jesus through faith. Recall the story of Abraham we read in chapter 4. "Abraham believed the LORD, and he credited it to him as righteousness" (Genesis 15:6). Paul explains that verse this way: "Now to the one who works, pay is not credited as a gift, but as something owed. But to the one who does not work, but believes on him who justifies the ungodly, his faith is credited for righteousness" (Romans 4:4-6). When we believe that God punished our sin in the sinless Christ on the cross, that belief (faith) is credited for righteousness. Though we are ungodly, God justifies us (declares us to be righteous) when we trust in Jesus's person and work. Through faith, we are united to Christ such that our sin was credited to him on the cross, and his righteousness is credited to us.

THE CROSS: GOD'S "WEAKNESS"

Speaking of the cross as God's instrument of salvation, Paul wrote, "God's foolishness is wiser than human wisdom, and God's weakness is stronger than human strength" (1 Corinthians 1:25). Once more, we encounter a statement so astounding we might call it heresy were it not found in Scripture! Whatever does he mean?

In verse 17, Paul told the Corinthians that Christ sent him to preach the gospel—"not with eloquent wisdom, so that the cross of Christ will not be emptied of its power." Paul refused to embrace methods the world calls *strength*, because doing so stripped the cross of its power. Why? God determined to showcase his power and wisdom in a way that would "destroy the wisdom of the wise and...set aside the intelligence of the intelligent" (verse 19). No worldly system of strength or wisdom ever achieved reconciliation with God. The world's power and wisdom prove only to be impotence and folly. In this way, "God made the world's wisdom foolish" (verse 20). However, "God was pleased to save those who believe through the foolishness of what is preached" (verse 21).

To the unbelieving world, the cross is foolishness: "The Jews ask for signs and the Greeks seek wisdom" (verse 22). The Jews demanded a miraculous sign as evidence that Jesus was the Messiah—particularly signs of a strong, conquering Messiah.[42] "Let the Messiah, the King of Israel, come down now from the cross, so that we may see and believe" (Mark 15:32). The Greeks sought a worldview communicated with rhetorical ingenuity and finesse by a distinguished figure whose gravitas and savvy commanded high fees and received lavish praise. But Paul says, "We preach Christ crucified, a stumbling block to the Jews and foolishness to the Gentiles" (1 Corinthians 1:23). To the Gentiles, the idea of a condemned and executed criminal being the locus of God's power in the world was ridiculous and uncivilized. Thus, the Roman soldiers mocked him as "the King of the Jews."

To the Jews, a cursed Messiah was a contradiction in terms—like "imprisoned deliverer" or "dead life-giver." The cross was to the Messiah what a bathroom was to the Holy of Holies—a blasphemous combination! God's anointed would come to deliver them from the curse, not to be cursed! Thus, they objected when Pilate had a sign hung on the cross reading, "Jesus of Nazareth, the King of the Jews" (John 19:19-22). How could God's King be under God's curse? In this way, "the word of the cross is foolishness to those who are perishing" (1 Corinthians 1:18). But that same message—Christ crucified—"is the power of God to us who are being saved" (verse 18).

"Yet to those who are called, both Jews and Greeks, Christ is the power of God and the wisdom of God" (verse 24). Those effectively called by God see the cross for what it is. In the crucified Messiah, God's wise plan culminated in his power working to destroy sin,

---

42. For example, see Matthew 12:39-40; 16:1-4; Luke 11:16, 29-32; John 2:18-22; 6:30.

death, and the devil. The cross is "the power of God and the wisdom of God, because God's foolishness is wiser than human wisdom, and God's weakness is stronger than human strength" (verses 24-25). We expect Paul to write, *God's wisdom is wiser, and God's power is stronger.* But he does not, for God's work does not belong in the same categories as human wisdom and strength. He won't allow Christ crucified to be measured by human metrics. It's in a category of its own, unlike anything this world has ever seen, and so the world cannot touch, judge, or thwart it. The weakest thing—an executed and cursed man—is wiser and more potent than anything the world could conceive. Such language invites believers to remember how God makes his power available to us. The "weakness" of God—Christ crucified—is the power of God to salvation![43]

THE CROSS: GOD'S GLORY ON FULL DISPLAY

To say that the cross manifests God's power and wisdom is to say that the cross displays God's glory. That's what John wanted his readers to see when he wrote that Jesus revealed the God whom "no one has ever seen" (John 1:18). When we see Jesus's glory, we behold the "grace and truth" Moses could not see (verses 14-17). Where, when, and how does John see that happening?

In John 12:27-28, while speaking about his crucifixion, Jesus said, "Now my soul is troubled. What should I say—Father, save me from this hour? But that is why I came to this hour. Father, glorify your name." To this, the Father replied, "I have glorified it, and I will glorify

---

43. "Weakness becomes the circuit through which strength is conveyed, and what seems to be foolish—the message of the cross—becomes the vehicle by which wisdom is transmitted. Power is not displayed fundamentally through amazing signs and wonders but through a crucified man, a person robbed of all dignity who was exposed to the most degrading death conceived of in the Graeco-Roman world." Thomas R. Schreiner, *1 Corinthians: An Introduction and Commentary*, ed. Eckhard J. Schnabel, Tyndale New Testament Commentaries, vol. 7 (London: InterVarsity Press, 2018), 71.

it again" (verse 28). Then Jesus told the crowd, "This voice came, not for me, but for you. Now is the judgment of this world. Now the ruler of this world will be cast out. As for me, if I am lifted up from the earth I will draw all people to myself" (verses 30-32). Then John adds, "He said this to indicate what kind of death he was about to die" (verse 33). This passage indicates three things that would happen in Christ's crucifixion. We'll review them in reverse order.

First, in the cross God was casting out the ruler of the world. God promised a deliverer who would strike the head of the serpent.[44] "The Son of God was revealed for this purpose: to destroy the devil's works" (1 John 3:8). Satan's ultimate weapon is our sin. He can't harm us eternally, but he can tempt us to sin, which brings guilt deserving God's eternal wrath.[45] Satan is the accuser who points at our guilt and demands that God damn us accordingly.[46] But, in Christ, God "erased the certificate of debt, with its obligations, that was against us and opposed to us, and has taken it away by nailing it to the cross" (Colossians 2:14). In Christ crucified, our sin and guilt are removed—and Satan is unable to accuse us effectively. In this way, God "disarmed the rulers and authorities and disgraced them publicly; he triumphed over them in him" (verse 15). No one expected that the long-awaited Champion would crush the serpent while being so weak—naked and dead on a cross.

Second, in the cross God was judging the world. To see the cross is to see God's final declaration about sin. It's a foretaste of the judgment to be rendered on the last day against those who won't repent and believe. For those who believe, the cross is the good news that our sin has been judged (and cannot be judged again). Therefore, "there is now no condemnation for those in Christ Jesus" (Romans

44. Genesis 3:15.
45. Romans 1:18; 5:9; Ephesians 5:6; Colossians 3:6.
46. Revelation 12:10.

8:1). We need not fear judgment, for we have been judged already in Christ crucified. In the weakness of the cross, God has triumphed over the world.

Ultimately, in the cross God was glorifying his name. No aspect of God's glory was absent at the cross. To put it positively, all of God's glory was present in the cross. His love, grace, mercy, wrath, justice, holiness, power, wisdom, and every other divine attribute were present and working together in that moment in such a way that we will never stop praising God over it. The weakness of a crucified Messiah will forever be the centerpiece of our worship of the Triune God.[47] The condescension of Christ crucified is the theme of our song![48]

CHRIST LIVES OUT OF THE POWER OF GOD

"He was crucified out of weakness, but he lives out of the power of God" (2 Corinthians 13:4).[49] Christ's crucifixion isn't the end of the story. Just as he lived a life of faith by the power of the Spirit, God's power raised him from the dead. In 1 Timothy 3:16, Paul described the resurrection as Christ being "vindicated in the Spirit." To *vindicate* means "to demonstrate to be morally right, prove to be right."[50] That was necessary because the world, seeing Christ crucified out of weakness could draw false conclusions—he was a fraud, a failure, cursed by God for his own sin. But Jesus Christ our Lord "was declared to be the Son of God in power according to the Spirit of holiness by his resurrection from the dead" (Romans 1:4 ESV). God's power raised Jesus to vindicate him—to declare him to be in the right as the beloved Son in whom the Father is well pleased.

---

47. See Revelation 5:9-10, 12; 11:15-18; 15:3-4; 19:6-8.

48. Philippians 2:5-11; Colossians 1:15-20.

49. As translated by Mark Seifrid in *The Second Letter to the Corinthians*, 478.

50. Robert W. Yarbrough, *The Letters to Timothy and Titus*, ed. D.A. Carson, Pillar New Testament Commentary (Grand Rapids: Eerdmans, 2018), 222.

The resurrection vindicates Jesus by proving the effectiveness of his ministry of weakness. If the Messiah is still dead, then he remains cursed. If the curse remains on him, he has not ended the curse. If the curse isn't satisfied, then our debt isn't paid in full. If our debt is not paid, then the gospel is a lie. "If Christ has not been raised, then our proclamation is in vain, and so is your faith" (1 Corinthians 15:14). If the Messiah is still dead, then Satan has not been cast out and his power to accuse us of sin remains. "If Christ has not been raised, your faith is worthless; you are still in your sins" (verse 17). If the Messiah is dead, death still reigns and will reign over us: "Those, then, who have fallen asleep in Christ have also perished" (verse 18). If the Messiah is still dead, our faith is as pathetic as the world said Jesus was. "If we have put our hope in Christ for this life only, we should be pitied more than anyone" (verse 19). The cross without the resurrection is terrible, horrible, no good, very bad news.

But the word of the cross is beautiful, delightful, excellent, very good news, for "Christ has been raised from the dead, the firstfruits of those who have fallen asleep" (verse 20). His resurrected body is the first physical portion of the new heavens and earth—incorruptible, glorious, powerful, and spiritual.[51] Like the world to come, his body cannot and shall not pass away. As the first harvest of the resurrection, Jesus's resurrection shows and guarantees what we who hope in him will be like on the final day. "For if we died with him, we will also live with him" (2 Timothy 2:11).

Jesus has risen and "has gone into heaven and is at the right hand of God with angels, authorities, and powers subject to him" (1 Peter 3:22). He ascended into heaven and received all authority—but he has not forgotten his weak brothers and sisters who long to be "set free from the bondage to decay into the glorious freedom of God's

---

51. See 1 Corinthians 15:42-44.

children" (Romans 8:21). The Lamb who was slaughtered stands "at the right hand of God and intercedes for us" (verse 34) and with the Spirit "helps us in our weakness" (verse 26).

———

For we do not have a high priest who is
unable to sympathize with our weaknesses,
but one who has been tempted in every
way as we are, yet without sin.
Therefore, let us approach the throne of grace with boldness,
so that we may receive mercy and find
grace to help us in time of need.

HEBREWS 4:15-16

CHAPTER 11

WEAKNESS IN THE CHURCH

I will most gladly boast all the more about my
weaknesses, so that Christ's power may reside in me.

2 CORINTHIANS 12:9

My high school principal and a favorite teacher were engaged in conversation standing on either side of the otherwise empty hallway. I excused myself as I passed between them in a hurry to get somewhere. I wasn't ten feet past when I heard the principal say, "What do you think of that young man?"

"Impressive," the teacher replied. "I look forward to seeing what becomes of him."

"Me too," the principal agreed. "Whatever he does, he'll be a success."

At the time, that conversation filled me with pride. I'd set out to build an impressive résumé of accomplishments in high school, racking up awards and honors along the way. Evidently, in the eyes of those two, I'd succeeded. Though their words filled me with satisfaction, they also landed with almost overwhelming pressure. It wasn't enough to shine in a few areas in high school. Now I had to excel in all of life for the rest of my life. I couldn't show my face at that school again unless I was impressive. To be average would let them down. The memory of that hallway conversation played in my mind whenever I returned for a sibling's graduation or on summer break from college. I was ashamed to show my face without having an accomplishment to boast about. That shame increased exponentially after I became a pastor.

I entered ministry with great confidence in my flesh. I expected that if I applied myself to thorough Bible study, wrote and delivered excellent sermons, and did all the right things, then my ministry would flourish, people would celebrate me, and God would be pleased. (Dear reader, I'm an idiot.) The ministry didn't live up to my naive and proud expectations. I certainly wasn't making a name for myself. The churches I pastored weren't thriving; they were falling apart. Hurting members brought me problems I couldn't solve (and that I likely made worse!). I was an inexperienced and unskilled leader who was terrified of conflict but confident in himself. I too often responded with impatience, irritation, pride, fear, and too little love. Inwardly, I was anxious, depressed, afraid, and despairing of life itself. Here's how I described just one dark night during that period:

> I knelt on the floor of my study all night, my forehead pressed into the carpet, my fists pressed against my temples. I pulled my hair and wept until I fell asleep, exhausted. Waking in a fetal position, I remembered where I was and what I faced and begged, "Lord, please…please…please… send someone else."
>
> I pressed my face into the floor and sobbed, no longer able to pray with words. Tears and snot and saliva soaked my beard and the carpet. Alone in the darkness, I didn't care.
>
> A faint light shone through the blinds but the rising sun did not bring hope. I wiped my face and tasted blood. Weeping face down through the night, the capillaries in my

nose had broken and bled into the cream carpet. Time was up. I had to shower. I had to dress. I had to go to church. I had to preach.

In the early morning light, I knelt with rags and carpet cleaner and scrubbed the spot until it changed from crimson to white. The words of the prophet repeated in my head, "Though your sins are as scarlet, they shall be white as snow."

Although that was the last time I bled into the carpet, it was not the last time I met Sunday morning with a breakdown. I didn't want to preach. I didn't want to pastor. I didn't want to live.[1]

I knew I was a failure, and I suspected everyone else knew it too. I didn't want to show my face at my alma mater—neither high school nor seminary! I didn't even want to show my face in church. I wanted to crawl into a hole and die.

I eventually concluded that I wasn't strong enough to be a pastor. I didn't have the intelligence, gravitas, thick skin, and charisma to succeed. It took a strong pastor to build a strong church. So I quit. I was too weak to be a good pastor—and deeply ashamed of that fact. And, once again, I couldn't have been more wrong. I wasn't too weak to be a good pastor. As Jesus would show me, I wasn't weak enough.

TO BECOME GREAT
YOU MUST BECOME SMALL

Too often, the bride of Christ has been wooed away by personalities and platforms that do "large things famously and fast."[2] She strays

---

1. Eric Schumacher, "Giving Up the Stage: From Childhood, I Longed to Serve God," *Fathom Mag*, April 22, 2019, https://www.fathommag.com/stories/giving-up-the-stage.

2. Zack Eswine, *The Imperfect Pastor* (Wheaton, IL: Crossway, 2015), Kindle ed., 23.

from her first love to commit adultery with wealth, power, performance, and celebrity. Like Adam and Eve, she sometimes thinks it's not enough to belong to God—she wants his glory for herself.

At least twice, Jesus found his disciples arguing about "who was the greatest of them" (Luke 9:46).[3] Even worse, the debates happened immediately after Jesus predicted his crucifixion![4] On one occasion:

> James and John, the sons of Zebedee, approached him and said, "Teacher, we want you to do whatever we ask you." "What do you want me to do for you?" he asked them. They answered him, "Allow us to sit at your right and at your left in your glory" (Mark 10:35-37).

When the other ten overheard the conversation, "they began to be indignant with James and John" (verse 41). (No fair seeking a promotion unless everyone gets to apply!) Seeing their self-promotion, Jesus seized the opportunity to teach about greatness in his upside-down and backward kingdom.

Jesus said to them, "You know that those who are regarded as rulers of the Gentiles lord it over them, and those in high positions act as tyrants over them. But it is not so among you" (verses 42-43). In this world, people use greatness to get others to serve them, exploiting their power to benefit themselves at the cost of others. But, Jesus insists, it's not like that in his kingdom. "On the contrary, whoever wants to become great among you will be your servant" (verse 43). In his kingdom, the one who wants to be big must become small. Yes, "whoever wants to be first among you will be a slave to all" (verse 44). A *slave to some* might have his own slaves. A *slave to all* has no one

---

3. Matthew 18:1-5; Mark 9:33-37.
4. See Matthew 17:22-23; 18:1-5; 20:17-19, 20-28; Mark 9:30-32, 33-37; Mark 10:32-24, 35-45; Luke 9:43-45, 46-48; 22:14-23, 24-30.

beneath him—he's everyone's slave, the lowest of the low! In Christ's kingdom, the highest status goes to the person with the lowest status. This implies that the King will be the most humiliated slave. Jesus made it explicit: "For even the Son of Man did not come to be served, but to serve, and to give his life as a ransom for many" (verse 45).

"The Son of Man did not come to be served." Paul explains that this way: "Christ Jesus, who, existing in the form of God, did not consider equality with God as something to be exploited" (Philippians 2:5-6). The Son existed eternally as God. Though he was in a high position, he did not exploit his status to be served by his subjects. Instead, Jesus came to serve—"he emptied himself by assuming the form of a servant, taking on the likeness of humanity" (verse 7). He set aside the prerogatives of his divine position to become a human servant.

How did Jesus serve? As he said himself, "To give his life as a ransom for many." Paul put it this way: "When he had come as a man, he humbled himself by becoming obedient to the point of death—even to death on a cross" (verses 7-8). This was voluntary humiliation—he came to give his life, and when he had come, he humbled himself. He served by giving "his life as a ransom for many."

Christ crucified became the preeminent slave—the one and only slave to all. No one in the kingdom will ever have a lower status than Christ himself—for only he became a slave to everyone in the kingdom by giving his life as a ransom for theirs. There's no greater state of weakness than to be dead under God's curse. Jesus became the weakest of the weak—weakness par excellence in service to others.

What resulted from his service? The slave to all became first in the kingdom.

> For this reason God highly exalted him
> and gave him the name

that is above every name,

so that at the name of Jesus

every knee will bow—

in heaven and on earth

and under the earth—

and every tongue will confess

that Jesus Christ is Lord,

to the glory of God the Father (Philippians 2:9-11).

The risen and ascended Jesus received first place, being highly exalted by God and bestowed with the greatest of all names. Why? "For this reason"—that is, because he humbled himself to the point of death on a cross as a ransom for sinners. Because Jesus became the lowest, God made him the highest. One day, every creature in every realm will glorify God the Father by bowing and confessing that the once-crucified slave, the now-risen Jesus Christ, is Lord over God's kingdom. To become the greatest, Jesus made himself the smallest.

WEAKNESS IS THE WAY

Apart from Jesus, no one confronted and dismantled the church's lust for earthly glory more thoroughly and capably than the apostle Paul in his letters to the church in Corinth. Their lust for worldly strength provoked him to godly jealousy: "I have promised you in marriage to one husband—to present a pure virgin to Christ" (2 Corinthians 11:2). Yet he feared that their minds "may be seduced from a sincere and pure devotion to Christ" (verse 3).

"The fundamental problem with the congregation was pride and worldliness."[5] They rejected the values of the cross to embrace the values of their culture. In 1 Corinthians, we find that rivalries existed

---

5. Thomas R. Schreiner, *1 Corinthians: An Introduction and Commentary*, ed. Eckhard J. Schnabel, Tyndale New Testament Commentaries, vol. 7 (London: InterVarsity Press, 2018), 15.

among them as divisions of the church identified with Paul, Apollos, Peter, and even Christ (1:11-12). Instead of receiving the gospel they'd proclaimed, the church members judged their rhetorical abilities and picked tribes, entranced by "eloquent wisdom" (verse 17). Their worship of strength led them to boast in sexual immorality (5:1-6; 6:12-20), enter frivolous lawsuits (6:1-11), and mistreat the poor at the Lord's Supper (11:17-34). Craving social status, they wanted to be seen in pagan temples eating meat sacrificed to idols (chapters 8–11). They misused spiritual gifts to serve themselves instead of others (chapters 12–14). In sum, the Corinthians rejected the power of "Christ crucified," preferring strength the world valued. Unfortunately, Paul's letter didn't end the problem. In 2 Corinthians, he defended himself against "super-apostles" who preached a false gospel rooted in confidence in the flesh and not in Christ crucified out of weakness.

In both letters, Paul demonstrates God's design for weakness in the Christian life, relentlessly returning to God's power present in the weakness of the cross. For Paul, Christian living requires following Jesus in faith, rejecting the values of the world, and embracing the Christ crucified out of weakness, which is the locus of God's power. In what follows, we'll consider seven ways Paul encourages us to embrace weakness in the Christian life.[6]

1. Believe that the weakness of Christ crucified is God's power to save.

In previous chapters, we discussed what must be stated again: "God was pleased to save those who believe through the foolishness of what is preached" (1 Corinthians 1:21). The message of Christ

---

6. For an excellent and more thorough examination of Paul's theology of weakness in the gospel and Christian living, I highly recommend two books from D.A. Carson: *A Model of Christian Maturity: An Exposition of 2 Corinthians 10–13* (Grand Rapids: Baker Books, 1984) and *The Cross and Christian Ministry: Leadership Lessons from 1 Corinthians* (Grand Rapids: Baker Books, 2003). I owe much of what follows to these volumes.

crucified is "the power of God and the wisdom of God" (verses 23-24). So, for Paul, the whole of the Christian life is lived "by faith in the Son of God, who loved me and gave himself for me" (Galatians 2:20). Since the gospel "is the power of God for salvation to everyone who believes," all of God's saving righteousness is revealed and received entirely through faith in Jesus (Romans 1:16-17). To put our hope in anything else is to forfeit God's saving power! Will the church preach this today?

2. Imitate the weakness of Christ.

To be an apostle was to be conformed to the image of Christ crucified. "God has displayed us, the apostles, in last place, like men condemned to die" (1 Corinthians 4:9). But the way of weakness isn't limited to Jesus's apostles. Paul's gospel ministry birthed the church in Corinth. As their "father in Christ Jesus through the gospel," he expects his "dear children" to grow up to look like him: "I urge you to imitate me" (verses 14-16). Paul sent Timothy to the Corinthians for that purpose. "He will remind you about my ways in Christ Jesus, just as I teach everywhere in every church" (verse 17).

There is no incongruity between what Paul teaches everywhere in every church and his ways in Christ Jesus. His ways and his teaching inseparably correspond. The Corinthians didn't need more theology; they needed to be shaped by what Paul taught them! What did he teach? "I decided to know nothing among you except Jesus Christ and him crucified" (2:2).

> That is more than a creedal statement; it sets out Paul's priorities, his lifestyle, and, in this context, his style of ministry. If he really holds that God has supremely disclosed himself in the cross and that to follow the crucified and risen Savior means dying daily, then it is preposterous to

adopt a style of ministry that is triumphalistic, designed to impress, calculated to win applause.[7]

What example does the church set and call people to imitate today?

3. Consider your weakness when God called you.

Understanding that "God's weakness is stronger than human strength" requires remembering your own weakness when God saved you. "Brothers and sisters, consider your calling: Not many were wise from a human perspective, not many powerful, not many of noble birth" (1 Corinthians 1:26). The Corinthian church included converts who were well respected in the surrounding culture. But there were not many. It seems the bulk of the church were the despised and rejected of the world. This was by God's design.

> Instead, God has chosen what is foolish in the world to shame the wise, and God has chosen what is weak in the world to shame the strong. God has chosen what is insignificant and despised in the world—what is viewed as nothing—to bring to nothing what is viewed as something, so that no one may boast in his presence (verses 27-29).

Paul's logic is as follows: God wants to show that no human ever has any reason to boast before him. Therefore, he delights to save those that the world considers weak, foolish, insignificant, and despised. If these are saved alongside the wise, powerful, and noble of the world, then it's apparent that a higher status in the world makes no difference to God. So no one may boast in God's presence as though what they were somehow mattered. "It is from him that you are in Christ

---

7. D.A. Carson, *The Cross and Christian Ministry: Leadership Lessons from 1 Corinthians* (Grand Rapids: Baker Books, 2003), 38.

Jesus" (verse 30). We may not boast that we were wise, wealthy, or strong enough to gain a standing in Christ. God put us there.

Christ Jesus "became wisdom from God for us—our righteousness, sanctification, and redemption" (verse 30). Paul isn't content to say that God made us wise, righteous, holy, or redeemed—or even that he gave us these things. For then we might boast that we are these things (even if God is to thank for it), praying like the Pharisee: "God, I thank you that I'm not like other people—greedy, unrighteous, adulterers, or even like this tax collector" (Luke 18:11). Instead, Paul insists that Christ Jesus became these things for us. We are not these things—Christ is—and we're "in him" by God's work.

Where is our wisdom? Christ. Where is our righteousness? Christ. Where is our holiness? Christ. Where is our redemption? Christ. Christ Jesus—and he alone—is the entirety of our wisdom, righteousness, sanctification, and redemption. He became these things in the weakness of human flesh—and we're in him only by God's grace. Therefore, "Let the one who boasts, boast in the Lord" (1 Corinthians 1:31). Does today's church remember where she came from?

4. Reject any methodology that empties God's weakness of its power.

Paul reminds the Corinthians that when he came to them with the gospel, "I decided to know nothing among you except Jesus Christ and him crucified" (1 Corinthians 2:2). Paul is describing the *how* of his ministry. He didn't come "with brilliance of speech or wisdom" (verse 1), but "in weakness, in fear, and in much trembling" (verse 3). In Paul's thought, the Christian's medium is their message because the message determines the medium. The *how* of the messenger is as crucial as the *what* of the message, because when the world's means and manners are employed, the cross of Christ is "emptied of its power" (1:17 ESV).

The Corinthian culture placed a high value on words of wisdom, caring as much (or more) about the form of communication as the content. A speaker that didn't adopt their valued methods and manners was rejected as not worth listening to.

> Speakers were prized and praised in the Graeco-Roman world, and they were assessed by their rhetorical brilliance. Handbooks were written on correct rhetorical style by ancient writers such as Quintilian and Cicero. Probably the Corinthians were assessing Paul and Apollos based on their rhetorical effectiveness and brilliance. There is probably also a sociological component here (cf. 1:26-28), for brilliant rhetoric would appeal especially to the beautiful and the rich.[8]

Paul repeatedly emphasizes that he didn't adopt the cherished rhetorical style when he preached the gospel in Corinth.

- "For Christ did not send me to baptize, but to preach the gospel—not with eloquent wisdom" (1:17).
- "I did not come with brilliance of speech or wisdom" (2:1).
- "My speech and my preaching were not with persuasive words of wisdom" (verse 4).

That wasn't because Paul lacked the ability to meet standards. His letters exhibit his intelligence and mastery of language. His recorded speeches in the book of Acts prove his ability—although he was known to put a listener to sleep![9] Nor was it because Paul was culturally insensitive or inflexible: "I have become all things to all people, so that I may by every possible means save some" (9:22).

---

8. Schreiner, *1 Corinthians*, 65.
9. See Acts 20:7-12.

So why did Paul preach without eloquent wisdom when he knew they would be offended by its absence? It was a strategic choice "to adopt a more restrictive course, even though he was cutting across the stream of cultural expectations."[10] Paul rejected eloquent wisdom "so that the cross of Christ will not be emptied of its effect" (1:17). The English Standard Version puts it more starkly, "be emptied of its power," which isn't so blunt as "be made void" (NASB95). If the gospel is "the power of God for salvation" (Romans 1:16), how could it be *emptied* of its power? The gospel is *made void* when it's no longer the gospel.

The gospel is God's power of salvation to those who *believe* (Romans 1:16; 1 Corinthians 1:21). Believing means trusting in Christ crucified, resting your faith on God's power in the cross. If hearers "become entranced with the skill and the power of the speaker," then they "fail to grasp the message of the cross."[11] In that case, they have heard and believed not the gospel of Christ but another gospel (the good news of style and skill). Therefore, their faith is "based on human wisdom" and not "on God's power" (1 Corinthians 2:5). That is why Paul "self-consciously distanced himself from the rhetorical pomp of his day."[12] Is today's church willing to follow suit?

5. Live in a way that demonstrates the Spirit's power.

Paul chose to live in such a way that God's power was present and active, "with a demonstration of the Spirit's power" (1 Corinthians 2:4). Elsewhere, Paul tells the Corinthians that Christ "was crucified in weakness, but he lives by the power of God" (2 Corinthians 13:4). In the same way, he says, "we also are weak in him, but in dealing with you we will live with him by God's power" (verse 4). That

10. Carson, *The Cross and Christian Ministry*, 34.
11. Schreiner, *1 Corinthians*, 65.
12. Carson, *The Cross and Christian Ministry*, 35.

certainly involves the empowerment of God's indwelling Spirit, but it's more than that. It involves how he lives and ministers.

"We do not wage war according to the flesh, since the weapons of our warfare are not of the flesh" (10:3-4). God has given us powerful weapons. But they're not worldly weapons—"the kinds of tools of the trade relished by the intruders: human ingenuity, rhetoric, showmanship, a certain splashiness and forwardness in spiritual pretensions, charm, powerful personal charisma."[13] Therefore, Paul won't face his opponents on their terms. Theirs is the wrong war, waged in the wrong way.

Our weapons "are powerful through God for the demolition of strongholds" (verse 4). What are they? The answer is implied in how they work. "We demolish arguments and every proud thing that is raised up against the knowledge of God" (verses 4-5). These weapons destroy arguments and proud things that oppose the knowledge of God. Let's dissect that thought.

What does Paul mean by *the knowledge of God*? A few verses later he writes, "So let the one who boasts, boast in the Lord" (verse 17). He's quoting Jeremiah 9:24: "But the one who boasts should boast in this: that he understands and knows me—that I am the LORD." Paul's *boast in the Lord* is shorthand for boasting that you understand and know the Lord. So *knowledge of God* in 10:5 is synonymous with *boasting in the Lord* in 10:17. By *Lord*, Paul means specifically the Lord Jesus (2 Corinthians 1:2, 3, 14; 8:9; 11:31). By *boast*, Paul means basing one's faith on God's power displayed in Christ crucified (see 1 Corinthians 1:26–2:5). So, to summarize, *the knowledge of God* means "faith in Christ crucified."

So Paul's weapons destroy *arguments* and *proud things* that oppose faith in Christ crucified. What arguments and proud things do that?

---

13. D.A. Carson, *A Model of Christian Maturity: An Exposition of 2 Corinthians 10–13* (Grand Rapids: Baker Books, 1984), Kindle ed., 65.

Throughout both 1 and 2 Corinthians, Paul battles systems of thought that value earthly wisdom and strength. These *proud things* are anything that teaches or urges human beings to put their faith in something other than Jesus.

How does Paul go about demolishing such things? Every time, he preaches and applies the gospel. The powerful weapons of our warfare are the message of the cross proclaimed in the power of the Spirit through a gospel-shaped messenger. What weapon is the church using today?

6. Don't be afraid to appear weak.

At the center of the super-apostles' criticism of Paul (and the Corinthians' wavering fidelity to him and his gospel) was the charge that Paul was *weak*. He didn't measure up to the standards of "those who take pride in outward appearance rather than in the heart" (2 Corinthians 5:12).

The super-apostles complained that "his physical presence is weak" (10:10). Only one description of Paul's appearance has been preserved: "a man small of stature, with a bald head and crooked legs, in a good state of body, with eyebrows meeting and nose somewhat hooked, full of friendliness; for now he appeared like a man, and now he had the face of an angel."[14] He was a short, bald, bow-legged, hooked-nose man with a unibrow, whose only redeeming physical quality was his "good state of body," due, no doubt, to his extensive travels and manual labor. Only his overflowing "friendliness" gave him the face of an angel. Paul received the "thirty-nine lashes" five times, was beaten with rods three times, was stoned once, and endured many sleepless nights, sometimes in the cold and without clothing (11:24-27). We can't begin to picture the mass of scars and crooked bones

---

14. A. Malherbe, "A Physical Description of Paul," *Harvard Theological Review* 79, no. 1-3 (1986): 170–175.

that characterized him after recovering from such injuries without the aid of modern medicine.

Paul wasn't a specimen of human strength and beauty. But then again, neither was Jesus, who "didn't have an impressive form or majesty that we should look at him, no appearance that we should desire him" (Isaiah 53:2). But that's of no concern to Paul (or Jesus). "For the training of the body has limited benefit, but godliness is beneficial in every way, since it holds promise for the present life and also for the life to come" (1 Timothy 4:8). Christ's kingdom isn't so pathetic as to be threatened by unimpressive men.

The super-apostles complained that "his public speaking amounts to nothing" (2 Corinthians 10:10). This does not faze Paul: "I consider myself in no way inferior to those 'super-apostles.' Even if I am untrained in public speaking, I am certainly not untrained in knowledge. Indeed, we have in every way made that clear to you in everything" (11:5-6). He didn't need the world's strength to make the gospel clear.

The super-apostles complained about his weak social status. Paul asks, "Did I commit a sin by humbling myself...because I preached the gospel of God to you free of charge?" (verse 7). Paul accepted financial support from churches and sometimes solicited support.[15] In fact, he insisted on gospel ministers' right to be paid by those they serve, as did Jesus.[16] So why does Paul refuse their patronage when he knows it will offend them? To demolish a stronghold of cultural idolatry that opposed the gospel.

The super-apostles operated in a cultural system that weighed the worth of preachers by the size of their income and audience. (Sound familiar?)

---

15. See 2 Corinthians 11:8-9; Philippians 4:10-15; Romans 15:24.
16. See 1 Corinthians 9; Luke 9:3-4; 10:4-7; 3 John 5-8.

Traveling teachers in the first century, professional sophists and rhetoricians, did not normally work with their hands. The best of them avoided begging, even if some manual work was required; but the ideal was to make a good living from teaching itself. The more famous the teacher, the more he could charge, and the more students would attach themselves to him and count it a privilege to pay his fee. Thus in many ways a teacher's status could be assessed by the price he could command, much as a figure on modern college or political lecture circuit can be ranked by the size of his fee.[17]

Refusing to be paid (or paid well) was tantamount to undervaluing yourself and your message. Antiphon said of Socrates, "If you set any value on your own society, you would insist on getting the price for that too. It may well be that you are a just man because you do not cheat people through avarice; but wise you cannot be since your knowledge is not worth anything."[18] The super-apostles used this logic to argue that Paul's apostleship was worthless because his speaker fee was zero.

Paul understood these standards to be forms of idolatry, which were opposed to the knowledge of God in Christ. So long as they judged him by what amounted to a false gospel, he would do the opposite. He destroyed these satanic strongholds, "arguments and every proud thing that is raised up against the knowledge of God," by knowing nothing among them except Christ crucified. They could not reject Paul's weakness without also rejecting "the grace of our Lord Jesus Christ" (2 Corinthians 8:9). If Paul's humility is

---

17. Carson, *A Model of Christian Maturity*, Kindle ed., 120.
18. As quoted in Carson, *A Model of Christian Maturity*, Kindle ed., 121.

wrong, then so is Jesus, who "though he was rich, for your sake he became poor, so that by his poverty you might become rich" (verse 9). Paul won't allow himself to be accepted in an idolatrous system since that would communicate that the message he brings belongs to that system as well.

Jesus looked weak. Paul wasn't afraid to appear weak. Is today's church willing to look weak to keep the gospel central?

7. *Boast about your weaknesses so that Christ's power may reside in you.*

In Greco-Roman culture, "citizens and soldiers, without embarrassment and as a social convention, outdid one another in boasting of military and political achievements."[19]

> There was even a kind of stylized way of writing up such a brag-sheet, a technique modern scholars refer to as "well-known encomiastic conventions." Augustus Caesar, for instance, wrote an eulogy in his own honor, an encomium that listed his many accomplishments (the so-called *Res gestae Divi Augusti*). Augustus is careful to include numbers: once I did this, three times I did that, many times the other.[20]

Such boasting stood at the center of the super-apostles' triumphalism, a technique they used to invalidate Paul in the eyes of the Corinthians.

Paul deeply disdained the idea of commending himself. "For it is not the one commending himself who is approved, but the one the Lord commends" (2 Corinthians 10:18). In his mind, boasting is the talk of fools. Yet he no doubt feels the tension of Proverbs 26:4-5:

---

19. Paul Barnett, *The Message of 2 Corinthians: Power in Weakness*, The Bible Speaks Today (Downers Grove, IL: InterVarsity Press, 1988), 172.

20. Carson, *A Model of Christian Maturity*, Kindle ed., 144.

> Don't answer a fool according to his foolishness
> or you'll be like him yourself.
> Answer a fool according to his foolishness
> or he'll become wise in his own eyes.

Paul refuses to become a fool by answering the super-apostles according to their foolishness. Yet, if he does not answer them according to their foolishness, they will remain wise in the eyes of the Corinthian church and continue to lead them away from Christ. He has no choice but to answer them according to their folly, at least outwardly.[21] "I have been a fool; you forced it on me" (2 Corinthians 12:11).

His discomfort is palpable as he begins his boasting: "In whatever anyone dares to boast—I am talking foolishly—I also dare" (11:21). He insists that he matches the super-apostles in Jewish credentials, which he elsewhere described eloquently before discarding as dung.[22] What follows next is as ironic as it is unexpected, so much so that Paul says he's "talking like a madman" (verse 23). We expect him to step to the microphone and remind the convened how many churches he's planted, pastors he's trained, people he's discipled, and books he's penned. Instead, he boasts about the shameful weaknesses obvious in his ministry history:

---

21. See 2 Corinthians 11:1, 16-17.

22. Philippians 3:4-11: "If anyone else thinks he has grounds for confidence in the flesh, I have more: circumcised the eighth day; of the nation of Israel, of the tribe of Benjamin, a Hebrew born of Hebrews; regarding the law, a Pharisee; regarding zeal, persecuting the church; regarding the righteousness that is in the law, blameless. But everything that was a gain to me, I have considered to be a loss because of Christ. More than that, I also consider everything to be a loss in view of the surpassing value of knowing Christ Jesus my Lord. Because of him I have suffered the loss of all things and consider them as dung, so that I may gain Christ and be found in him, not having a righteousness of my own from the law, but one that is through faith in Christ—the righteousness from God based on faith. My goal is to know him and the power of his resurrection and the fellowship of his sufferings, being conformed to his death, assuming that I will somehow reach the resurrection from among the dead."

Five times I received the forty lashes minus one from the
Jews. Three times I was beaten with rods. Once I received
a stoning. Three times I was shipwrecked. I have spent a
night and a day in the open sea. On frequent journeys, I
faced dangers from rivers, dangers from robbers, dangers
from my own people, dangers from Gentiles, dangers in the
city, dangers in the wilderness, dangers at sea, and dangers
among false brothers; toil and hardship, many sleepless
nights, hunger and thirst, often without food, cold, and
without clothing (verses 24-27).

This isn't the one-upmanship of pastors hoping to impress one
another as they swap stories over boxed lunches at the SUPERAPOS-
TLES™ conference. Sufferings in themselves have no value. Instead, he
shrewdly unveils the sheer absurdity of their boasting.

The super-apostles boast of triumph, but Paul bears on his body
"the marks of Jesus" (Galatians 6:17). Triumphant living isn't the
hallmark of an apostle, for "we always carry the death of Jesus in
our body, so that the life of Jesus may also be displayed in our body"
(2 Corinthians 4:10). Being "transformed" into Christ's image "from
glory to glory" (3:18) does not make a believer outwardly impressive,
"for we who live are always being given over to death for Jesus's sake,
so that Jesus's life may also be displayed in our mortal flesh" (4:11).
God didn't entrust the gospel to impressive specimens of eloquence
and strength. The treasure of "God's glory in the face of Jesus Christ"
is placed in fragile "clay jars, so that this extraordinary power may
be from God and not from us" (verses 6-7).

To the aforementioned weaknesses, Paul adds, "There is the daily
pressure on me: my concern for all the churches. Who is weak, and
I am not weak? Who is made to stumble, and I do not burn with
indignation?" (11:28-29). The authenticity of his ministry isn't found

in his long tenure at a church that loves him, where wealthy patrons lavish him with luxury. He is riddled with anxiety over the churches he's planted, which are often weakened by suffering and stumble into sin through false teaching. Sometimes they reject him! Such is the case in Corinth. Yet he does not forsake them. Instead, he burns with anger that they would be afflicted. He empathizes deeply with their weaknesses and is willing to weaken himself through whatever means necessary to love and strengthen them.

Paul's list so far might be seen as triumphal boasting: "Look at all the dangerous daring circumstances I pressed through and overcame!" In this way, these experiences would be testimonies to Paul's strength in the flesh. But he wants nothing to do with such a conclusion. So he adds a capstone of humiliating weakness. "If boasting is necessary, I will boast about my weaknesses" (verse 30). It is as though he says, "Mark my point—this is a real, genuine, unvarnished weakness, not triumphal bragging masquerading under humble language!" Still, he knows what he's about to share is so shameful it's almost unbelievable. So he opens with an oath, swearing to its truthfulness: "The God and Father of the Lord Jesus, who is blessed forever, knows I am not lying" (verse 31).

The weakness, also recorded in Acts 9:23-25, was one of Paul's first experiences as an apostle. He'd set out for Damascus "breathing threats and murder against the disciples of the Lord," a zealous Pharisee, intent on seeing Christians arrested, imprisoned, and executed (Acts 9:1-2). But, on the road to Damascus, the risen Lord Jesus knocked him off his high horse, transformed his heart, and appointed him as his "chosen instrument to take my name to Gentiles, kings, and Israelites" (verses 2-19). Paul remained in Damascus for some time, growing stronger and preaching Jesus in the synagogues, "proving that Jesus is the Messiah" (verses 20-22). Then, as Paul now recalls, "a ruler under King Aretas guarded the city of Damascus in order to arrest me. So I was let down in a basket through a window in the wall and escaped from his hands" (2 Corinthians 11:32-33).

It's easy for us to retell that story as a hero's daring and narrow escape—a triumph! Paul did not. He recounted it with deep shame. One of the highest honors in the Roman Empire was the *corona muralis* (wall crown), awarded to the first soldier to go over the wall into an enemy city—an act requiring incredible strength and courage.[23] "Paul's point is devastatingly plain; he was first down."[24] He ran away—and is deeply ashamed over it.

It's not as though Paul does not have any glorious highs to speak of. He experienced visions and revelations of the Lord, even being "caught up to the third heaven" (12:1-2). But he's too humble to mention himself and forbidden to speak of what he saw and heard (verse 4). In response to these "extraordinary revelations," Paul received a further weakness: "Therefore, so that I would not exalt myself, a thorn in the flesh was given to me, a messenger of Satan to torment me so that I would not exalt myself" (verse 7). What this thorn is we're not told. Paul only reveals two things.

First, the thorn involved demonic affliction—"a messenger of Satan to torment me." Second, it was given so that he would not exalt himself. Surely, that's not Satan's motivation. Paul has already asserted that the self-exaltation in Corinth is Satan's work![25] What Satan intended for evil, Jesus was using for good. Paul pleaded with the Lord three times for the thorn to be removed (verse 8). But Jesus—who knows what it means to hear *no* in agonizing prayer—declined the request with this encouragement: "My grace is sufficient for you,

23. David E. Garland, *2 Corinthians*, The New American Commentary, vol. 29 (Nashville: B&H Publishers, 1999), 506.

24. E.A. Judge, "The Conflict of Educational Aims in NT Thought," *Journal of Christian Education* 9 (1966): 45.

25. See 2 Corinthians 11:14-15.

for my power is perfected in weakness" (verse 9). Jesus allowed Paul to experience ongoing satanic torment so that his powerful grace could be displayed to its fullest extent in Paul's weakness.

Then Paul writes, "Therefore I…" In other words, "Because Jesus's powerful grace is fully displayed in the context of my most painful and shameful experiences, here is what I do…"

How would you finish that sentence? "I pray even harder for God to remove my weaknesses." "I accept my weaknesses." "I patiently endure my weaknesses."

Once again, Paul's perspective surprises everyone: "Therefore, I will most gladly boast all the more about my weaknesses, so that Christ's power may reside in me" (verse 9). Paul is happy to boast more about his weaknesses—because when he does, Christ's power dwells in him. Lest we miss the point, he doubles down: "So I take pleasure in weaknesses, insults, hardships, persecutions, and in difficulties, for the sake of Christ" (verse 10). These manifold weaknesses please him because their presence benefits the cause of Christ. "For when I am weak, then I am strong" (verse 10). Paul takes delight in being weak and telling others about it because that's the context in which he's strong.

Are we in the church willing to boast about our shameful weaknesses to show Christ's glorious power? Does the church take pleasure in humiliation for Christ's sake? Are we willing to believe it (and live like it) when Jesus promises, "My grace is sufficient for you, for my power is perfected in weakness"?

CHAPTER 12

WEAKNESS IN THE NEW CREATION

Worthy is the Lamb who was slaughtered
to receive power and riches
and wisdom and strength
and honor and glory and blessing!

Revelation 5:12

I'm writing this final chapter in the early hours of July 4. Later today, our family will join our nation in observing Independence Day. It dawns on me that Independence Day is a holiday entirely limited to this present world. We will not celebrate independence in the age to come. Indeed, we will celebrate freedom! We will forever praise King Jesus, "who loves us and has set us free from our sins by his blood, and made us a kingdom, priests to his God and Father—to him be glory and dominion forever and ever" (Revelation 1:5-6). But freedom and independence are two different things. We will be free from sin and death in Christ! But we are—and always will be—entirely dependent on God in Christ for that freedom.

REMEMBER WEAKNESS

At the beginning of this book, we defined weakness as the inability to act or produce an effect. We noted that God—and God alone—is not weak.

No one created God. His existence—past, present, and future—owes itself to nothing. He depends on nothing. Nothing started him. Nothing sustains him. He has no need, weakness, or vulnerability. Nothing can end him. He simply is.

Only God is independent. We are entirely and eternally dependent on God.

It is natural to wonder how weakness will feature in the world to come. We might even question whether there can be weakness in the new heavens and new earth. After all, describing our resurrection from the dead, Paul writes, "Sown in corruption, raised in incorruption; sown in dishonor, raised in glory; sown in weakness, raised in power; sown a natural body, raised a spiritual body" (1 Corinthians 15:42-44). How could we be described as weak if we are raised in power?

We are helped by remembering the three categories of weakness we've considered—relative, consequential, and natural. *Relative weakness* describes the contrasting degrees of weakness between creatures—some are weaker or stronger than others. The bulk of our study has focused on the other two categories. *Consequential weakness* refers to weaknesses introduced or magnified by the Fall, which include both our moral weakness (sin) and our mortal weakness (our susceptibility to disease, decay, death, and the consequences of the Fall). *Natural weakness* refers to our good weaknesses, which are ours by God's design and by being creatures (not the Creator). In this chapter, we will consider these latter two categories of weakness, along with the "weakness of Christ crucified," as these relate to the new heavens and new earth.

CONSEQUENTIAL WEAKNESS

In chapter 2, we looked at weakness in the Fall. Through the deadly deception of the serpent, the woman and then the man believed the lie that they were strong enough to live independently from God. They took the fruit and ate it, and with that first sin, a host of consequential weaknesses flooded their lives. The Lord promised a Redeemer who would crush the head of the serpent and, by extension, save God's people from the consequences of sin. In this section, we'll briefly look back at these consequential weaknesses and consider the significance of their absence in the world to come.

Consequence #1: Knowledge of Nakedness

Before the Fall, "both the man and his wife were naked, yet felt no shame" (Genesis 2:25). After the Fall, "the eyes of both of them were opened, and they knew they were naked" (3:7). Awareness of nakedness represented an awareness of their guilt and awareness that they now lived in a dangerous world, one in which they needed protection. They understood they were weak—vulnerable to harm from each other, their environment, and the God they offended. In mercy, the Lord slaughtered an animal and "made clothing from skins for the man and his wife, and he clothed them" (verse 21). Then the Lord sent them "away from the garden of Eden" (verses 23-24). Eventually, those garments wore out, and Adam and Eve died.

In his mercy, God sent Jesus, "the Lamb of God, who takes away the sin of the world," to be "slaughtered" (John 1:29; Revelation 5:9). "Through faith," we are "clothed with Christ" (Galatians 3:26-27). In Christ Jesus, we are "free from the law of sin and death" (Romans 8:2), sanctified (1 Corinthians 1:2), given grace (verse 4), and forgiven (Ephesians 4:32). We "are all sons of God in Christ Jesus" (Galatians 3:26). We are clothed "in Christ Jesus," who is our "wisdom…righteousness, sanctification, and redemption"

(1 Corinthians 1:30). "In Christ," we are "a new creation," reconciled to God (2 Corinthians 5:17-19) and seated with him "in the heavens" (Ephesians 2:6). We are being transformed into Christ's image as we "put on the Lord Jesus Christ" (Romans 13:14), which is "to put on the new self" (Ephesians 4:24).[1] To wage spiritual warfare, we "put on the full armor of God" (6:10-18), which is everything God is for us in Christ.

Our new clothing is not merely spiritual but also physical. Paul speaks of our present physical body as "our earthly tent" that can be destroyed by death, leaving us "naked" (2 Corinthians 5:1-3). As our bodies suffer the curse, we groan in this mortal tent, not wanting to "be unclothed" (verse 4). But God has prepared for us a new body, "our heavenly dwelling," which will be clothed when "mortality" is "swallowed up by life" (verse 4). God gives us his Spirit as a sort of down payment, promising that our new bodies are on their way (verse 5). But on the last day, the risen Lord Jesus Christ will return to "transform the body of our humble condition into the likeness of his glorious body" (Philippians 3:21). Every ache, pain, disease of the curse—and death itself—will disappear from us forever. At that moment, "we will all be changed, in a moment, in the twinkling of an eye, at the last trumpet. For the trumpet will sound, and the dead will be raised incorruptible, and we will be changed. For this corruptible body must be clothed with incorruptibility, and this mortal body must be clothed with immortality" (1 Corinthians 15:51-53). And then, just as God drove Adam and Eve from the garden in Eden, he brings us into a new garden, where we will see his face and worship him forever (Revelation 22:1-5). "Thanks be to God, who gives us the victory through our Lord Jesus Christ!" (1 Corinthians 15:57).

---

1. See also Colossians 3:10-12.

Consequence #2: The Delusion of Self-Sufficiency

After the Fall, Adam and Eve foolishly believed they could save themselves from the consequences of sin through their works and wisdom. Moral weakness deludes us into thinking we are strong. We see this as they fashion leaves into loincloths, attempt to hide from God, and point the finger at others as though to transfer guilt. But this will not be the case in the end.

When all Christ's people are gathered before his throne, they will cry out in a loud voice, "Salvation belongs to our God, who is seated on the throne, and to the Lamb!" (Revelation 7:10). The vast multitude in heaven will say, "Salvation, glory, and power belong to our God, because his judgments are true and righteous" (Revelation 19:1-2). They declare together:

> Hallelujah, because our Lord God, the Almighty, reigns!
> Let us be glad, rejoice, and give him glory,
> because the marriage of the Lamb has come,
> and his bride has prepared herself.
> She was given fine linen to wear, bright and pure (verses 6-8).

Though the fine linen represents the righteous acts of the saints (verse 8), all the glory goes to the Lord because "she was given fine linen." The whole of salvation is a gift from God—"our sufficiency is from God" (2 Corinthians 3:5 ESV).

Consequence #3: Spiritual Disruption

Our moral weakness disrupts our relationship with God, resulting in profound separation from him. Adam and Eve were driven out of Eden, away from God's dwelling place. Their unbelieving son Cain "went out from the LORD's presence" (Genesis 4:16). For those who believe, however, our spiritual disruption has been mended and ended through Christ crucified out of weakness. By his blood, Jesus "purchased people for God" to make them the kings and priests to God (Revelation 5:9-10).

When the new heaven and earth are established, a loud voice will proclaim the new reality: "Look, God's dwelling is with humanity, and he will live with them. They will be his peoples, and God himself will be with them and will be their God" (21:3). The new city is a new and better Eden, where God and his people dwell in perfect harmony: "They will see his face" (22:4).

Consequence #4: A Depraved Nature

After the Fall, humans are born engulfed in moral weakness: "Every inclination of the human mind was nothing but evil all the time" (Genesis 6:5). Humans are so morally weak they are as able to do what is good as a leopard can change his spots (Jeremiah 13:23). But it is not so for God's people in the resurrection.

Outside the new Jerusalem are "the dogs, the sorcerers, the sexually immoral, the murderers, the idolaters, and everyone who loves and practices falsehood"—those whose nature is eternally depraved and morally weak (Revelation 22:15). But God's people are not outside the city, because they are no longer like that. They "washed their robes and made them white in the blood of the Lamb" so that they "may enter the city by the gates" (7:14; 22:14). As Christ's people, we will not be able to sin, because we "will be raised incorruptible, and we will be changed" (1 Corinthians 15:52). One day, we will stop sinning!

Consequence #5: Relational Disruption

Because our relationship with God was disrupted, so was our relationship with God's image (other humans). When we do not love God, we will not love our neighbor. But through the cross, hostility between kingdom citizens ends. Believers are "members of the same body, and partners in the promise in Christ Jesus through the gospel" (Ephesians 3:6). "There is no Jew or Greek, slave or free, male and female; since you are all one in Christ Jesus" (Galatians 3:28).

Nevertheless, sin disrupts our relationships as long as sin weakens us in these fallen bodies. That is why so many New Testament letters address ways Christians mistreat each other, even in the church! But when we are clothed in the incorruptible bodies of the resurrection, this relational weakness will be ended forever. On that day, we will each be fully mature in Christ and enjoy "unity in the faith and in the knowledge of God's Son" (Ephesians 4:13).

We are not told much about the relationship between individuals in the new heavens and the new earth. But what we are told points to a relationship of perfect peace. Jesus's blood purchased people for God "from every tribe and language and people and nation," and he has made them "a kingdom and priests to our God, and they will reign on earth" (Revelation 5:9-10). Those from diverse earthly backgrounds will be a single kingdom, a unified priesthood, and worship God together in one voice (7:9-10). God's people are a unified whole—a holy city, a bride, God's new humanity (21:2-3). "And they will reign forever and ever" (22:5). All this certainly requires unity of purpose and love for one another.

Consequence #6: Spiritual Warfare

At the Fall, the Lord told the serpent, "I will put hostility between you and the woman, and between your offspring and her offspring" (Genesis 3:15). Ever since, hostility has existed between God's people and "the ancient serpent, who is called the devil and Satan" (Revelation 12:9), between "God's children and the devil's children" (1 John 3:10). But this ancient spiritual warfare will be finally ended in the new creation.

Going to the cross, Jesus said, "Now the ruler of this world will be cast out" (John 12:31). Satan received a mortal wound through

Christ's crucifixion and resurrection. We battle the devil by being "firm in the faith" in Christ (1 Peter 5:8-9). We are assured that "the God of peace will soon crush Satan under your feet" (Romans 16:20).

> The salvation and the power
> and the kingdom of our God
> and the authority of his Christ
> have now come,
> because the accuser of our brothers and sisters,
> who accuses them
> before our God day and night,
> has been thrown down.
> They conquered him
> by the blood of the Lamb
> and by the word of their testimony;
> for they did not love their lives
> to the point of death (Revelation 12:10-11).

The ancient serpent is conquered and crushed under our feet when we love Christ more than life and trust in his blood. On the last day, Christ will defeat Satan and end our spiritual warfare forever, for we read, "The devil who deceived them was thrown into the lake of fire and sulfur where the beast and the false prophet are, and they will be tormented day and night forever and ever" (20:10).

Consequence #7: Painful Labor

After the Fall, life becomes painful.

> The ground is cursed because of you.
> You will eat from it by means of painful labor
> all the days of your life.

> It will produce thorns and thistles for you,
> and you will eat the plants of the field.
> You will eat bread by the sweat of your brow (Genesis 3:17-19).

Fulfilling our purpose to reign on earth is painful, frustrating, and seemingly futile. But in the resurrection, all such weakness is gone. The Lamb delivers us from the hostility of a cursed environment.

> They will no longer hunger;
> they will no longer thirst;
> the sun will no longer strike them,
> nor will any scorching heat.
> For the Lamb who is at the center of the throne
> will shepherd them;
> he will guide them to springs of the waters of life,
> and God will wipe away every tear from their eyes
> (Revelation 7:16-17).

In the new heaven and new earth, we will have constant access to the river of the water of life and the tree of life, invited and welcome always to partake freely (22:1-2, 17). We will not eat by the sweat of our brow, for "there will no longer be any curse" (verse 3). We will "reign forever and ever" (verse 5) without "grief, crying, and pain… because the previous things have passed away" (21:4).

Consequence #8: Decay and Death

After the Fall, the first humans were told, "You are dust, and you will return to dust" (Genesis 3:19). "The wages of sin is death" (Romans 6:23). Death is the ultimate form of physical weakness, the absence of life itself. But in the new world, this weakness shall be banished entirely: "For if we died with him, we will also live with him" (2 Timothy 2:11). "For just as in Adam all die, so also in Christ all will be made alive" (1 Corinthians 15:22).

When Jesus raises us from the dead, "when this corruptible body is clothed with incorruptibility, and this mortal body is clothed with immortality...Death has been swallowed up in victory" (verse 54). Death will die at the judgment seat of Christ, being "thrown into the lake of fire," which is the "second death" (Revelation 20:14). In the new heaven and new earth, "death will be no more" (21:4).

Consequence #9: Eternal Death

Physical death pales compared to the eternal death in body and soul that awaits those who rebel against God. In the end, the unbelieving will be raised from the dead to be judged and condemned to "eternal punishment" (Matthew 25:46), "the second death, the lake of fire" (Revelation 20:14; 21:8), where "their worm will never die, their fire will never go out" (Isaiah 66:24). This is why Jesus said, "Fear him who has authority to throw people into hell after death. Yes, I say to you, this is the one to fear!" (Luke 12:5). Still, Jesus also promised, "If anyone keeps my word, he will never see death" (John 8:51). This is the confident hope of those who obey the word of the gospel.

Jesus promises those who conquer (by faithfully trusting in his finished work[2]):

- "To the one who conquers, I will give the right to eat from the tree of life, which is in the paradise of God" (Revelation 2:7).

- "Be faithful to the point of death, and I will give you the crown of life" (verse 10).

- "The one who conquers will be dressed in white clothes, and I will never erase his name from the book of life but

---

2. See Revelation 12:11.

will acknowledge his name before my Father and before his angels" (3:5).

- "I will freely give to the thirsty from the spring of the water of life. The one who conquers will inherit these things" (21:6-7).

It is true: "Death will be no more" (verse 4). All we have to look forward to is life that lasts forever and ever:

> Then he showed me the river of the water of life, clear as crystal, flowing from the throne of God and of the Lamb down the middle of the city's main street. The tree of life was on each side of the river, bearing twelve kinds of fruit, producing its fruit every month. The leaves of the tree are for healing the nations, and there will no longer be any curse. The throne of God and of the Lamb will be in the city, and his servants will worship him. They will see his face, and his name will be on their foreheads. Night will be no more; people will not need the light of a lamp or the light of the sun, because the Lord God will give them light, and they will reign forever and ever (22:1-5).

NATURAL WEAKNESS

Removing bad weakness (consequential weakness) means that only good weakness (natural weakness) remains. Natural weakness is good because God designed us with weakness—and "God saw all that he had made, and it was very good indeed" (Genesis 1:31).

Chapter 1 observed six areas where we depend entirely on God: our place, presence, purpose, provision, protection, and partners. In the new heavens and new earth, we will remain entirely dependent on God for all these things.

In the new world, we depend entirely on God for our place.

"In the beginning God created the heavens and the earth" (Genesis 1:1). We didn't make it; we couldn't make it. He made it—and he continues to sustain it. Apart from his power, we have no place to live. When "the first heaven and the first earth" have "passed away," there will be "a new heaven and a new earth" (Revelation 21:1). The one on the throne declares, "Look, I am making everything new" (verse 5). He is making it, not us. Apart from his power, we have no place to live.

In the first creation, "the LORD God planted a garden in Eden, in the east, and there he placed the man he had formed," the special place where he dwelt with them (Genesis 2:8). In the new creation, there will be a new "holy city, the new Jerusalem," about which we are told: "Look, God's dwelling is with humanity, and he will live with them. They will be his peoples, and God himself will be with them and will be their God" (Revelation 21:2-3). The new Jerusalem will be a new Eden—a garden-city where the tree of life grows.

> Then he showed me the river of the water of life, clear as
> crystal, flowing from the throne of God and of the Lamb
> down the middle of the city's main street. The tree of life
> was on each side of the river, bearing twelve kinds of fruit,
> producing its fruit every month (22:1-2).

There will be no "temple in it, because the Lord God the Almighty and the Lamb are its temple" (21:22). Perfect, personal fellowship between God and his people will be restored in this special place: "They will see his face" (22:4). Our new place does not exist by our power, for we are "looking forward to the city that has foundations, whose architect and builder is God" (Hebrews 11:10). We will depend on God for our place eternally.

In the new world, we depend entirely on God for our presence.

In the first creation, "God created man" (Genesis 1:27). "The LORD God formed the man out of the dust from the ground and breathed the breath of life into his nostrils, and the man became a living being" (2:7). He sustains humans: "The life of every living thing is in his hand, as well as the breath of all humanity" (Job 12:10). We did not make ourselves. We do not sustain ourselves.

In the new creation, we will exist because the Triune God will raise our bodies from the dead and continually sustain us.

- Father: "God raised up the Lord and will also raise us up by his power" (1 Corinthians 6:14).

- Son: "Everyone who sees the Son and believes in him will have eternal life, and I will raise him up on the last day" (John 6:40).

- Spirit: "He who raised Christ from the dead will also bring your mortal bodies to life through his Spirit who lives in you" (Romans 8:11).

We will depend entirely on God for our presence eternally.

In the new world, we depend entirely on God for our purpose.

In the first creation, God determined humanity's purpose both when he created them and when he placed them in the garden:

- "Then God said, 'Let us make man in our image, according to our likeness. They will rule the fish of the sea, the birds of the sky, the livestock, the whole earth, and the creatures that crawl on the earth'" (Genesis 1:26).

- "God blessed them, and God said to them, 'Be fruitful, multiply, fill the earth, and subdue it. Rule the fish of the sea, the birds of the sky, and every creature that crawls on the earth'" (verse 28).

- "The LORD God took the man and placed him in the garden of Eden to work it and watch over it" (2:15).

Humans did not determine why they existed. God gave humanity its mandate to be rulers on earth and priests to him.

In the new creation, God determines humanity's purpose (which is the same!). Jesus purchases people for God by his blood and makes "them a kingdom and priests to our God, and they will reign on the earth" (Revelation 5:10). Yes, "they will reign forever and ever" (22:5). We did not, do not, and will not determine our purpose. We will depend entirely on God for purpose eternally.

In the new world, we depend entirely on God for our provision.

In the first creation, the Lord said, "Look, I have given you every seed-bearing plant on the surface of the entire earth and every tree whose fruit contains seed. This will be food for you, for all the wildlife of the earth, for every bird of the sky, and for every creature that crawls on the earth—everything having the breath of life in it—I have given every green plant for food" (Genesis 1:29-30). Even after the Fall, "he gives food to every creature" (Psalm 136:25).

In the new creation, he gives us the river of the water of life and the tree of life and invites us to eat (Revelation 21:6; 22:1-2, 17). We will eternally depend entirely on God for our satisfying, life-sustaining food and drink.

In the new world, we depend entirely on God for our protection.

In the first creation, God instructed his people, warning them about the lethal consequences of eating from the forbidden tree. They could not know this apart from his protection.

In the new creation, we will live with God in an imperishable, incorruptible, and unassailable fortress city—a strong picture of God's protection (Revelation 21:9-21). Only one thing appears vulnerable: "Its gates will never close" (verse 25). Open gates allow enemies in! But the gates will not close "because it will never be night there" (verse 25). We will walk in the safety of the glory of God shining in Christ, which always illuminates the city (verses 23-24). "Nothing unclean will ever enter it, nor anyone who does what is detestable or false" (verse 27). We will not be under the threat of harm in the city because "outside are the dogs, the sorcerers, the sexually immoral, the murderers, the idolaters, and everyone who loves and practices falsehood" (22:15). *Outside* is an understatement, because, at the last judgment, God will cast our every last enemy into the lake of fire (20:10-15). We will depend entirely on God for our protection eternally.

In the new world, we depend entirely on God for our partners.

In the first creation, God noted, "It is not good for the man to be alone. I will make a helper corresponding to him" (Genesis 2:18). The man could not rule the earth solo—God blessed man and woman with that reign. The man needed a helper. He could not make one himself. He depended entirely on God to provide her.

In the new creation, we will neither be alone nor fulfill our calling alone. "Look, God's dwelling is with humanity, and he will live with them. They will be his peoples, and God himself will be with them and will be their God" (Revelation 21:3). In the new heaven and the new earth, "the marriage of the Lamb has come" (19:7). We will be wed to Christ for eternity, married partners fulfilling our purpose. God's people "will reign forever and ever" (22:5). But they will not reign alone, for "the kingdom of the world has become the kingdom of our Lord and of his Christ, and he will reign forever and ever" (11:15). Christ and his bride will reign together for eternity. God has given us himself in Christ. We will depend entirely on God for our partner—himself—eternally.

We will be weak—entirely dependent on God—forever. "Amen! Come, Lord Jesus!" (22:20).

THE WEAKNESS OF CHRIST CRUCIFIED

In the first chapter, we learned that weakness isn't a bug in the universe's design; it's a feature. Weakness reminds us that God designed life to be lived by faith. Weakness is God's good gift because it's the context in which he gives us himself. Weakness matters because it's the backdrop against which God displays his strength. It is on that last point that I want to conclude this book.

Our weakness is the backdrop against which God displays his strength. His strength, we've seen, is made perfect in our weakness. So we delight in remaining weak forever so that God's strength might be displayed in us forever! But God's strength displayed in our weakness is not quite the center of God's glory in eternity—that honor belongs to Christ's weakness. As we have seen, the supreme display of God's power and glory is in Christ crucified out of weakness.[3]

The cross was not an unpleasant but necessary experience of weakness to be momentarily endured and then forgotten, like a root canal or a colonoscopy. God did not raise Jesus from the dead and say, "Thanks for your work, Son. I know it was unpleasant and shameful. We'll never bring it up again." No, even as he lives by the power of God, exalted in glory, his crucifixion out of weakness is continually brought to the forefront of his praise. The weakness of Christ crucified was the centerpiece of God's glory in history. And the weakness of Christ crucified shall be the centerpiece of God's glory in eternity.

---

3. 2 Corinthians 13:4, see pages 196 and 211.

As John opens Revelation, he prays for grace and peace to come to his readers "from Jesus Christ, the faithful witness, the firstborn from the dead and the ruler of the kings of the earth" (1:5). This description is how John sees Jesus now, in his exalted state. His first descriptor, "the faithful witness," refers to what we saw in Hebrews 12:1-2. In the "large cloud of witnesses," Jesus is the witness par excellence because he is the one who perfected faith by trusting God when he endured the cross, despising the shame, before he became "the firstborn from the dead." John sees Jesus's glory through the lens of crucifixion. And he should! For he gives glory "to him who loves us and has set us free from our sins by his blood" by the weakness of crucifixion (Revelation 1:5).

John reminds his readers:

> Look, he is coming with the clouds,
> and every eye will see him,
> even those who pierced him.
> And all the tribes of the earth
> will mourn over him.
> So it is to be. Amen (verse 7).

They will mourn because the one who comes in power is the one they crucified in weakness. Jesus's glory shines in the light of his death.

In Revelation 4, John looks into the throne room of heaven, which is filled with awe-inducing splendor to which creatures and elders never stop responding in worship. John sees the scroll of history in the hand of the one seated on the throne and weeps "because no one was found worthy to open the scroll or even to look in it" (5:4). But then one of the elders says to him, "Do not weep. Look, the Lion from the tribe of Judah, the Root of David, has conquered so that he is able to open the scroll and its seven seals" (verse 5).

John is told to look at a conquering lion—the Davidic King! This figure is worthy to approach the throne, take the scroll, and open the scroll. So his glory must surely match the one on the throne! Given the throne room's terrifying glory, this figure must be a sight to behold—if one can look at him at all!

When John looks at the conquering lion, what does he see? "Then I saw one like a slaughtered lamb standing in the midst of the throne" (verse 6). Yes, he had "seven horns and seven eyes," but he was one "like a slaughtered lamb." He didn't just look like a lamb. He looked like a slaughtered lamb. It is evident that he had been put to death—and he is worthy to approach the throne of glory.

Jesus's "slaughtered lamb" appearance isn't accidental to his worthiness—it's the central reason for his worthiness. For the creatures and elders who never stop praising the Lord God, the Almighty, fell down before the Lamb and sang a new song:

> You are worthy to take the scroll
> and to open its seals,
> because you were slaughtered,
> and you purchased people
> for God by your blood
> from every tribe and language
> and people and nation (verses 8-9).

Then "countless thousands, plus thousands of thousands" of angels around the throne agreed:

> Worthy is the Lamb who was slaughtered
> to receive power and riches
> and wisdom and strength
> and honor and glory and blessing! (verses 11-12).

Then "every creature in heaven, on earth, under the earth, on the sea, and everything in them" said,

> Blessing and honor and glory and power
> be to the one seated on the throne,
> and to the Lamb, forever and ever! (verse 13).

What does this scene show us about Jesus? It shows us that Jesus's slaughteredness is the reason for his worthiness in the throne room of heaven. "You are worthy...because you were slaughtered" (verse 9). "Worthy is the Lamb who was slaughtered" (verse 12). "Blessing and honor and glory and power be to the one seated on the throne and to the Lamb" (verse 13).

The most prominent title for Jesus in Revelation's glorious visions is "the Lamb," first seen as a slaughtered lamb standing. It is the Lamb who:

- reigns over the outworking of history (6:1)
- brings wrath on God's enemies (6:16)
- gathers God's redeemed multitude (7:9)
- possesses salvation (7:10)
- makes his saints' robes white through his blood (7:14)
- is at the center of the throne, shepherding his persecuted people (7:17)
- makes us, as brothers and sisters, able to conquer (12:11)
- authored the book of life (13:8)
- stands on Mount Zion (14:1)
- is followed wherever he goes by the redeemed of humanity (14:4)

- oversees the execution of God's wrath (14:10)

- conquers the antichrist's kings "because he is Lord of lords and King of kings" (17:14)

- marries the bride (19:7, 9; 21:9)

- replaces the temple (21:14)

- is the lamp of God's glory (21:23)

- sits on God's throne in the new Jerusalem (22:1-3)

In all that Revelation reveals about heaven and the world to come, Jesus is only referred to as the Lion once (5:5). The purpose of calling him the Lion who has conquered is to highlight, by way of contrast, that he is "one like a slaughtered lamb standing in the midst of the throne" (verse 6).

It is not too much to say that the central display of God's glory is Christ crucified out of weakness. The new Jerusalem "does not need the sun or moon to shine on it, because the glory of God illuminates it, and its lamp is the Lamb" (21:23). What is a lamp? It's a device for giving light. The light resides in it and emanates from it. To illuminate a room, you light a lamp and put it on a lampstand. God's glory is the only light that illuminates the new creation. The lamp from which God's glory emanates is the Lamb. The risen, glorified body of Jesus Christ, which looks like it had been slaughtered in weakness, is the centerpiece of God's glory forever. If we shall walk in the glory of Christ crucified forever, let us learn to walk in it now.

A LEGACY OF WEAKNESS

He must increase, but I must decrease.

JOHN 3:30

Looking back over a book you've written is a bit like looking back over your life. You see what you did, you know what you should have done, and it's far too late to do anything about it.

This book on weakness is weak. I can't begin to count its flaws: too little application, too much content in each chapter, too dense for the average reader, and too insubstantial for the academic. I'm most ashamed to admit that it's too weak on my weakness. I opened too many chapters with "safe" stories—illustrations of youthful weakness that risk relatively nothing in their retelling. Nevertheless, I have confidence that the Lord will use this book in readers' lives because I've seen how he used it in mine.

I leave this work a changed man. I find myself less confident in my own strength and more confident in the Lord's. I'm less tolerant of arrogance, pride, and boasting—especially in myself. I'm taking more risks in ministry and obedience because I'm more convinced of Jesus's gracious willingness to be my strength in every weakness. Part of that means I've grown more confident in owning my shortcomings. What I want to have in the end—and give to you—is less of my illusions of strength and more of God's sovereign kindness in the face of Jesus Christ.

Chapter 11 opened with a peek into one of my many dark nights of the soul. I wrote that piece because a friend challenged me to chronicle something I'd failed at and then submit it for publication. I'm thankful she did. Yet, when I look back on that article, I feel embarrassed—not in what I wrote but in what I didn't. I chickened out and failed to be fully vulnerable. There was a darker night I didn't think I could survive sharing—the night I ripped my Bible to shreds.

Those Saturday nights of deep darkness plagued me with increasing intensity. I stayed up late, laboring at sermons—not so I could better feed the sheep but to avoid criticism and garner praise. Crafting a sermon manuscript is long, hard work—countless hours of writing and rewriting. It's even worse when you're laboring to do the impossible: to write the "perfect" sermon every week. The disparagements of unappeasable critics tormented me. I wearied myself with study and writing so my sermons would be unassailable. I had supporters whom I feared disappointing with an average sermon. Ultimately, in my mind, I was developing a legacy—a catalog of full sermon manuscripts that moved verse by verse through the Bible. I couldn't leave a gap in that by preaching from notes!

I hated the place I was in—the place I'd put myself in. I hated the goals I'd set that kept me from sleep for no reason other than my pride. I hated my weakness—my inability to be good enough to make everyone happy. I hated the idols that controlled me and my unwillingness to renounce them. I hated the broader pastoral culture that encouraged me to boast about such empty credentials. I hated the ministry. I hated myself. And I questioned why God wouldn't do something to help me. Filled with frustration, anger, despair, and desperation, I wanted it all to end. I wanted someone, something to be destroyed so that it could all be over and I could rest.

I looked down and saw the Bible I'd studied daily and preached from every Sunday for over a decade. The leather on the spine was worn smooth from my grip. The pages were discolored from my thumbs. I'd determined to preach from that Bible for fifty years—and then, in my old age, leave it to a child or grandchild as the centerpiece of the legacy ministry I built. I saw that, and I hated it—not the Bible per se, but the terrible, overwhelming, soul-crushing thing it represented in my heart.

Without thinking, I picked it up and tore it in two. But two pieces weren't enough. I ripped out whole sections of pages, tearing them again and again until translucent, onionskin confetti covered the floor. When I saw it, I hated myself. I kicked one of the louvered office doors, expecting it to swing open and shut. Instead, it popped out of its hinges and crashed to the floor. I followed it, completely undone.

The middle-of-the-night crash woke Jenny. I could hear her coming down the stairs and didn't know what to expect—anger, disgust, scolding. But I only heard a deep sigh—"Oh, Eric"—that sounded like the grace of Jesus. She knelt next to me and listened with compassion. She prayed for me and told me to go to bed and sleep. Then she retrieved a gallon-sized ziplock bag and slowly collected every last piece of my Bible.

Somehow, I preached something at church the following day, deeply aware that all I had was the grace of God in Christ. After church, I pulled one of our elders aside at small-group lunch and asked if we could talk. We sat in my office, and through sobs, I told him everything. I didn't know if I'd get fired, be asked to resign, or be shamed as a disappointment. Whatever was coming, I deserved it and would receive it.

Only I didn't deserve what was coming. He sat there quietly and listened. He wasn't ashamed of me. Tears wet his cheeks as he told me he loved me and reminded me of the grace of Jesus. Then he sent me home to rest. He gathered and informed the elder team to see that I was cared for. Eventually, with their support, I quit—leaving the ministry for a season to rest and recover.

It wasn't until writing this book that I understood the depth of Jesus's human weakness—and, therefore, the depth of his love. His voluntary humiliation enabled him to empathize with me in my weakness. Did Jesus not experience the shameful weakness of a night in torment? "Being in anguish, he prayed more fervently, and his sweat became like drops of blood falling to the ground" (Luke 22:44). What a picture I now see! There is Jesus, weak and in anguish, being made "like his brothers and sisters in every way" (Hebrews 2:17). There is Jesus, in his weakness, being "tempted in every way as we are" (4:15). There is Jesus, feeling the same torment as me, "yet without sin" (verse 15). There is Jesus, succeeding where I failed! And why? "To make atonement for the sins of the people" (2:17). He suffered weakness without sin to save me from mine. Jesus didn't become weak so that he could condemn me when I failed, but to be "a **merciful** and faithful high priest" (verse 17, emphasis added). He became weak to "sympathize with our weaknesses" (4:15).

It wasn't until the end of this book that I understood how deeply I was loved and sustained by Christ that night (and countless others). I now see that Jesus viewed me not with wrath and disappointment but with mercy and tender sympathy. Jesus didn't turn his face away, ashamed of me. Because he was made "perfect through sufferings," Jesus isn't ashamed to call me "brother" (2:10-11). He became weak like me to help me on that night and a thousand more. He came in weakness so I could go to him in boldness. He reigns from a "throne of grace," which I can approach in confidence, knowing that I will certainly "receive mercy and find grace to help [me] in time of need" (4:16).

I wish I could say that my inner turmoil has gone away. I wish I could say I haven't had another night as dark as that one. God has helped and strengthened me in many ways and through many means. But I still feel the thorns of insecurity, inadequacy, dread, darkness, and despair. They haunt me relentlessly. I still feel pangs of fear and anxiety *every time* I go to church, get up to preach, or meet with fellow church members. I've hoped and prayed it would disappear, but the Lord has not allowed that. I'm sure Satan delights in it. But what Jesus has done is teach me to respond to the thorn's prick by calling on him in faith. He has repeatedly shown me that his power really is perfected in my weakness. That's why I'm now willing to share my weakness with you—both my embarrassing story and my feeble book. I know that Christ loves and strengthens me in my weakness, and I want you to know that grace too.

I still have that Bible in the same ziplock bag my wife gathered it into that night. One day I will give it to my children. I planned to give it to them after preaching from it for fifty years. It was to be my legacy. It's still my legacy. Only now, it will be handed down as a testimony of my weakness and the relentless, gracious, merciful power of Christ, my strength. I can think of nothing better to leave to them—and you—than my weakness and the Lord, my strength.

Now, dear reader, may the Father bless you
with the grace to confess your weakness
and to receive his abundant strength
through faith in his Son, Jesus,
in the power of his Holy Spirit.
Amen.

ACKNOWLEDGMENTS

Jesus Christ—I'll never get over the fact that you became like me in every way (except you never sinned). You voluntarily humiliated yourself, taking on the full weakness of human nature—even becoming *weaker* than me by submitting to death under God's curse—so that you could be my strength. Thank you. Thank you. Thank you.

The Apostle Paul—Thank you for writing honestly about your weaknesses. You showed me that you were every bit as weak as I am. Therefore, I can trust that the Lord who empowered your ministry is at work in me. Christ really is our everything, isn't he!

Jenny and family—You've suffered more than anyone because of my weaknesses. And yet you love me. Thank you.

Paul Tripp—Thank you for encouraging me to write this book (and volunteering the foreword)! Your Christlike willingness to befriend and pour yourself into younger brothers is a treasure.

Kyle Hatfield—You championed this project from the moment you saw the proposal. Thank you for believing in its value, bearing with my weaknesses, and all you've done to help bring it to fruition.

Michael Felkins—Thank you for encouraging me to write. And thanks for being a pastor who isn't afraid to admit weakness so that God's power might be displayed.

Grand Avenue Baptist Church—Thanks for loving this weak brother and for praying me through this project.

Tom Schreiner—Thank you for your feedback and dialogue, and for being a wonderful example of humility and faith in Jesus.

Emily Jensen and Jared von Kamp—Thanks for reading early drafts of chapters, providing feedback, and encouraging me to keep writing.

Eric Schumacher is an author, podcaster, songwriter, and has served in pastoral ministry for over two decades. He is currently the pastoral ministry director for the Baptist Convention of Iowa.

Along with Elyse Fitzpatrick, he is the coauthor of *Worthy* and *Jesus and Gender* (2023 winner of the Spiritual Formation Award of Merit from the Christianity Today Book Awards). He is the sole author of *Ours* and *My Last Name*. Eric currently interviews guests on the Nothing is Wasted podcast and has hosted the Worthy podcast (with Elyse Fitzpatrick). He also serves on the board of directors for Walk With You, a nonprofit organization dedicated to supporting families who have experienced the loss of a child.

Eric and his wife, Jenny, live in Iowa with their five children.

Connect with Eric at emschumacher.com
or on social media @emschumacher

To learn more about Harvest House books and
to read sample chapters, visit our website:

www.HarvestHousePublishers.com

HARVEST HOUSE PUBLISHERS
EUGENE, OREGON